S0-BMU-099

Existentialism and Phenomenology:

A Guide for Research

Existentialism and Phenomenology:

A Guide for Research

by

Leonard Orr

The Whitston Publishing Company
Troy, New York
1978

Library of Congress Catalog Card Number 77-93782

ISBN 0-87875-141-6

Printed in the United States of America

FOREWORD

Dis-covering Existentialism

by Joseph Buttigieg
New Mexico State University

Bibliography, strictly speaking, means simply the writing of books; it is, in other words, a description of a specific activity. This meaning has, however, become obsolete and in so far as the term 'bibliography' describes an activity, it is the activity of writing books about books. More frequently the term 'bibliography' refers to a list of titles by and about a particular author, or dealing with a common topic; a list, that is, which shares most of the characteristics of a catalog. Those who study bibliography do not learn how to write books, and only rarely do they educate themselves in the history of writing, printing, binding, etc. A typical college course in bibliography instructs students in the most efficient ways of locating sources of information, and gathering that information. One is taught how to compile a bibliography as the first necessary step in any scholarly endeavor, most especially in research projects. The act of compiling a bibliography is itself a research activity, but it preceded the actual research it is intended to support. This task is lightened by the accessibility of bibliographies already prepared to assist the student or scholar in his work. Not only do bibliographies abound, but they are also easy to locate or trace thanks to the availability of bibliographies of bibliographies. These books on books on books testify to the proliferation of aids at the disposal of the researcher. Yet, bibliographies as we know them and use them are a relatively new phenomenon. Probably, the earliest use of the word 'bibliography' in its most common current sense does not go farther back than 1869, when W. Rowlands published his *Cambrian Bibliography* (this is the first instance cited by the *OED*). Since then bibliographies have become commonplace and used as a matter of course. One expects to find a bibliography on virtually any subject, no matter how specialized. Such bibliographies are not always adequate or satisfactory, but even so they might still serve some purpose or save the researcher some time. Those long engaged in research work are generally extremely adept at using bibliographies efficiently and fruitfully. Ultimately, of course, a bibliography is like every other tool; it can be good or poor, depending on the competence of its maker and the skill of its user.

A bibliography, then, is a tool to which the investigator turns for basic information, generally at the very outset of his investigation. It makes available to him a record of the existing 'literature' on his topic. From it he derives a list of papers, journals, books which address the subject or problem that interests him. He then moves on to acquiring and reading those works, and his studies are under way. The bibliography, in this case, functions as a pointer, a labor saving device, a convenient tool. Once it has served its purpose the tool is discarded or shelved. The user of the bibliography rarely spends time reflecting on the nature and properties of the bibliography itself. He handles the bibliography as a piece of equipment; he perceives it as (to use Heideggerian language) something ready-at-hand. For, generally, the tool attracts attention to itself only when it breaks down, malfunctions, or fails to perform according to expectations. When a breakdown occurs, when the bibliography for some reason or other falls short of one's expectations or does not provide the help one anticipated from it, then one is led to focus one's attention on the bibliography itself, as a thing—one can then see it as something present-at-hand. Such an occurrence brings to the fore questions and considerations otherwise held in abeyance. A new awareness takes over. One feels the need to examine the principles which guide the compilation of a bibliography, the assumptions which lie behind the divisions into sections and categories within a bibliography, the methods which govern choice, the grounds on which certain judgements are based. Thus, for instance, one starts to take a closer look at, and even question, the accepted division into periods (usually by century) which almost always characterizes general literature bibliographies. Bibliographies organized according to topic also give rise to similar fundamental questions. Why is a particular topic abstracted? Why this subject heading rather than another? Does not a bibliography of existentialism assume that there is such a thing as existentialism which can be differentiated from romanticism, anti-Hegelianism, modernism, etc.? And, how has one decided what to include under the heading of existentialism? Is phenomenology a separate area, or is it to be treated as an important corollary of existentialism; or are the two inseparable? One need not await the breakdown of the bibliography as a tool in order to raise these issues; indeed they should be held in the foreground by anybody dealing with the subject. The compiler of the present bibliography had to take these and many other questions into account, and he had to answer them before he embarked on the actual project of compiling the bibliography. His answers formed, unavoidably, the presuppositions upon which the compilation is based and from which it took its present form. At the same time, it is certain that in the course of the actual preparation of the bibliography certain choices and decisions had to be made which called at least some of the presuppositions into question, and thus modified the procedure even while it was being carried out.

The compiler, therefore, had to grapple with fundamental issues before he could ever set out to prepare his bibliography. He must have started with a good understanding of existentialism; otherwise he could not have even contemplated the project. Between the intention to prepare this guide and the actual preparation of it, however, he went through a very complex and significant process. Confronted by the immediacy of choice and the necessity to exercise his judgement, he had to not only bring his understanding of existentialism to bear upon his decisions, but he opened that understanding to the possibility of modification, severe challenge, and perhaps even radical revision. The good bibliographer who approaches his task with openness and generosity—the marks of authentic exploration—cannot rely on received notions. The author of this guide embarked on the risky journey of interpretation, from which he could have steered clear by preparing a bibliography on Sartre, or Heidegger, or Jaspers, or on all three Instead we have a bibliographic guide to existentialism, and this immediately places the compiler in an interpretative role; a role in which one's own prior understanding of a subject is placed at risk. But such a risk is a *sine qua non* for anyone genuinely interested in exploring any branch of human knowledge. The choice is quite simple: one either relies on and accepts what is handed down, or else one engages what is received in a dialectical dialogue of rational inquiry. Only when the latter course is adopted is there the possibility of genuine dis-covery. A smug acceptance of received notions inevitably causes the forgetting and obscuring of the radical sources of human inquiry. The authentic scholar and researcher must be forever engaged in an unending process of exploration which does not lead to a final goal, but rather keeps un-covering that which is constantly in danger of being forgotten. In T. S. Eliot's words:

> We shall not cease from exploration
> And the end of all our exploring
> Will be to arrive where we started
> And know the place for the first time.

The "end" of which Eliot speaks is no end at all, for it marks the beginning of yet another journey in the interpretative (i.e. hermeneutic) circle. What really matters, though, is not the attainment of the end but the return which enables us to see what we already know for the first time.

There is, of course, no point at which this interpretative cycle stops—it is an incessant process of disclosive repetition, an open ended dialectic which aims not at the closure of synthesis but at the revelation of that which is all too often in danger of falling into oblivion. Repetition of this kind wards off forgetting. This is a notion of tremendous importance in existentialist thought, as evidenced by its centrality in the writings of, among others, Kierkegaard and Heidegger. Nevertheless, those who study and write about existentialism run the peril of falling into the error of reducing the whole intellectual movement to a fixed definition, or a set of carefully formulated axioms. The temptation is very strong to explain existentialism in such a way as to make it graspable, even marketable. The desire to achieve mastery by crystallizing a concept, by naming it, by pinning it down (i.e. by fixing it "in a formulated phrase") threatens to overwhelm the authentic search for understanding. Hence the work of the bibliographer might have the unintended effect of obviating its user's need to ask those fundamental questions which the bibliographer himself asked. It is essential, if existential thought is to be truly understood, that this bibliographic guide does not become for its user a handy Baedeker, a convenient chart which imposes a sense of organization and order over an immensely complex and confusing field. Rather, it should be seen as opening vast areas waiting to be explored; or, better still, it should be the occasion for a serious commitment to encounter existentialist thought once again and come to know it anew. Indeed, the time has come to retrieve existentialist thought from the clichés which submerge the fundamental questions it raises, questions which seem to be receding into the background even while the word 'existentialism' gains wider currency.

The need to re-open the discussion on the radical questions brought to the fore by existentialist thinkers is a real one, for a number of reasons. First of all, the terms 'existentialism' and 'existentialist' have for a long period of time, particularly in the 1950's and 60's, been used loosely and indiscriminately. They came to characterize little more than an ill-defined and amorphous fad. It was, for a time, fashionable to declare oneself an existentialist. Also, and largely as a direct consequence of this fashion, several words and phrases associated with existentialist thought—words or phrases like '*Angst*' and 'dread', 'authentic', 'bad faith', 'alienation', '*malaise*', etc.—have become clichés. There utterance is seldom accompanied by an awareness of their real significance in their original context. Further, it has become habitual to talk and write about existentialism without paying much attention to the basic existentialist texts. College courses on 'Existentialism' are frequently taught with reading lists which include nothing other than novels and plays. Philosophic rigor tends to fall by the wayside and give way to the pleasantries of a superficial, content-oriented type of literary analysis. A philosophic thrust which sought to shake the foundations of western thought is now frequently, though by no means always, approached with astounding suavity and detachment. Existentialism has been rendered 'safe.' The ease with which explanations are offered in introductory essays and certain handbooks has diluted the sense of the acuteness of the existentialist's dis-ease in the face of the contingent world into which he finds himself thrown. Existentialism has, perhaps, been domesticated, its sting has been removed, its challenge muted.

It is not entirely surprising that this has occurred in the Anglo-American *milieu,* for existentialist thought emerged almost entirely from the European continent. The most important works appeared in alien languages and they seemed to address none of the issues which for long have preoccupied the majority of British and American philosophers. Existentialism has little in common with the empiricist and positivist traditions long prevalent in the English speaking world. This does not mean that it has been ignored, but certainly the writings of Heidegger, to take only one example, have attracted much less attention in England and North America (but most especially in England) than they have in continental Europe. Several attempts were made, even as far back as the 40's, to explain existentialism to an English speaking audience. But these have been, for the most part, sketchy efforts written, generally, from well-entrenched positions. In 1947, for example, F. C. Copleston published two essays, "What is Existentialism?" and "Existentialism and Religion," in which he offers his readers a fairly good description of the basic ideas set forth by existentialists. In both instances, however, it is obvious that his position *vis-a-vis* existentialism is determined *a priori* by his intent to defend theism and by his scholastic orientation. Whatever understanding of existentialism emerged from such treatments could not have been very sympathetic. Many of the earliest essays in English betray a hostile insularity and impart incomplete and distorted versions of existentialist thought. Furthermore, existentialism has received the enthusiastic attention of several writers who are not themselves trained in philosophy, and this has contributed to a popularization which engenders further distortion and misunderstanding.

Not all the works on existentialism in English offer partial or distorted views. Some excellent studies have been produced by English and American authors on existentialism in general as well as on individual existentialist philosophers. These works do not, however, necessarily enjoy the widest circulation, nor are they always the more easily available ones. Moreover, the better books on the subject tend to be difficult and require concentration and perseverance from the reader. This is necessarily so, for the writings of Kierkegaard, Nietzsche, Heidegger, Jaspers, Sartre (excluding the plays, novels, and journalistic pieces), Marcel, Merleau-Ponty, and others are anything but simple either in what they treat or in the way they treat it. They are sustained arguments and presentations of the kind one expects in serious philosophical investigation. It would be as reasonable to call for an 'easy' explanation of Heidegger as it would be to call for a popular version of Kant's or Hegel's work. Kant and Hegel, though, never became 'fashionable' in the way Sartre, for example, did. There was never a popular market for Kant or Hegel, whereas existentialism is a topic that sells well. College courses on Hegel attract a dedicated few, while courses on existentialism (often offered by literature departments who would never dream of devoting a whole course to the study of Hegelianism and neo-Hegelianism, notwithstanding the fact that such a subject has a direct bearing on the study of literature and critical theory) draw huge crowds. Many of those who pack the classes which expose them to the joys of reading *Nausea, The Stranger, The Plague, Notes from Underground, Waiting for Godot, The Trial,* etc. are curiosity seekers looking for something 'different' and would never enroll in a course that offers them the opportunity to take a close and disciplined look at *Concluding Unscientific Postscript, Being and Time,* and *Being and Nothingness.* It is, therefore, easy to see why Sartre and Camus are almost household words on the university campuses. Their novels and plays have a vast readership and a student familiar with *Nausea* and *The Stranger* is easily led to foster the illusion that he is versed in the basic tenets of existentialism. In this way the term 'existentialism' becomes meaningless, as a mass of vague notions are lumped together with little discrimination and distinction.

For a good example of the type of writing on existentialism which encourages the undisciplined thinking that has hastened the forgetting of the radical features of existentialist thought, one need only turn to Hayden Carruth's introduction to the New Directions edition of *Nausea.* Carruth's essay is relatively brief and, therefore, one can hardly expect to find much detailed analysis in it. Nonetheless, the generalizations which abound in the essay, although not grossly inaccurate, tend to be misleading and foster the sort of vague general ideas which are ultimately devoid of any substance. After a brief explanation of how and when existentialism, in spite of initial opposition, emerged as a significant intellectual movement, Carruth proceeds to advise the reader that the word 'Existentialism' should not be used as a defining term. There are too many variants of 'Existentialism' and some existentialists refuse to be described as such. "Nevertheless," Carruth asserts, "we go on calling them Existentialists, and we are quite right to do so: as long as we use the term as a proper name, an agreed-upon semanteme, it is as good as any, or perhaps better, for signifying what unites the divergent interests." What follows is a three paragraph history of existentialism from its roots to the present. In this very brief account Carruth manages to associate so many figures and movements with existentialism that one is led to wonder whether there is anything at all distinctive about it—except, perhaps, its antirationalism. Citing William Barrett's *Irrational Man* as his source (or maybe simply as a corroborative authority), Carruth finds that

> the Existentialist impulse is coeval with the myths of Abraham and Job; it is evident in the pre-Socratic philosophies of Greece, in the dramas of Aeschylus and Euripedes, in the later Greek and Byzantine culture of mystery; and it is a thread that winds, seldom dominant but always present, through the central European tradition: the Church Fathers, Augustine, the Gnostics, Abelard, Thomas, and then the extraordinary Pascal and the Romantic tradition that took up his standard a century later. And in the Orient, concurrently, the entire development of religious and philosophical attitudes, particularly in the Buddhist and Taoist writings, seems to us now to have been frequently closer to the actual existence of mankind than the rationalist discourses of the West.

Such sweeping, all-embracing statements cannot but blur everything by putting it out of focus. If, indeed, the "Existentialist impulse" has been clearly present throughout virtually the entire history of western and eastern thought, then why does Heidegger find it necessary to undertake the task of destroying (in his sense of the word) the history of western philosophy in order to bring to light that which it has covered over? What needs to be shown is not the fact that some periods in the history of the west manifested ideas and gave rise to movements which bear resemblance to those of other periods, but rather that the fundamental question of the meaning of Being has in the course of our history been forgotten. The existentialist thinkers propose to bring this question out into the open after an inordinately long period of concealment.

In his treatment of the more recent exponents of existentialism Carruth is equally generous in admitting people to the fold. He names Heidegger, Jaspers, Marcel, and Sartre as the major existentialist philosophers. One is surprised by his omission of Merleau-Ponty, especially since he finds the space to mention Ortega, Buber, Berdyaev, and Whitehead—thinkers who "have been influenced by the main factors of Existentialist concern." Nowhere is there any mention of Husserl. In his views on literature Carruth is even less discriminating.

> In literature many, or even most, of the chief modern authors have been, consciously or not, Existentialists; certainly the tradition is very strong in the line of development represented by Kafka, Unamuno, Lawrence, Malraux, Hesse, Camus, and Faulkner. Even a writer as far removed as Robert Frost from the centers of self-conscious Existentialism joins in this alignment, as we see when we reread such poems as "The Census Taker" and "Stopping by Woods."

One rereads "Stopping by Woods" in search of an existentialist impulse (or the mere hint of any such thing) and one is left perplexed. What is not perplexing in the light of such statements, though, is why Charles Olson, whose poetry reflects so many of the views and insights found in Husserl and Heidegger, denied being an existentialist.

Hayden Carruth is, obviously, more than merely sympathetic to existentialist thought, but in his eagerness to find traces of it everywhere he loses sight of its true character. He claims that most of the major modern authors have been existentialists. This is clearly an exaggeration. There are, naturally, many areas of concern shared by numerous modern novelists and existentialist thinkers—the frightening reality of change, the collapse of man's ordered vision of the universe, the overwhelming sense of *ennui,* the dehumanizing effects of positivism. Novelists like John Galsworthy, Virginia Woolf, E. M. Forster, Ford Madox Ford, and a host of others gave prominence to such themes in their writings. But to associate them in any way with existentialism is seriously misleading. These Modernist novelists embraced an aestheticism which the existentialist philosophers regard as totally untenable. The Modernist impulse to spatialize time runs counter to the existentialist view of *Dasein* (i.e. man-in-the-world) grounded in temporality. It is highly significant that many Modernist writers found in Byzantine art (in which Carruth also detects the presence of an existentialist impulse) a perfect model for their iconic as opposed to temporal imagination. Their dedication to closed form and to the autotelic nature of the work of art was firm. The writings of Kierkegaard, Heidegger, and Sartre present a serious challenge to these Modernist tenets, and this challenge is likely to silenced by those who search so avidly for thematic similarities that they forget about the paramount importance of the role played by the handling of form. In fact, Carruth's notion of novelistic form appears to be in line with the dicta of New Criticism and is certainly not informed by an existentialist position. When he writes about the novel that "it is a self-consistent and dynamic whole," Carruth echoes an orthodox Modernist stance and misses the opportunity, which presents itself in his introductory remarks, to dwell on the radical departures in critical and literary theory brought about by existentialist thought.

Existentialism has received the attention of many writers whose primary concern is literature. There are several reasons for this. For one thing, many existentialist philosophers have written extensively on literature and some have even produced literary works of their own. Kierkegaard, many of whose writings are novelistic in form, contributed an immensely valuable study, *The Concept of Irony.* Heidegger's interest in Hölderlin, Trakl, and Rilke emerges vividly in his work, and his *Poetry, Language, Thought* is of immediate interest (as, in fact, all his other works have reason to be) to the interpreter of literature. Sarter has produced volumes of literary studies apart from his famous *What is Literature?* Hans-Georg Gadamer, Heidegger's follower, has authored a work, *Truth and Method,* which nobody engaged in critical and literary analysis can afford to ignore. These are merely a few examples. Existentialism also exercised a strong influence on literature because the writings of Kierkegaard, Heidegger, Jaspers, Sartre, Marcel, etc. touch upon matters of special interest to the novelist and dramatist. As Iris Murdoch points out, "The 'world' of *The Concept of Mind* is the world in which people play cricket, cook cakes, make simple decisions, remember their childhood and go to the circus, not the world in which they commit sins, fall in love, say prayers or join the Communist Party." The contemporary novelist would find it hard to discover source material in A. J. Ayer, Gilbert Ryle, or P. F. Strawson. The works of Kierkegaard and Sartre, on the other hand, could supply him with many points of departure. In addition to all this, Husserl's call for a return "to the things themselves," from which stems the phenomenology so central to the work of Heidegger, Sartre, and Merleau-Ponty, is echoed by a number of post-modern poets. These poets might not have been familiar with Husserl or any of the philosophers who heeded his call. Those readers, however, who come to Stevens,

Williams and Olson with the new awareness sparked by the post-Hegelian phenomenologists are in a position to read their poetry in a more meaningful, more open, and more sympathetic manner.

The impact of existentialism on literary studies has been notable and to a large degree salutary. The stranglehold of New Criticism has been loosened, and new approaches to the theory of interpretation and to literary history have been developing. In the creative field, the novel, drama, and poetry have entered into areas long left unexplored. The predictions that the collapse of the center which once held our world together will bring with it the death of the novel have, so far, been proved wrong. The new philosophy does, indeed, call all in doubt, but it has not yet reduced all to silence. But these developments have also been accompanied by an outburst of meaningless jargon and by irresponsible popularization. As a consequence, the rhetoric of existentialist thought is in danger of losing its significance. Terms are bandied around much too readily. The expression 'existentialist' has itself been rendered hollow by essayists who write of the 'existentialist novel' and the 'existentialist hero.' Dostoevsky's underground man, Sartre's Roquentin, Camus' stranger, sometimes even Kafka's Gregor Samsa have all been labelled as 'existentialist man.'

Yet, Roquentin is not 'existentialist man' at all, and whether *Nausea* is an 'existentalist novel' is at least debatable. Roquentin, like Dostoevsky's underground man, and in many respects like Tolstoy's Ivan Ilych, is a person who has reached a *cul-de-sac.* These characters, and many others like them who populate modern fiction and drama, embody the predicament of modern western man who has reached a blank wall against which his dead metaphysical tradition is useless. As a result, Roquentin and the underground man have no choice but to face despair; unless, of course, they take refuge in the dulled consciousness of the anonymous mass. They choose to turn in towards themselves and make of their despair the very sustenance that keeps them alive–they close themselves off from the world and retreat into their little corners. "I savour this total oblivion into which I have fallen," Roquentin writes. They create their own separate miserable worlds and survive but cultivating and feeding upon their misery. They are comfortable and at home when the world around them manifests its ugliness. They even try to transform their misery into a work of art. Roquentin and the underground man, seen in this way, are romantic figures. Their creators, however, do not espouse their cause, although they sympathize with their quandry. Neither Roquentin nor the underground man is an exponent of existentialist theory; they are not the fictional spokesmen of philosophers; they are not the personifications of an idea. Rather, they are examples of the modern condition, they are concrete manifestations of the bankruptcy of the western tradition. They represent, in fact, the starting point from which existentialist thought emerges. The dead end they encounter is the dead end of western metaphysics. Their cry of despair is the cry of modern man who has run out of escape routes and is forced to confront the failure and collapse of a tradition on which he has relied for so long. This tragic state of affairs is not brought about by the existentialist philosopher. The existentialist philosopher is the one who takes cognizance of this disease and redirects the attention of western man to the very ground of his being and makes him ask again the most basic of questions—the question of what it means to be.

The renewal of this question constitutes the main concern of existentialism. As existentialism receives wider and wider attention, however, there is the very real likelihood that its primary concern be forgotten. Explanations and elucidations of the admittedly difficult writings of existentialist philosophers tend to dilute the immediacy of the fundamental question. The question that was asked once needs to be asked again and it must remain a question which opens the way to investigation. And this investigation, unlike that of a detective, must remain forever open. The temptation to resort to conclusive assertion has to be resisted. One would like to assert quite simply that the quintessence of existentialism rests in the conviction that existence is prior to essence. But that will not do, for it comes too close to being a fixed definition which stills the disquiet roused by the Being-question itself. Existentialism is not a metaphysical theory that one can apprehend from a safe distance and explain. Existentialist theory cannot be mapped out; it is not homogeneous and it is not a system. It is, instead, an investigative process, an exploration. One does not so much observe existentialism as enter into it. It seems, though, that much more effort has been spent in discussing the merits and nature of the existentialist philosophy than in the pursuit of the meaning of Being. This is true of Anglo-American studies, in which some historians of philosophy express uncertainty as to whether existentialism is a school of philosophy worthy of discussion. John Passmore, for example, in *A Hundred Years of Philosophy,* opens his chapter entitled "Existentialism and Phenomenology" in the following manner:

> If, working within my self-imposed limitations, I were to make no reference whatsoever to existentialism, I could not justly be rebuked. For one thing, it has been quite without influence on the main trends in contemporary British philosophy; for another thing, in so far as it has been discussed, existentialism has been taken seriously as a stimulus to ethico-religious thinking, rather than as a metaphysics. Professional philosophers, for the most part, dismiss it with a contemptuous shrug.
>
> Yet there would be a certain cowardice in ignoring it completely, welcome, in some respects, as that decision would be. Existentialism lies on the periphery of British philosophical consciousness; it stands, to British philosophers for Continental excess and rankness.

Passmore is, self-admittedly, articulating the typical English attitude. He narrates the history of philosophy from the perspective of the British philosophical tradition. He is by no means an unprejudiced onlooker and his work has serious shortcomings. On the other hand, can there possibly be a truly objective view? Does not one necessarily bring to any discussion a set of presuppositions and expectations?

A valid discussion of existentialist philosophy must have for its starting point an analysis of those very presuppositions one brings to it. This means that one must start with a study of that tradition and those writings which have helped fashion one's notions about existentialism. The present bibliographic guide is an excellent starting point for any study of this kind. Even before leaving its pages in search of the books it lists, one learns a number of very important facts. It might be surprising for some to discover, for instance, that several works dealing with existentialism appeared in English before the major existentialist texts were translated. The length of time separating the publication of *Sein und Zeit* and its availability in translation as *Being and Time* is astounding. The first edition of Heidegger's *magnum opus* came out in 1927; the first complete English version went on sale in 1962. Before this major text was obtainable in English, though, some rather substantial books on Heidegger were being read by an Anglo-American audience. Indeed, existentialism was already being attacked and distorted, as in Bobbio's *The Philosophy of Decadentism,* the full English version of which appeared in 1948. Sartre's *L'Etre et le Neant* was published in 1943. It took thirteen years to have an English version. In the meantime, an essay by Ayer in *Horizon* (1945), Irish Murdoch's *Sartre* (in which, incidentally, some very interesting, though brief, comparisons are drawn between Sartre's ideas and the positions of major British philosophers), Desan's *The Tragic Finale,* as well as other writings had already started to fashion the English reader's ideas on Sartre. Merleau-Ponty's *Phenomenology of Perception* could be read in English in 1962, seventeen years after its original publication. Jaspers and Marcel, on the other hand, sparked a quicker response, probably because their works were of interest to theologians, and modern theology has had close affinities with the roots of existentialism. By the time *Being and Nothingness* appeared in paperback in England (University Paperbacks brought it out in 1969), existentialism was already being pronounced dead. Mary Warnock concludes her introduction to the volume in a tone reminiscent of a *post-mortem.*

> Perhaps it is right, therefore, to regard *Being and Nothingness* as the culmination of a mood—anti-rational, anti-scientific and anti-political. The book itself seems to me to be of tremendous power and interest; and the history of existentialism in general to have a certain fascination, particularly in its manner of converting the scientific aims of Husserl, in psychology and perception, into something so different yet so recognizable. But the time has come to consider existentialism as a part of the history of philosophy, not as a means of salvation nor as a doctrine of commitment. And, as for Sartre himself, we must realize that he is no longer an existentialist at all.

Although one cannot readily agree with Mary Warnock and affirm that existentialism is just another chapter in the history of philosophy, one can intuit a sense in which she is correct. Existentialism has, in a way, been dead since the moment it became an '-ism.' What we might be witnessing at present, as the word 'existentialism' is bandied around so indiscriminately, and as works about existentialism continue to proliferate is its burial. The voluminous writing *about* existentialism may be removing us farther and farther from existentialist thinking. As Heidegger very pertinently observes in his *Letter on Humanism,* " '-isms' have for a long time now been suspect. But the market of public opinion continually demands new ones. We are always prepared to supply the demand. Even such names as 'logic,' 'ethics,' and 'physics' begin to flourish only when original thinking comes to an end. During the time of their greatness the Greeks thought without such headings. They did not even call thinking 'philosophy.' Thinking comes to an end when it slips out of its element." One can understand, in the light of this remark, why Heidegger refused to be labelled an existentialist. So, what needs to be resurrected or reawakened is not so much existentialism itself, as the inquiry into the meaning of Being which the philosophers commonly referred to as existentialist declared as their project. This does not necessarily entail the abandonment of the term 'existentialism.' The term, however, needs to be revitalized; it needs to be rescued from the status of a cliche; it has to be understood anew in order that the project it stands for can be revived. What is called for, in short, is a Heideggerian destruction of the history of existentialism.

Anybody undertaking a care-ful study of existentialism is situated in a position analogous, in several ways, to that of Heidegger at the outset of *Being and Time.* Heidegger opens his book with a quotation from Plato.

> "For manifestly you have long been aware of what you mean when you use the expression '*being*'. We, however, who used to think we understood it, have now become perplexed."

He then goes on:

> Do we in our time have an answer to the question of what we really mean by the word 'being'? Not at all. So it is fitting that we should raise *anew the question of the meaning of Being.* But are we nowadays even perplexed at our inability to understand the expression 'Being'? Not at all. So first of all we must reawaken an understanding for the meaning of this question.

In a similar fashion one asks: Do we really understand what we really mean by the expression 'existentialism'? What is 'existentialism'? In order to answer such a question one must, before anything else, clear the ground of all the received notions and the distortions which cloud one's understanding. The task of destroying or, to use Derrida's term, deconstructing the history of existentialism is a task of the highest priority. And this destruction is not inspired by a negative impulse. Like Kierkegaard's attack on Christianity it is necessary for other than negative reasons. Before he could establish a proper relationship with Christianity, Kierkegaard had to liberate it from the encrustments which over the centuries had obscured its true meaning. There is, of course, a big difference between Kierkegaard's assault on the Christian tradition and the proposed destruction of the history of existentialism. Kierkegaard sought his salvation in the Christian faith. Existentialism is not a faith and it promises no salvation.

Nonetheless, existentialism needs to be dis-covered for a very important reason. A destruction of existentialism will lead us back to *the most basic of questions,* and it will set us on the way towards an understanding of the meaning of Being. The publication of this bibliographic guide is a good occasion to set out.

PREFACE

The more than two-thousand works listed here indicate the volume of material published on Existentialism. Three-quarters of the way into the twentieth century, it can be said without hesitation that Existentialism has become the major philosophy of our time. But the vast literature on the subject is, to a great extent, either inaccesible to the researcher who does not read French or German, or is scattered through hundreds of magazines, scholarly journals, and books, many of which are out-of-print.

There are bibliographies of works on Existentialism in French and German and other languages: they are noted in this Bibliography and in the index. The lists restricted to sources in English, however, are either very short or very dated. The major Bibliography used in the United States prior to this listing is Kenneth Douglas' *A Critical Bibliography of Existentialism* (The Paris School, *Yale French Studies,* Monograph No. 1), published in 1950. This Bibliography instead concentrates on works between 1950 and 1976, and has a much expanded scope.

This listing is intended to be practical, therefore, rather than historical. Not listed are works which are selections of primary sources listed here under the names of the authors and the books in which they originally appeared, newspaper or popular magazine articles, privately printed works, works in languages other than English, obituaries, and other such materials. Works by major Existential thinkers not on Existentialism, are not included. For example, Sartre's *On Cuba* and Buber's writings on the hasidim are not included in this Bibliography.

The books and articles are listed alphabetically by author's last name, and each item is numbered. At the end of the Bibliography itself is an Index divided into the following categories: Bibliographies, Buber and Jewish Existentialism, Camus, Christian Existentialism, Existentialism and Education, Heidegger, Husserl, Introductions and Anthologies, Kierkegaard, Literature and Literary Criticism, Merleau-Ponty, Nietzsche, Phenomenology, Existentialism and Political and Economic Systems, Existentialism and Psychology, and Sartre. The numbers in the index refer to item numbers, not page numbers. In this way, it is hoped that this bibliography will become a useful research tool for those interested in seriously studying any of the complex questions of Existentialism.

Where necessary, works have been annotated or cross-indexed, for clarity or as a description of contents.

In addition to the hundreds of books, bibliographies, checklists, and journals consulted, I received valuable aid and advice from my colleagues Sarah Roden (who did most of the indexing), Theodore Billy, Lawrence Shorr, Daniel Fraustino, and Dwight Linder.

Professors Joseph Buttigieg and William V. Spanos provided the impetus for this project, and created much of my interest in Existentialism. They constantly lent me books and articles, and spent many hours discussing the subject with me. This Bibliography is dedicated to them.

Leonard Orr
The Ohio State University
November 15, 1977

Contents

Foreword, by Joseph Buttigieg v

Preface xxi

Introduction 1

Bibliography 13

Subject Index 191

INTRODUCTION

Heidegger's Re-Collection of the Question of the Meaning of Being (Seinsfrage)

by Leonard Orr
The Ohio State University

> Man obviously is a being. As such he belongs to the totality of Being—just like the stone, the tree, or the eagle. To "belong" here still means to be in the order of Being. But man's distinctive feature lies in this, that he, as the being who thinks, is open to Being, face to face with Being; thus man remains referred to Being and so answers to it. Man *is* essentially this relationship of responding to Being, and he is only this.[1]

> Everything we talk about, everything we have in view, everything towards which we comport ourselves in any way, is being; what we are is being, and so is how we are. Being lies in the fact that something is, and in its Being as it is; in Reality; in presence-at-hand; in subsistence; in validity; in Dasein; in the 'there is'.[2]

It may seem retrogressive, in this fiftieth anniversary year of the publication of *Being and Time,* to return to the question of the meaning of Being Heidegger poses throughout that work, the question which he made his project to answer throughout the rest of his life. Yet, as Jarava Lal Mehta recently observed of *Being and Time,* "the main *problem* of the work, in the service of which the analysis of human existence was conducted, was largely overlooked."[3] For the most part, research in existential thinking has been diverted into the periphery of the Being-question, as though that question was finally answered for all time by Heidegger's pioneering work.

In the Preface to *Being and Time* Heidegger notes, "Do

we in our time have an answer to the question of what we really mean by the word 'being'? Not at all. So it is fitting that we should raise anew *the question of the meaning of Being.*" Immediately, in the preface, this question is given as the fundamental inquiry for man, without hinting yet what all the complexities and ramifications of the question are.

What is the meaning of the question of Being? How is it to be answered? Why should it be answered? Does it matter? Is this ontological investigation important?

The question is an ancient one, a primoridal inquiry. Why does Heidegger not feel it has been answered or, at least, that the answer has been intuited by men throughout history? Mehta realizes that "to raise the problem of Being is for Heidegger no act of homage to a hallowed tradition or indulgence in the academic pastime of speculating about abstractions; it is rather to raise the most vital and concrete of all questions."[4] This might, at first glance, not be obvious to all. But it is Heidegger's interpretation that all philosophical thinking stems from this inquiry. The most ancient thinkers who have left written records, or the Greeks in the Western intellectual tradition, do indeed begin with the Being-question. Prior to Plato, in the fragments of Heraclitus, Parmenides, and others, philosophy was involved in the ontological inquiry and questions were raised about the meaning and Being of the universe and of man in the world. After Socrates and Plato, the investigation was *ontic* rather than *ontological,* and the "particular" was analyzed rather than the Being which underlies all entities as beings. Joseph Kockelmans is correct in pointing out that "Heidegger sees the fundamental mistake of traditional metaphysics in the fact that since Plato philosophers have forgotten or neglected the essential difference between being and Being."[5] Thus, when Heidegger precedes his re-asking of the Being-question with a quote from Plato's *Sophist* the quotation acts "as a reminder that in classical metaphysics the battle of the giants over the Being of what is, has already broken out."[6] Therefore, for Heidegger and those who follow him,

> The question of Being is. . .essentially and intrinsically a historical one, requiring both a critical, regressive analysis or "destruction" of the history of ontology as well as a reconstruction of that history in the light of the deeper

> and more original understanding of Being and of man in his relationship to Being acquired in the course of the inquiry.[7]

This is the rationale behind Heidegger's lengthy restatement and reformulation of the question and the need for the rapid destruction of the Western ontotheological tradition. Destruction is not, in Heidegger, a strictly negative act but rather functions as a ground for a "calling into question" of previous assumptions. This calling into question forces the inquirer to re-examine and re-evaluate his "knowledge" and to see through the various "coverings" which his acculturation has allowed him to place over what is and so mask it. Magda King writes that "Heidegger claims to give philosophy a new start, but it is not at all evident where the newness of his question lies. It strikes us rather as the revival of an old question that has gone out of fashion."[8] This is indeed how the re-asking of the Being-qeuestion would strike the inquirers who have casually assumed that the Being-question has been answered, or else is not very important. But since it is fundamental and primordial the Being-question not only can never be "out of fashion," but *must always be continually re-asked.*

Therefore we note that the ancient Ionian philosophers, both the metaphysical monists and the metaphysical pluralists, begin with the arguments over the nature of the ontologically real: what *is* the material universe? is it made up of one substance or many? does it have one state or is it in transition, that is to say, is there both permanence and change or one or the other? Thus Xenophanes of Colophon raises the question of whether everything which is has reached its true state and full development, or whether it is in motion towards becoming what its full development will be; in other words, whether there is Being alone or becoming alone. Xenophanes identified God with the one Being, an unchanging entity which underlies all things and which is synonymous with the universe.

This questioning of Xenophanes on Being and Becoming was answered in two ways. Heraclitus of Ephesus, in his process philosophy, regarded the universe as something which was ceaselessly changing from one state to another (the figurative matter which makes up the universe was fire), and so for Heraclitus, the answer was that there is only Becoming; Being is an ideal which cannot actually exist. Xenophanes' God as one unchanging, eternal, permanently underlying Being becomes in Heraclitus' cosmology the *Archē* (originator, beginning, force, genesis, motion), the start of perenniel process. Parmenides took the opposite point of view. For him, Becoming and Not-Being were equally impossible concepts: there could only be Being. Thinking was necessarily thinking about things-which-are. Then ontology in Parmenides, as Montgomery Furth tells us, "is not 'confined' to either of our two distinct concepts, that of existence and that of being something-or-other in the sense of having such-and-such properties. . .rather, these notions are impacted or *fused* in the early Greek concept of being."[9] Kierkegaard severely criticized Spinoza in particular and the post-Socratics in general for re-separating this "fused" concept of Being. Parmenides claimed then that there was only Being; this Being is changeless and universal. The Atomist philosopher Leucippus of Abdera argued, in opposition to Parmenides, that non-Being (or Not-Being) is as real and important as Being, but we see his solely material interpretation of these modes. Being is the things which are, entities, Leucippus aruges. Entities are made of Atoms (indivisible elements) which must have room to move about. That is to say, Being must move in and be bounded by something and this something must be other than Being, and therefore is Not-Being. Because we must see that there *is* Not-Being, Not-Being is Something which exists. The Pythagoreans soon followed with a theory that Being as permanent or ultimately real must *be* Numbers, or the mathematical. Their argument was that mathematical laws seem to govern or dictate shape and design of physical objects and such intangibles as music; even though the entities under analysis constantly change the mathematical hypotheses and axioms remain, alone, permanent. Therefore, mathematics defines and delimits reality or Being.

Of these early thinkers, Heidegger is most attracted to Parmenides from *Being and Time* on. In the late collection, *On Time and Being,* Heidegger meditates on a poem by Parmenides which "was the first to reflect explicitly upon the Being of beings" and idiosyncratically interprets a passage:

> . . .but you should learn all:
> the untrembling heart of unconcealment, well-rounded
> and also the opinions of mortals,

lacking the ability to trust what is unconcealed.

Aletheia, unconcealment, is named here.[10]

Heidegger consistently interprets the Greek word for truth, *Aletheia,* as "unconcealment" or "uncovering that which has been covered over." By this he means the removal or, at least, the "bracketting" of received assumptions about Being in order to see Being as it is; this type of truth-seeing is consistent with the Husserlian "return to the things themselves." Being must be opened up so that the inquirer can confront it; it must be "disclosed." " 'Disclosure of being' means the unlocking of what forgetfulness of being closes and hides."[11] The early philosophers we have just spoken about, Heidegger claims, were close to Being and kept asking and thinking about the Being-question. This forgetting of the Being-question (*Seinsforgessenheit*) is post-Socratic and indicates the decline of authentic thinking and disclosure of Being. Parmenides encourages originative thinking about being through investigative inquiry. Furth explains that "the type of 'enquiry,' *dizēsis,* which Parmenides has in mind, is of a very large kind indeed: some enormous *Seinsfrage* that would be expressed, *is it*? (answer, *it is*); or again, *what is*? (answer, *what is*)."[12] Socrates believed in this method of inquiry to disclose truth; indeed, his famous *maieutic* or dialectic method is based on the idea (it is interesting that Heidegger, according to Walter Biemel, Hannah Arendt and others, always used and excelled in the "Socratic method" of teaching in his seminars). Socrates did not give a student answers to a question or problem, but instead would relentlessly ask and re-ask one question after another, returning to former questions but receiving new answers built on the accumulated questions, until finally the student perceived the answer to the question himself. The idea behind this was that all answers are innate and need only to be drawn out from the person through his covering assumptions. This is guiding reason behind the constant redefinition of terms in the "Socratic method."

But Socrates' own followers got away from this: they concentrated on giving answers instead of asking questions. One of the first things they did after Socrates' death was to add Socrates' notion of the Good to the earlier, Eleatic, ideas of Being until Being came to be solely identified with the Good, thus subjecting Being to a moral onus prior to complete ontological analysis. The Being-question as an issue was further clouded by Plato's *Ideal* in which he makes the differentiation between the ontologically real or *Ontos* (Being as a permanent and sublime object, and the phenomena empirically observable which is a representation of the Ideal or *Ontos* and is constantly striving to attain identification with the Ideal (or, in other words, is always Becoming). This Platonic idea of the two states (which we might see as Being and being), a "heavenly" state and an earthly or everyday state, became immediately popular because of the way it combines and answers both Heraclitus and Parmenides. Plato also delineated certain qualities of the two states: space and time, for example, in this ontology, exist only in the phenomenal or earthly world, and not in the Ideal. This is in contradiction, Heidegger claims, to the earliest Greek notions of Being in which time is the horizon of Being and its ground. Being was thought of as the presence of what is present (*einai*), or "to-be-present" (*Anwesen*).

By the time of Aristotle, who, like Plato, identified Being with "true statements" and not-being with "false statements"[13], Being in its originative mode as "presence" or as that-which-*is*, ceased as a concept. The Being-question was held to be a dead issue although it had never been satisfactorily treated. Moreover the post-Socratic wrenching apart of Being into an atemporal and aspatial Ideal and an upwardly mobile empirical world which is an imitation or representation of the eternal ultimate reality, overtook the Western tradition and closed it off entirely to the Being-question. Also, Plato and Aristotle still left impacted or fused existence and essence and Being as meaning cognition or perception of the phenomena, facts exploited by such philosophers as Descartes. It was not until Søren Kierkegaard, in two works of 1844, that the Being-question was once again properly raised and an attempt was made to separate existence and essence. First, in the *Philosophical Fragments,* Kierkegaard criticizes Spinoza and the other rationalists who do not make these distinctions, and then, in *The Concept of Dread,* he emphasizes that "all things and all circumstances have an essence-aspect and a being-aspect, contingency[14] is fate's being-aspect, whereas its essence comes under necessity, which is characteristic of all essence determinants."[15]

Until Heidegger, however, Hegel overshadowed Kierkegaard, and the Being-question was hidden over still further.

Hegel's attraction to triadic structuring caused him to see three possibilities with relation to existence: Being, Becoming, and Nothing.

> The notion of Being is chosen by Hegel as the beginning of his logical Dialectic because an acknowledgement of Being. . .seems to him the simplest and most fundamental of thinking approaches. . .Hegel is conscious of some paradox in making Pure Being his absolute beginning. The system he is about to develop forms a closed, and not an open series, and this would seem to preclude it from having an absolute beginning.[16]

Hegel systematized the idea of mediation: any two contradictory and hostile elements may be forced together (*aufgehoben*) and reconciled to a medial position. Therefore, starting with the contradictions of Being and Nothing, in his *Encyclopaedia,* he sees Becoming as the mediation. The Heraclitean solution is a simple way for Hegel to dismiss the bothersome concepts of Being and Nothing by the transitory, fleeting Becoming. Hegel did not have to analyze either Being or Nothing because he believed that "acknowledgement of mere Being always occurs at the level of simple sense-certainty."[17] Hegel in fact comes to see Being and Nothing as one and the same, as abstractions removed from reality. Separate, they do not exist for there is no change or process in Hegel's "pure" Being or Nothing, and what does not change cannot be. Becoming is the mode of Hegel's "momentum" because as one thing becomes, it *is,* and simultaneously something else (whatever it was before it became) ceases to be. So Becoming provides the momentum. J. N. Findlay notes that "this notion of Becoming does nothing, however, to remedy the *emptiness* which is alike characteristic of pure Being and all-exclusive Nothing: it becomes, perhaps, a two-edged, vibrant emptiness, but it remains as void of content as ever."[18]

But the most interesting idea in Hegel's "ontology" is the belief that we innately realize what Being is through "simple sense-certainty" because this widely held point-of-view, Heidegger says, is the main reason for the forgetting or dismissing of the Being-question.

> . . .A dogma has been developed which not only declares the question about the meaning of Being to be super-

> fluous, but sanctions its complete neglect. It is said that 'Being' is the most universal and emptiest of concepts. As such it resists every attempt at definition. Nor does this . . .concept require any definition, for everyone uses it constantly and already understands what he means by it.[19]

The verb "is" and the infinitive "to be" are the most common verb-variatns in English and almost every other Western language. Mehta reminds us that "the fact that we always have a certain understanding of Being, and that, nevertheless, the meaning of Being is shrouded in darkness, only goes to establish the necessity of raising again the problem of what 'Being' means."[20] It is something of a privilege man possesses, to be able to confront and question the meaning of Being. In Aristotle and Descartes man is defined as the thinking animal; in Heidegger man would be defined as the being who may ask the *Seinsfrage.* Joseph Kockelmans explains:

> By saying of a table that it is, one wants to express that once it is made, it is definitively determined in its being. Of itself, the table cannot change and has no possibility to relate itself either toward itself or other be-ings. There are no possibilities at all for it. For man, however, the situation is entirely different. In his being man is not determined once and for all. His being is distinguished from that of things precisely in that it can always be further realized. By seizing his given possibilities freely in a certain way, he arrives at the way of being proper to him.[21]

Therefore descriptions of Being and "how it stands with Being" must be entirely different than descriptions of entities, or the inquirer will be lead away from the originative nature of Being into those assumptions which prevent Being from actual discovery and meaningful recollection. This questioning of the meaning of Being should not exist solely in abstract thinking, as in Hegel. Kierkegaard reminds us of this in the *Concluding Unscientific Postscript:* "Because abstract thought is *sub specie aeterni,* it ignores the concrete and the temporal, the existential process, the predicament of the existing individual arising from his being a synthesis of the temporal and the eternal situated in existence. . ."[22] The task is to confront Being. In speaking of

the *Seinsfrage,* Heidegger asks rhetorically in *Being and Time,* "Does it simply remain—or is it at all—a mere matter for soaring speculation about the most general of all generalities, *or is it rather, of all questions, both the most basic and the most concrete*?"[23] Almost thirty years later Heidegger responded to his own question in *An Introduction to Metaphysics:*

> Because the understanding of being resides first and foremost in a vague, indefinite meaning, and yet remains certain and definite; because, accordingly, the understanding of being, with all its rank, remains obscure, confused, and hidden, it must be elucidated, disentangled, and torn from its concealment. This can be done only if we inquire *about* this understanding of being which we are first accepted as a mere fact—if we put it into question.[24]

NOTES

[1]Martin Heidegger, *Identity and Difference,* tr. Joan Stambaugh (New York: Harper and Row, Torchbooks, 1969), p. 31.

[2]Martin Heidegger, *Being and Time,* tr. John Macquarrie and Edward Robinson (New York: Harper and Row, 1962), p. 26.

[3]Jarava Lal Mehta, *Martin Heidegger: The Way and the Vision,* rev. ed. (Honolulu: University Press of Hawaii, 1976), p. 29.

[4]*Ibid.,* p. 90.

[5]Joseph J. Kockelmans, *Martin Heidegger: A First Introduction to His Philosophy* (Pittsburgh: Duquesne University Press, 1965), p. 165.

[6]Mehta, p. 28.

[7]*Ibid.,* p. 355.

[8]Magda King, *Heidegger's Philosophy: A Guide to His Basic Thought* (New York: Macmillan Co., 1964), pp. 5-6.

[9]Montgomery Furth, "Elements of Eleatic Ontology," in A. P. D. Mourelatos, ed., *The Pre-Socratics: A Collection of Critical Essays* (New York: Doubleday/Anchor Press, 1974), p. 243.

[10]Martin Heidegger, "The End of Philosophy" in *On Time and Being,* tr. Joan Stambaugh (New York: Harper and Row, 1972), p. 67.

[11]Martin Heidegger, *An Introduction to Metaphysics,* tr. by Ralph Manheim (New Haven: Yale University Press, 1959), p. 16. See William B. Macomber, *The Anatomy of Disillusion: Martin Heidegger's Notion of Truth* (Evanston: Northwestern University Press, 1967) for the most complete analysis of Heidegger's "re-collection" of *aletheia.*

[12]Furth, p. 248.

[13]See W. D. Ross, ed. and tr., *Aristotle: Selections,* rev. ed. (New York: Barnes and Noble, 1966), pp. 53, 60, and elsewhere.

[14]This "contingent" aspect has a continuity in the writings of Dostoyevsky, Nietzsche, and Sartre, and in Heidegger's analysis of "throwness."

[15]Gregor Malantschuk, *Kierkegaard's Thought,* tr. by H. V. and E. H. Hong (Princeton: Princeton University Press, 1971), pp. 267-268.

[16]J. N. Findlay, *Hegel: A Re-Examination* (New York: Oxford University Press Paperback, 1976), pp. 153, 154.

[17]*Ibid.,* p. 155.

[18]*Ibid.,* p. 158.

[19]Heidegger, *Being and Time,* p. 21.

[20]Mehta, p. 88.

[21]Kockelmans, p. 142.

[22]Søren Kierkegaard, *Concluding Unscientific Postscript to the Philosophical Fragments,* tr. by D. F. Swenson and Walter Lowrie (London, 1941), p. 267.

[23]Heidegger, *Being and Time,* p. 29.

[24]Heidegger, *An Introduction to Metaphysics,* p. 70.

1. Abbagnano, Nicola. *Critical Existentialism,* tr. and ed. by Nino Languilli (New York: Anchor Books, 1969).

2. –, "Outline of a Philosophy of Existence," *Philosophy and Phenomenological Research,* IX (1948), pp. 200-211.

3. Abel, Lionel. "Albert Camus, Moralist of Feeling," *Commentary,* XXXI, 2 (February, 1961), pp. 172-175.

4. –, "The Existence of Jews and Existentialism," *Politics,* VI (1949), pp. 37-40.

5. –, "Sartre vs. Lévi-Strauss: Who are the Radicals Today?" *Commonweal,* LXXXIV (June 17, 1966), pp. 364-368.

6. Abraham, Claude K. "Caligula: Drama of Revolt or Drama of Deception?" *Modern Drama,* V, 4 (1963), pp. 451-453.

7. Abrams, Fred, "Sartre, Unamuno, and the 'Hole Theory'," *Romance Notes,* V, 1 (1963), pp. 6-12.

8. Adamczewski, Zygmunt, "Martin Heidegger and Man's Way to Be," *Man and World,* I (1968), pp. 363-379.

9. –, "On the Way to Being (Reflecting on Conversations with Heidegger)" in John Sallis, ed., *Heidegger and the Path of Thinking* (Pittsburgh, Duquesne University Press, 1970), pp. 12-36.

10. Adams, J. L. *Paul Tillich's Philosophy of Culture, Science, and Religion* (New York: Harper and Row, 1965).

11. Adkins, Arthur W. H., "Heidegger and Language," *Philosophy,* XXXVII (1962), pp. 229-237.

Takes issue with many of Heidegger's etymological investigations into primordial (i.e., Pre-Socratic) meanings of important terms.

12. Adler, F., "The Social Thought of Jean-Paul Sartre," *American Journal of Sociology,* LV (1949), pp. 284-294.

13. Adorno, T. W., "On Kierkegaard's Doctrine of Love," *Studies in Philosophy and Social Science,* VIII (1940), pp. 413-429.

14. Agus, Jacob. *Modern Philosophies of Judaism* (New York: Behrman's Jewish Book House, 1941).

    Contains very good sections on Buber's dialogic Jewish existentialism.

15. Ahlstrom, Sidney E., "The Continental Influence on American Christian Thought Since World War I," *Church History,* XXVIII (1958), pp. 256-272.

16. Aiken, Henry David, "Introduction to *Zarathustra,*" in Robert Solomon, ed., *Nietzsche: A Collection of Critical Essays* (New York: Anchor Press, 1973), pp. 114-130.

17. –, "The Revolt Against Ideology," *Commentary,* XXXVII, 4 (April, 1964), pp. 29-39.

18. Albérès, R.-M. *Jean-Paul Sartre: Philosopher Without Faith,* tr. by Wade Baskin (New York: Philosophical Library, 1961).

19. Alderman, Harold G. *Heidegger and the Overthrow of Philosophy,* Ph.D. diss., Tulane University (1968).

20. –, "Heidegger on Being Human," *Philosophy Today,* XV (1971), pp. 16-29.

21. –, "Heidegger on the Nature of Metaphysics," *Journal of the British Society for Phenomenology,* III (1971), pp. 12-22.

22. —, "Heidegger: The Necessity and Structure of the Question of Being," *Philosophy Today,* XIV (1970), pp. 141-147.

23. —, "Heidegger's Critique of Science," *The Personalist,* L (1969), pp. 549-558.

24. —, "The Work of Art and Other Things," in Edward G. Ballard and Charles E. Scott, eds., *Martin Heidegger in Europe and America* (The Hague: Martinus Nijhoff, 1973), pp. 157-170.

25. Aler, Jan, "Heidegger's Conception of Language in *Being and Time*," in Joseph J. Kockelmans, ed., *On Heidegger and Language* (Evanston: Northwestern University Press, 1972), pp. 33-64.

26. Alexander, I. W., "Jean-Paul Sartre and Existentialist Philosophy," *Cambridge Journal,* I (1948), pp. 720-736.

27. —, "What is Phenomenology?" *Journal of the British Society for Phenomenology,* I (1970), p. 3.

28. Allen, Edgar Leonard, "The Challenge of Nietzsche," *London Quarterly and Holborn Review* (1953), pp. 206-210.

29. —, "Existentialism," *Adelphi,* II (1948), pp. 157-160.

30. —, "Existentialism and Christian Faith," *Congregational Quarterly* (April, 1949), pp. 156-164.

31. —. *Existentialism from Within* (Westport: Greenwood Press, 1973).

32. —, "Existential Sacramentalism," *Religion in Life,* XXII (1953), pp. 364-370.

33. —. *Freedom in God: A Guide to the Thought of Nicholas Berdyaev* (New York: Philosophical Library, 1951).

34. —, "Introduction to Kierkegaard," *Durham University Journal,* XXXVI (1943), pp. 9-14.

35. —, "Justification and Self-Justification in Sartre," *Theology Today*, XVIII (1961), pp. 150-158.

36. —, "Kierkegaard and Karl Marx," *Theology*, XL (1940), pp. 117-121.

37. —. *Kierkegaard: His Life and Thought* (Nott, 1935).

38. —, "Pascal and Kierkegaard," *London Quarterly and Holborn Review*, CLXII (1937), pp. 150-164.

39. —. *The Self and its Hazards: A Guide to the Thought of Karl Jaspers* (London: Hadder and Stoughton, 1953).

40. Allers, R. *Existentialism and Psychiatry* (Springfield: C. C. Thomas, 1961).

41. —, "Heidegger on the Principle of Sufficient Reason," *Philosophy and Phenomenological Research*, XX (1959-1960), pp. 365-373.

42. —, "The meaning of Heidegger," *The New Scholasticism*, XXXVI (1962), pp. 445-474.

43. —, "On Darkness, Silence, and the Nought," *The Thomist*, IX (1946), pp. 515-572.

44. Allison, Henry E., "Christianity and Nonsense," *Review of Metaphysics*, XX (1967), pp. 432-460.

45. —, "Kierkegaard's Dialectic of the Religious Consciousness," *Union Seminary Quarterly Review*, XX (1965), pp. 225-233.

46. Allport, G. *Becoming* (New Haven: Yale University Press, 1955).

47. —, "Comment on Existentialism and Psychology," *Existential Inquiry*, 1 (1960), p. 6.

48. Alter, Jean V., "Faulkner, Sartre, and the Nouveau Roman," *Symposium*, XX (1966), pp. 101-112.

49. Altizer, Thomas J., "The Influence of Nietzsche upon Contemporary Theology," *Emory University Quarterly,* XVI (1960), pp. 152-163.

50. Alvarez de Vayo, J., "Politics and the Intellectual," *The Nation* (September 28, 1946), pp. 346-349.

51. Ames, Van Meter, "Existentialism and the Arts," *Journal of Aesthetics and Art Criticism,* IX (1951), pp. 252-256.

52. –, "Fetishism in the Existentialism of Sartre," *Journal of Philosophy,* XLVII (1950), pp. 407-411.

53. –, "Mead and Sartre on Man," *Journal of Philosophy,* LIII (1956), pp. 205-219.

54. Anderson, Adele B. *The Political Implications of Jean-Paul Sartre's Concept of Freedom and Responsibility,* Ph.D. diss., Claremont Graduate School (1968).

55. Anderson, Betty C., "The Melville-Kierkegaard Syndrome," *Rendezvous,* III (1968), pp. 41-53.

56. Anderson, D., "Images of Man in Sartre and Camus," *Modern Churchman,* VIII (October, 1964), pp. 33-45.

57. Anderson, J. M., "On Heidegger's Gelassenheit: A Study in the Nature of Thought," *Journal of Existentialism,* V (1964-1965), pp. 339-351.

58. Anderson, Thomas C., "Is a Sartrean Ethics Possible?" *Philosophy Today,* XIV (1970), pp. 116-140.

59. –, "Neglected Sartrean Arguments for the Freedom of Consciousness," *Philosophy Today,* XVII (1973), pp. 28-38.

60. Andreas-Salomé, Lou. *Nietzsche* (New York: Gordon and Breach, 1960).

61. Anonymous, "Absurdiste," *New Yorker,* XXII (April 20, 1946), pp. 22-23.

62. –, "Choose, Leap, and Be Free," *Times Literary Supplement,* XLV (March 9, 1946), pp. 109-111.

63. Ansbacher, R., "The Third Viennese School of Psychotherapy," *Journal of Individual Psychology,* XV (1959), pp. 236-237.

64. Ansbro, John J., "Kierkegaard's Gospel of Suffering," *Philosophical Studies,* XVI (1967), pp. 182-192.

65. Arbaugh, George B. and George E. *Kierkegaard's Authorship: A Guide to the Writings of Kierkegaard* (Rock Island, Illinois: Augustana College Library, 1967).

66. Arendt, Hannah, "French Existentialism," *The Nation* (February 23, 1946), pp. 226-228.

67. –, "Jaspers as Citizen of the World," in Paul Schilpp, ed., *The Philosophy of Karl Jaspers* (New York: Tudor Pub. Co., 1957), pp. 539-550.

68. –, "What is Existenz Philosophy?" *Partisan Review* (Winter, 1946).

69. Arnaud, Pierre, "Aftermath—A Young Philosopher's View," tr. by Derek Aiken, *Yale French Studies,* XVI (1955), pp. 106-110.

70. Arnold, M. and J. A. Gasson. *The Human Person* (New York: Ronald Press, 1954).

See esp. Chapter XVI, "Logotherapy and Existential Analysis."

71. Arnou, René, "Existentialism in France Today," *The Modern Schoolman,* XXIV (1946-1947), pp. 193-199.

72. Aron, Raymond. *Marxism and the Existentialists* (New York: Harper and Row, 1969).

73. Aronson, A. R. *Art and Freedom in the Philosophy of Jean Paul Sartre,* Ph.D. diss., Brandeis University (1968).

74. –, "Interpreting Husserl and Heidegger: The Root of Sartre's Thought," *Telos,* V (1972), pp. 47-67.

75. Ashmore, J., "Existentialist Themes in Stephen Greene," *College Art Journal,* XVII (1958), pp. 160-170.

76. Attwater, D. *Modern Christian Revolutionaries* (New York: Devin-Adair Co., 1947).

77. Atwell, John E., "Existence Precedes Essence," *Man and World,* II, 4 (1969), pp. 580-591.

78. –, "Sartre's Conception of Action and his Utilization of *Wesenschau,*" *Man and World,* V, 2 (1972), pp. 143-157.

79. Auden, W. H., "Knight of Doleful Countenance," *New Yorker* (May 25, 1968), pp. 141-142, 146-148, 151-154, 157-158.

80. Awerkamp, D., "Heidegger and the Problem of God," *Duns Scotus Philosophical Association,* XXIX (1965), pp. 75-97.

81. Ayer, A. J., "Albert Camus," *Horizon,* XIII, 75 (March, 1946), pp. 155-168.

82. –, "The Definition of Liberty: Jean-Paul Sartre's Doctrine of Commitment," *The Listener* (November 30, 1950), pp. 633-634.

83. –, "Jean-Paul Sartre," *Horizon,* XII (1945), pp. 12-26.

84. –, "Reflexions on Existentialism," *Modern Languages,* XLVIII (March, 1967), pp. 1-12.

85. Babbage, S. Barton, "Soren Kierkegaard," *Evangelical Quarterly* (January, 1943), pp. 56-72.

86. Bachelard, Suzanne. *A Study of Husserl's Formal and Transcendental Logic,* tr. by Lester E. Embree (Evanston: Northwestern University Press, 1968).

87. Badt-Strauss, Bertha, "Martin Buber," *The Jewish Spectator,* XIII (May, 1948), pp. 22ff.

88. Bailey, Anthony, "The Isolated Man," *Commonweal,* LXVII, 4 (October, 1957), pp. 91-93.

89. Bailey, Roland. *What is Existentialism? The Creed of Commitment and Action* (London: S.P.C. K., 1950).

90. Bailiff, J. D. *Coming to Be: An Interpretation of the Self in the Thought of Martin Heidegger,* Ph.D. diss., Pennsylvania State University (1966).

91. Baillie, John. *Our Knowledge of God* (New York: Charles Scribner's Sons, 1939).

Pp. 161, 201-239, deal with Buber.

92. Bain, J. M. *Soren Kierkegaard: His Life and Religious Teaching* (London: Student Christian Movement Press, 1935).

93. Ballard, Edward G., "A Brief Introduction to the Philosophy of Martin Heidegger," *Tulane Studies in Philosophy,* XII (1963), pp. 106-151.

94. –, "Heidegger's View and Evaluation of Nature and Natural Science," in John Sallis, ed., *Heidegger and the Path of Thinking* (Pittsburgh: Duquesne University Press, 1970), pp. 37-64.

95. – and Charles E. Scott, eds. *Martin Heidegger in Europe and America* (The Hague: Martinus Nijhoff, 1973).

96. –, "On the Pattern of the Phenomenological Method," *Southern Journal of Philosophy,* VIII (1970), pp. 421-431.

97. Bannan, John F. *The Philosophy of Merleau-Ponty* (New York: Harcourt, Brace, 1967).

98. –, "The Psychiatry, Psychology, and Phenomenology of Sartre," *Journal of Existential Psychiatry,* I (1960),

pp. 176-187.

99. Bannerjea, Devendra, "The Indian Origin of Nietzsche's Theory of the Eternal Return," *German Life and Letters,* VII (1954), pp. 161-169.

100. Barnes, Hazel, "Adler and Sartre: A Comment," *Journal of Individual Psychology,* XXI, 2 (1965).

101. –. *An Existentialist Ethics* (New York: Alfred Knopf, 1967).

102. –, "Balance and Tension in the Philosophy of Camus," *The Personalist,* XLI, 4 (October, 1960), pp. 433-447.

103. –, "Introduction" to Jean-Paul Sartre's *Being and Nothingness* (Philosophical Library, 1956).

Barnes was Sartre's translator for this work, and her introduction provides a good grounding for the reading of all Sartrean philosophy.

104. –, "Jean-Paul Sartre and the Haunted Self," *Western Humanities Review,* X (1956), pp. 119-128.

105. –, "Jean-Paul Sartre and the Outside World," *Chicago Review,* XV (1961), pp. 107-112.

106. –, "Literature as Salvation in the Work of Jean-Paul Sartre," *American Catholic Philosophical Association Proceedings,* XXXIX (1965), pp. 53-68.

107. –. *The Literature of Possibility: A Study in Humanistic Existentialism* (Lincoln: University of Nebraska Press, 1959).

108. –, "Measure of Magnificence," *Prairie Schooner,* XXIV, 2 (1960), pp. 115-119.

109. –, "Modes of Aesthetic Consciousness in Fiction," *Bucknell Review,* XII, 1 (1964), pp. 82-93.

110. –. *Sartre* (London: Quartet Books, 1974).

111. –, "Transcendence Toward What: Is the Universe Like Us?" *Religious Humanism,* IV (Winter, 1970), pp. 11-14.

112. Barral, Mary Rose. *Merleau-Ponty: The Role of the Body-Subject in Interpersonal Relations* (Pittsburgh: Duquesne University Press, 1965).

113. Barrett, Cyril, "Soren Kierkegaard: An Exception," *Studies,* XLV (1956), pp. 77-83.

114. Barrett, William, "The End of Modern Literature: Existentialism and Crisis," in Morton D. Zabel, ed., *Literary Opinion in America* (New York: Harper, 1951), pp. 749-756.

115. –. *Irrational Man: A Study in Existential Philosophy* (New York: Doubleday, 1958).

Since its publication, this work has been *the* introductory source on Existentialism. It is clear and without the overwhelming jargon which is the major boundary in the introductory texts on Existentialism. Barrett begins by providing an overview of the major themes of Existentialism, gives a history of the sources of Existential thought, and then has general essays of about thirty pages each on Kierkegaard, Nietzsche, Heidegger, and Sartre. He then deals with the impact Existentialism has had in a number of fields.

116. –, "Talent and Career of Jean-Paul Sartre," *Partisan Review,* XIII (1946), pp. 237-246.

117. –. *What is Existentialism?* (New York: Grove Press, 1964).

118. Barry, J. L., "Sartre and Simone de Beauvoir," *Carleton Miscellany,* XXI (February-March, 1965), pp. 62-66.

119. Barth, Karl, "Kierkegaard and the Theologians," tr. by H. M. Rumscheidt, *Canadian Journal of Theology,* XIII (January, 1967), pp. 64-65.

120. Bartky, S. L., "Heidegger's Philosophy of Art," *British Jour-*

nal of Aesthetics, IX (1969), pp. 353-371.

121. –, "Originative Thinking in the Later Philosophy of Heidegger," *Philosophy and Phenomenological Research*, XXX (1969), pp. 368-381.

122. –. *A Study of 'Being' in the Philosophy of Heidegger*, Ph.D. diss., University of Illinois (1963).

123. Bartsch, Hans Werner, ed. *Kerygma and Myth: A Theological Debate*, tr. by Reginald H. Fuller, 2 vols. (London: S.P.C.K., 1960, 1962).

Bultmann, Jaspers and others on Heidegger's concept of demythologizing.

124. Barzun, Jacques, "Ça Existe: A Note on a New Ism," *The American Scholar* (October, 1946), pp. 449-454.

125. Bauer, George H. *Sartre and the Artist* (Chicago: Chicago University Press, 1969).

126. Baumgardt, D., "Rationalism and the Philosophy of Despair," *Sewanee Review*, LV (1947), pp. 223-237.

127. Baumgarten, Eduard, "The 'Radical Evil' in Jaspers' Philosophy," in Paul Schilpp, ed., *The Philosophy of Karl Jaspers* (New York: Tudor Pub. Co., 1957), pp. 337-368.

128. Bays, Gwendolyn, "Simone de Beauvoir: Ethics and Art," *Yale French Studies*, I, 1 (1948), pp. 106-112.

129. Beatty, Joseph, "Forgiveness," *American Philosophical Quarterly*, VII (1970), pp. 246-252.

130. de Beauvoir, Simone, "Jean-Paul Sartre: Strictly Personal," *Harper's Bazaar* (January, 1946), pp. 113, 158, 160.

131. –. *The Ethics of Ambiguity* (New York: Philosophical Library, 1948).

132. –, "An Existentialist Looks at Americans," *New York*

Times Magazine, XXV (May, 1947), pp. 51-54.

133. –, "Eye for Eye," *Politics*, IV (1947), pp. 134-140.

134. Beck, Maximilian, "Existentialism," *Philosophy and Phenomenological Research*, V (1944-1945), pp. 126-137.

135. –, "Existentialism, Rationalism, and Christian Faith," *Journal of Religion*, XXVI (1946), pp. 283-295.

136. –, "Existentialism Versus Naturalism and Idealism," *South Atlantic Quarterly*, XLVII (1948), pp. 157-163.

137. Beck, S. J., "Implication for Ego in Tillich's Ontology of Anxiety," *Philosophy and Phenomenological Research*, XLIV (1957), pp. 51-64.

138. Bedell, George C., "Kierkegaard's Conception of Time," *Journal of the American Academy of Religion.* XXXVII (1969), pp. 266-269.

139. Bedford, Mitchell. *Existentialism and Creativity* (New York: Philosophical Library, 1972).

140. Beebe, Maurice, "Criticism of Albert Camus: A Selected Checklist of Studies in English," *Modern Fiction Studies*, X, 3 (1964), pp. 303-314.

141. Behl, L., "Wittgenstein and Heidegger," *Duns Scotus Philosophical Association*, XXVII (1963), pp. 70-115.

142. Behrens, Ralph, "Existential 'Character-Ideas' in Camus' The Misunderstanding," *Modern Drama*, VII, 2 (1964), pp. 210-212.

143. Beis, R., "Atheistic Existentialist Ethos: A Critique," *Modern Schoolman*, XLII (1965), pp. 153-177.

144. Belkind, Allen J. *Jean-Paul Sartre in English: A Bibliographical Guide* (Kent: Kent State University Press, 1970).

145. Benda, Clemens, "The Existential Approach in Psychiatry,"

Journal of Existential Psychiatry, I (1960), pp. 24-41.

146. –, "Existentialism in Philosophy and Science," *Journal of Existenial Psychiatry,* I (1960), pp. 284-315.

147. –, "Language, Consciousness and Problems of Existential Analysis," *American Journal of Psychotherapy,* XIV (1960), p. 259.

148. Bentley, Eric, "Jean-Paul Sartre, Dramatist: The Thinker as Playwright," *Kenyon Review,* VIII (1946), pp. 66-79.

149. –, "A Note on French Existentialism (With a List of Camus' Writings)," *Books Abroad,* XX, 3 (Summer, 1946), pp. 264-264.

150. Benton, Richard. *The Aesthetics of Friedrich Nietzsche: The Relation of Art to Life,* Ph.D. diss., Johns Hopkins University (1955).

151. Berdyaev, Nikolai. *The Beginning and the End,* tr. by M. French (New York: Charles Scribner's Sons, 1957).

152. –. *The Destiny of Man,* tr. by W. Duddington (New York: Harper and Row, 1960).

153. –. *The Divine and the Human,* tr. by R. M. French (London: Geoffrey Bles, 1949).

154. –. *Dostoievski* (New York: Meridan, 1957).

155. –. *Dream and Reality: An Essay in Autobiography,* tr. by Katherine Lambert (New York: Collier, 1962).

156. –. *The End of our Time,* tr. by D. A. Atwater (Ann Arbor: University of Michigan Press, 1961).

157. –. *Fate of Man in the Modern World,* tr. by Donald Lowrie (Ann Arbor: University of Michigan Press, 1961).

158. –. *Freedom and the Spirit,* tr. by Oliver Clarke (New York: Scribner's, 1935).

159. –. *The Meaning of History,* tr. by George Reavey (Cleveland: Meridian, 1962).

160. –. *The Meaning of the Creative Act,* tr. by D. Lowrie (New York: Macmillan-Collier, 1955).

161. –. *Slavery and Freedom,* tr. by R. M. French (New York: Scribner's, 1944).

162. –. *Solitude and Society,* tr. by George Reavey (London: Geoffrey Bles, 1948).

163. –. *Spirit and Reality,* tr. by George Reavey (London: Geoffrey Bles, 1933).

164. –. *Towards a New Epoch* (London: Geoffrey Bles, 1949).

165. –. *Truth and Revelation,* tr. by R. M. French (New York: Collier, 1962).

166. Berger, Gaston. *The Cogito in Husserl's Philosophy,* tr. by Kathleen McLaughlin (Evanston: Northwestern University Press, 1972).

167. –, "The Different Trends of Contemporary French Philosophy," *Philosophy and Phenomenological Research,* VII (1946), pp. 1-11.

168. –. *Existentialism and Literature in Action: Two Lectures on Present-Day Problems in France* (Buffalo: University of Buffalo, 1948).

169. Bernstein, Richard J. *Praxis and Action: Contemporary Philosophies of Human Activity* (Philadelphia: University of Pennsylvania Press, 1971).

See particularly the chapter "Consciousness, Existence, and Action: Kierkegaard and Sartre," pp. 84-164.

170. Bertocci, Angelo P., "Camus' 'La Peste' and the Absurd," *Romantic Review,* XLIX, 1 (1958), pp. 33-41.

171. –, "Existential Phenomenology and Psychoanalysis," *The*

Review of Metaphysics, XVIII (1965), pp. 690-710.

172. Bettes, Joseph Dabney, ed. *Phenomenology of Religion: Eight Modern Descriptions of the Essence of Religion* (New York: Harper and Row, 1969).

173. Bieber, Konrad, "*Engagement* as a Professional Risk." *Yale French Studies,* XVI (1954), pp. 29-39.

Primarily on Camus.

174. Biemel, Walter. *Martin Heidegger: An Illustrated Study,* tr. by J. L. Mehta (New York: Harcourt, Brace Jovanovich, 1976).

Despite some interesting information of the young Heidegger, and Heidegger as a teacher, this study often seems rambling and overladen with jargon.

175. –, "Poetry and Language in Heidegger," in Joseph J. Kockelmans, ed., *On Heidegger and Language* (Evanston: Northwestern University Press, 1972), pp. 65-106.

176. Bigelow, Gordon E., "A Primer of Existentialism," *College English,* XXII (December, 1961), pp. 171-178.

177. Binion, Rudolph. *Frau Lou* (Princeton: Princeton University Press, 1968).

178. Binkley, Luther John. *Conflict of Ideals: Changing Values in Western Society* (New York: Van Nostrand, 1969).

179. Binswanger, Ludwig. *Being-in-the-World,* tr. by James Needleman (New York: Basic Books, 1963).

180. –, "The Case of Ellen West," "The Existential Analysis School of Thought," and "Insanity as Life–Historical Phenomenon and as a Mental Disease: The Case of Ilse," in Rollo May et al, eds., *Existence: A New Dimension in Psychiatry and Psychology* (New York: Basic Books, 1958).

181. –, "Existential Analysis, Psychiatry, and Schizophrenia," *Journal of Existential Psychiatry*, L (1960), pp. 157-166.

182. Birault, Henri, "Thinking and Poeticizing in Heidegger," in Joseph J. Kockelmans, ed., *On Heidegger and Language* (Evanston: Northwestern University Press, 1972), pp. 147-168.

183. Bixler, J. S., "The Failure of Martin Heidegger," *Harvard Theological Review*, LVI (1963), pp. 121-143.

184. –, "On Being Absurd," *The Massachusetts Review*, X (1969), pp. 407-412.

185. Blackham, Harold John. *Six Existentialist Thinkers* (New York: Harper and Row, 1959; London: Routledge and Kegan Paul Ltd., 1972).

Good introduction to Kierkegaard, Nietzsche, Jaspers, Marcel, Heidegger, and Sartre.

186. Blair, R. G., "Imagination and Freedom in Spinoza and Sartre," *Journal of the British Society for Phenomenology*, I (1970), pp. 13-16.

187. Blake, Patricia, "No Exit and Flies," *Partisan Review*, XIV (May-June, 1947), pp. 313-316.

188. Blakely, Thomas J., "Current Soviet Views on Existentialism," *Studies in Soviet Thought*, VII (1967), pp. 333-339.

189. Blamires, Henry. *The Tyranny of Time* (New York: Morehouse, 1965).

190. Blanshard, Brand, "Kierkegaard on Faith," *The Personalist*, XLIX (1968), pp. 5-23.

191. Blauner, J., "Existential Analysis: L. Binswanger's Daseinanalysis," *Psychoanalytic Review*, XLIV (1957), pp. 51-64.

192. Block, Haskell M., "Albert Camus: Towards a Definition of Tragedy," *University of Toronto Quarterly*, CXIX, 4 (1950), pp. 354-360.

193. Blondel, Maurice, "The Inconsistency of Jean-Paul Sartre's Logic," *The Thomist*, X (1947), pp. 393-397.

194. Bluestone, Natalie. *Time and Consciousness in Jean-Paul Sartre and William James*, Ph.D. diss., Johns Hopkins University (1962).

195. Bluhm, Heinz, "Nietzsche's Religious Development as a Student at the University of Bonn," *PMLA*, LII (1973), pp. 880-891.

196. –, "Nietzsche's Religious Development as a Student at the University of Leipzig," *Journal of English and Germanic Philology*, XLI (1942), pp. 490-507.

197. –, "Nietzsche's Final View of Luther and the Reformation," *PMLA*, LXXI (1956), pp. 75-83.

198. Blumenthal, G. *Andre Malraux: The Conquest of Dread* (Baltimore: The Johns Hopkins Press, 1960).

199. Boas, G., "Being and Existence," *Journal of Philosophy*, LIII (1956), pp. 748-759.

200. –. *Dominant Themes of Modern Philosophy* (New York: Ronald Press, 1957).

201. Bobbio, Norberto. *The Philosophy of Decadentism: A Study in Existentialism*, tr. by David Moore (Oxford: Basil Blackwell, 1948).

202. Boelen, Bernard Jacques Marie. *Existential Thinking: A Philosophical Orientation* (Pittsburgh: Duquesne University Press, 1968).

203. –, "Martin Heidegger's Approach to Will, Decision, and Responsibility," *Review of Existential Psychology and Psychiatry*, I (1961), pp. 197-204.

204. Bogen, James, "Kierkegaard and the 'Teleological Suspension of the Ethical'," *Inquiry,* V (1962), pp. 305-317.

205. –, "Remark on the Kierkegaard-Hegel Controversy," *Synthese,* XIII (1961), pp. 372-389.

206. Bollnow, Otto Friedrich. *Deutsche Existenzphilosophie: Bibliographische Einführungen in das Studium der Philosophie,* 23 (Bern: A Francke, 1953).

Not in English, but an excellent bibliography for further study in German Existentialism.

207. Bolman, Frederick de W., Jr., "Kierkegaard in Limbo," *Journal of Philosophy,* XLI (1944), pp. 711-721.

208. Boorsch, Jean, "Sartre's View of Cartesian Liberty," *Yale French Studies,* I, 1 (1948), pp. 90-96.

209. Borgmann, A., "Language in Heidegger's Philosophy," *Journal of Existentialism,* VII (1966-1967), pp. 161-180.

210. –, "Philosophy and the Concern for Man," *Philosophy Today,* X (1966), pp. 236-246.

211. –, "The Transformation of Heidegger's Thought," *The Personalist,* XLVII (1966), pp. 484-499.

212. Borowitz, E. G., "Existentialism's Meaning for Judaism," *Commentary,* XXVIII (1959), pp. 414-420.

213. Boss, Medard. *A Daseinanalytic Approach to the Psychopathology of the Phenomenon of Love* (New York: Grune and Stratton, 1949).

214. –. *Psychoanalysis and Daseinanalysis,* tr. by Ludwig B. Lefebre (New York: Basic Books, 1963).

215. Bossart, W. H., "Heidegger's Theory of Art," *Journal of Aesthetics and Art Criticism,* XXVII (1968-1969), pp. 57-66.

216. Bossert, B., "A Note on Heidegger's 'Opus One,'" *Journal of the British Society for Phenomenology,* I (1973), pp. 61-64.

217. Bowman, Frank, "Irredentist Existentialism: Fondane and Shestov," *Yale French Studies,* XVI (1954), pp. 111-117.

218. Brand, Gerd, "Intentionality, Reduction, and Intentional Analysis in Husserl's Later Manuscripts," in Joseph J. Kockelmans, ed., *Phenomenology: The Philosophy of Edmund Husserl and Its Interpretation* (New York: Anchor Press, 1967), pp. 197-220.

219. Brandes, George. *Friedrich Nietzsche,* tr. by A. G. Chater (London: Heinnemann, 1915).

220. Brandt, Frithoof, "The Great Earthquake in Soren Kierkegaard's Life," *Theoria,* XV (1949), pp. 38-53.

221. —. *Soren Kierkegaard 1813-1855: His Life—His Works,* tr. by Ann R. Born (Copenhagen: Det Danske Selskab, 1963).

222. Brandt, Rudolf, "Freud and Nietzsche: A Comparison," *Revue de l'Université d'Ottawa,* XXV (1955), pp. 225-234.

223. Brantl, George E. *The Tragic Commitment: An Essay in Existentialist Metaphysics,* Ph.D. diss., Columbia University (1957).

224. Braun, Sidney D., "Existentialism in the Classroom," *Modern Language Journal,* XXXIX, 7 (1955), pp. 348-355.

On teaching existentialism.

225. Brearley, Katherine, "The Theme of Isolation in Camus," *Kentucky Foreign Language Quarterly,* IX, 3 (1962), pp. 117-122.

226. Brée, Germaine. *Albert Camus* (New York: Columbia

University Press, 1964).

227. –, "Albert Camus and the Plague," *Yale French Studies,* VIII (1951), pp. 93-1000.

228. –. *Camus* (New Brunswick: Rutgers University Press, 1959, 1961).

229. –, ed. *Camus: A Collection of Critical Essays* (Englewood Cliffs: Prentice-Hall, 1962).

230. –. *Camus and Sartre: Crisis and Commitment* (New York: Delacorte Press, 1972).

231. –, "The Genesis of the Stranger," *Shenandoah,* XII, 3 (1961), pp. 3-10.

232. –, "Introduction to Albert Camus," *Yale French Studies,* IV, 1 (1950), pp. 27-37.

233. – and Margaret Guiton. *An Age of Fiction: The French Novel from Gide to Camus* (New Brunswick: Rutgers University Press, 1957).

Not specifically on existentialism, but includes useful analysis of Sartre as well as Camus.

234. –, "The Writer and Our Time: Malraux, Sartre, Camus," in Stanley Burnshaw, ed., *Varieties of Literary Experience* (New York: New York University Press, 1962), pp. 75-94.

235. Breisbach, Ernst. *Introduction to Modern Existentialism* (New York: Grove Press, 1962).

236. Bretall, R., ed. *A Kierkegaard Anthology* (Princeton: Princeton University Press, 1946).

237. Breton, S., "From Phenomenology to Ontology," *Philosophy Today,* IV (1960), pp. 227-237.

238. Brinton, Crane. *Nietzsche* (Cambridge: Harvard University Press, 1941; New York: Harper and Row, 1965).

239. Brock, Werner. *An Introduction to Contemporary German Philosophy* (Cambridge: Cambridge University Press, 1947).

240. –, Introduction and Notes to Martin Heidegger, *Existence and Being* (Chicago: Henry Regnery Co., 1949).

Brock supplies a 106-page summary of Heidegger's *Being and Time,* and shorter essays on each of the four essays by Heidegger translated in this volume: "Remembrance of the Poet," "Holderlin and the Essence of Poetry," "On the Essence of Truth," and "What is Metaphysics?"

241. Brockmann, Charles B., "Metamorphoses of Hell: The Spiritual Quandary in La Chute," *French Review,* XXXV, 4 (1962), pp. 361-368.

242. Brombert, Victor, "Camus and the Novel of the 'Absurd'," *Yale French Studies,* I, 1 (1948), pp. 119-123.

243. –. *The Intellectual Hero: Studies in the French Novel, 1880-1955* (Philadelphia: Lippincott, 1961).

244. Brookfield, C. M., "What was Kierkegaard's Task? A Frontier to be Explored," *Union Seminary Quarterly Review,* XVIII, pp. 23-35.

245. Broudy, H. S., "Kierkegaard's Doctrine of Indirect Communication," *Journal of Philosophy,* LVIII (1961), pp. 225-233.

246. –, "Sartre's Existentialism and Education," *Educational Theory,* XXI (1971), pp. 155-177.

247. Brown, J. L., "Chief Prophet of the Existentialists," *The New York Times Magazine* (February 2, 1947), pp. 20-21.

248. Brown, James. *Kierkegaard, Heidegger, Buber and Barth: Subject and Object in Modern Theology* (New York: Collier Books, 1962).

249. Brown, Stuart M., Jr., "The Atheistic Existentialism of Jean-Paul Sartre," *Philosophical Review,* LVII (1948), pp. 158-166.

250. Bruckberger, Raymond-Léopold, "The Spiritual Agony of Europe," *Renascence,* VII, 2 (1954), pp. 70-80.

251. Bruneau, Jean, "Existentialism and the American Novel," *Yale French Studies,* I, 1 (1948), pp. 66-72.

252. Bryant, D. S. *Bases for Educational Theory in the Philosophy of Jean-Paul Sartre,* Ph.D. diss., Stanford University (1966).

253. Bryant, R. H., "Albert Camus' Quest for Ethical Values," *Religion in Life,* XXIX (1960), pp. 443-452.

254. Buber, Martin. *Between Man and Man,* tr. by Ronald Gregor Smith (London: Routledge and Kegan Paul, 1947).

255. –, "Distance and Relation," tr. by Ronald Gregor Smith, *The Hibbert Journal,* XLIX (1951), pp. 105-113.

256. –. *Eclipse of God: Studies in the Relation between Religion and Philosophy* (New York: Harper, 1951; Harper Torchbook, 1957).

257. –. *Good and Evil: Two Interpretations* (New York: Charles Scribner's Sons, 1953).

258. –. *I and Thou,* tr. by Ronald Gregor Smith (Edinburgh: T. and T. Clark, 1937). Newly translated and with a Prologue and Notes by Walter Kaufmann (New York: Charles Scribner's Sons, 1970).

259. –. *Pointing the Way: Collected Essays,* tr. by Maurice S. Friedman (New York: Harper and Bros.; London: Routledge and Kegan Paul, 1956).

260. –. *Two Types of Faith,* tr. by Norman P. Goldhawk (London: Routledge and Kegan Paul, 1951; New York: Macmillan, 1952).

261. –, "What is Common to All," *Review of Metaphyscis,* XI (1958), pp. 359-380.

262. Bukala, C. R., "Sartrean Ethics: An Introduction," *New Scholasticism,* XLI (1967), pp. 450-464.

263. –, "Sartre's Dramatic Philosophical Quest," *Thought,* XLVIII (1973), pp. 79-106.

264. Bultmann, Rudolph. *Essays Philosophical and Theological,* tr. by James C. Grieg (London: S.C.M. Press, 1955).

265. –. *Kerygma and Myth,* tr. by Reginald Fuller (London: S.P.C.K., 1954).

266. –. *The Presence of Eternity* (New York: Harper & Bros., 1957).

267. Bunting, I. A., "Sartre on Imagination," *Philosophical Studies,* XIX (1970), pp. 236-254.

268. Burgelin, Pierre, "Existentialism and the Tradition of French Thought," *Yale French Studies,* XVI (1954), pp. 103-105.

269. Buri, F. *Theology of Existence,* tr. by H. H. Oliver and G. Onder (Greenwood, South Carolina: Attic Press, 1966).

270. Burke, David R. *An Examination of Jean-Paul Sartre's Conception of Freedom,* Ph.D. diss., Michigan State University (1966).

271. Burke, Edward L., "Camus and the Pursuit of Happiness," *Thought,* XXXVII (1962), pp. 391-409.

272. Burnier, Michel Antoine. *Choice of Action: The French Existentialists on the Political Front Line,* tr. by Bernard Murchland (New York: Random House, 1968).

273. Burton, Arthur, "The Clinician as Moralist," *Journal of Existential Psychiatry,* I (1960), pp. 207-219.

274. —, ed. *The Concept of Man: A Definition of Patient and Therapist* (New York: Basic Books, 1962).

275. —, "Schizophrenia and Existence," *Psychiatry,* XXIII (1960), pp. 385-394.

276. Busst, A. J. L., "A Note on the Eccentric Christology of Camus," *French Studies,* XVI, 1 (1962), pp. 45-50.

277. Cain, Seymour. *Gabriel Marcel* (New York: Hillary, 1963).

278. Cairns, Dorion, "Phenomenology," in V. Ferm, ed., *A History of Philosophical Systems* (London: Rider, 1958).

279. —, "Some Results of Husserl's Investigations," in Joseph J. Kockelmans, ed., *Phenomenology: The Philosophy of Edmund Husserl and Its Interpretation* (New York: Anchor Press, 1967), pp. 147-149.

280. Callan, Edward, "Auden and Kierkegaard: The Artistic Framework of *For the Time Being*," *Christian Scholar,* XLVIII (1965), pp. 211-223.

281. —, "Auden's *New Year Letter:* A New Style of Architecture," *Renascence,* XVI (1963), pp. 13-19.

282. Camele, A., "Martin Heidegger and the Meaning for Man," *Listening,* I (1966), pp. 140-149.

283. Campbell, Karlyn. *The Rhetorical Implications of the Philosophy of Jean-Paul Sartre,* Ph.D. diss., University of Minnesota (1968).

284. Campbell, R., "Lessing's Problem and Kierkegaard's Answer," *Scottish Journal of Theology,* XIX (1966), pp. 35-54.

285. Camus, Albert, "Art and Revolt," *Partisan Review,* XIX (1952), pp. 268-281.

286. —, "The Artist as Witness of Freedom," *Commentary,* VIII (1949), pp. 534-538.

287. –, "Between Yes and No," *Partisan Review,* XVI (1949), pp. 1090-1097.

288. –. *The Myth of Sisyphus* (New York: Vintage Books, 1955).

All of Camus' works of fiction and drama are available in the paperback Vintage editions.

289. –. *The Rebel: An Essay on Man in Revolt,* tr. by A. Bower (New York: Alfred Knopf, 1956).

290. –, "Reflections on the Guillotine," *Evergreen Review,* IV (1960), p. 12.

291. –. *Resistance, Rebellion, and Death,* tr. by Justin O'Brien (New York: Vintage Books, 1974).

292. Caputo, John D., "Being, Ground and Play in Heidegger," *Man and World,* III (1970), pp. 26-48.

293. –, "Heidegger's Original Ethics," *New Scholasticism,* XLV (1971), pp. 127-138.

294. –, "Meister Eckhart and the Later Heidegger: The Mystical Element in Heidegger's Thought," *Journal of the History of Philosophy,* XII, 4 (1974) and XIII, 1 (1975).

295. –, "The Rose is Without Why: An Interpretation of the Later Heidegger," *Philosophy Today,* XV (1971), pp. 3-16.

296. –. *The Way Back into the Ground: An Interpretation of the Path of Heidegger's Thought,* Ph.D. diss., Bryn Mawr University (1968).

297. Caradang, Amado I. *Jean-Paul Sartre and his Atheism,* Ph.D. diss., University of Notre Dame (1967).

298. Cardinal, Clive H., "Rilke and Kierkegaard: Some Relationships Between Poet and Theologian," *Bulletin of the Rocky Mountain Modern Language Association,* XXIII (1969), pp. 34-39.

299. Carlo, William E. *The Ultimate Reducibility of Essence to Existence in Existential Metaphysics* (The Hague: Martinus Nijhoff, 1966).

300. Carlson, Eric W., "The Humanism of Albert Camus, Plus a Review of Five Critiques of Camus," *The Humanist,* XX, 5 (1960), pp. 298-315.

301. Carnell, E. J. *The Burden of Soren Kierkegaard* (Grand Rapids: William B. Eerdmans Publishing Co., 1965).

302. Carr, David, "Husserl's Problematic Concept of the Life-World," *American Philosophical Quarterly,* VII (1970), pp. 331-339.

303. Carrol, O., "Sartre and Barth," *Philosophy Today,* IX (1965), pp. 101-111.

304. Catlin, G., "A Reply to Existentialism," *Papers of the Aristotelian Society,* XLVII (1947), pp. 197-224.

305. Celestin, George, "Kierkegaard and Christian Renewal," *Dominicana,* XLIX (1964), pp. 149-157.

306. Cerf, W. H., "An Approach to Heidegger's Ontology," *Philosophy and Phenomenological Research,* I (1940), pp. 177-190.

307. –, "Existentialist Mannerism and Education," *Journal of Philosophy,* LII (1955), pp. 141-152.

308. Chamberlin, John Gordon. *Toward a Phenomenology of Education* (Philadelphia: Westminster Press, 1969).

309. Champigny, Robert, "The Comedy of Ethics," *Yale French Studies,* XXV (1960), pp. 72-74.

310. –, "Existentialism in the Modern French Novel," *Thought,* XXXI (1956), pp. 365-384.

311. –, "God in a Sartrean Light," *Yale French Studies* (1953), pp. 81-87.

312. –, "Sartre and Christianity," *Renascence,* VII (1954), pp. 59 ff.

313. –. *Stage's on Sartre's Way: 1938-1952* (Bloomington: Indiana University Press, 1959).

314. –, "Way of Flesh," *Yale French Studies,* XI (1953), pp. 73-79.

315. Chaning-Pearce, M. *The Terrible Crystal: Studies in Kierkegaard and Modern Christianity* (New York: Oxford University Press, 1941).

316. Chapman, Harmon M., "Realism and Phenomenology," in John Wild, ed., *The Return to Reason: Essays in Realistic Philosophy* (Chicago: Henry Regnery Co., 1953), pp. 3-35.

317. Chari, C. T. K., "On the Dialectic of Swami Vivekenanda and Soren Kierkegaard: An 'Existential' Approach to Indian Philosophy," *Revue Internationale de Philosophie,* X (1956), pp. 315-331.

318. Charlesworth, Max. *Existentialists and Jean-Paul Sartre* (New York: Prior, 1976).

319. Chatterdon-Hill, Georges. *The Philosophy of Nietzsche* (London: Heath, Cranton, and Ouseley, 1914).

320. Chiaromonte, Nicola, "Albert Camus," *New Republic,* CXIV, 17 (April 29, 1946), pp. 630-633.

321. –, "Albert Camus and Moderation," *Partisan Review,* XV, 10 (October, 1948), pp. 1142-1145.

322. –, "Sartre Versus Camus: A Political Quarrel," *Partisan Review,* XIX, 6 (November-December, 1952), pp. 680-686.

323. Choron, Jacques. *Death and Western Thought* (New York: Collier Books, 1967).

324. Christensen, A. "Kierkegaard's Secret Affliction," *Harvard*

Theological Review, XLII (1949), pp. 255-271.

325. –, "*L' Etranger:* The Unheroic Hero," *College English,* XXIV, 3 (1962), pp. 235-236.

326. Christopher, P., "Heidegger, Hegel, and the Problem of 'Das Nichts.," *International Philosophical Quarterly,* VIII (1968), pp. 379-405.

327. Clancy, James, "Beyond Despair: A New Drama of Ideas," *Educational Theatre Journal,* XIII, 3 (1961), pp. 157-166.

328. Clark, A. F. B., "Jean-Paul Sartre: Philosopher and Novelist," *The Canadian Forum,* XXXVII (1958), pp. 269-271.

329. Clarke, Oliver F. *Introduction to Berdyaev* (London: Geoffrey Bles, Ltd., 1950).

330. Clive, Geoffrey. *The Broken Icon: Intuitive Existentialism in Classical Russian Fiction* (New York: Macmillan, 1962).

331. –, " 'The Teleological Suspension of the Ethical' in Nineteenth Century Literature," *Journal of Religion,* XXIV (1954).

332. –, "The Sickness Unto Death in the Underworld: A Study of Nihilism," *Harvard Theological Review,* LI (1958), pp. 133-167.

333. Closs, August, "Goethe and Kierkegaard," *Modern Language Quarterly,* X (1949), pp. 264-280.

334. Clough, Wilson O., "Camus' 'The Plague'," *Colorado Quarterly,* VIII, 4 (1959), pp. 389-404.

335. Coates, J. B. *The Crisis of the Human Person: Some Personalist Interpretations* (London: Longmans, Green & Co., 1949).

Pp. 32-35, 65-81, 158, 240-248 deal with Martin Buber.

336. –, "The Purpose of the Existentialist School," *Congregational Quarterly* (July, 1950), pp. 219-228.

337. Cochran, Arthur L. *Existentialists and God: Being and the Being of God in the Thought of Kierkegaard, Jaspers, Heidegger, Sartre, Tillich, Gilson, and Barth* (Philadelphia: Westminster Press, 1956).

338. Cohn, Georg. *Existentialism and Legal Science*, tr. by George H. Kendal (Dobbs Ferry, New York: Oceana Publishers, 1967).

339. Cohn, Robert Greer, "From Chretien to Camus: Plumes and Prisons," *Modern Language Notes*, LXXX, 4 (1965), pp. 601-609.

340. –, "Sartre-Camus Resartus," *Yale French Studies*, XXX (1962-1963), pp. 73-77.

341. –, "Sartre's First Novel: *La Nausée*," *Yale French Studies*, I, 1 (1948), pp. 62-65.

342. –, "Sartre versus Proust," *Partisan Review*, XXVIII (September-November, 1961), pp. 633-645.

343. Cohn, Ruby, "The Absurdly Absurd: Avatars of Godot," *Comparative Literature Studies*, II, 3 (1965), pp. 233-240.

344. Cole, J. Preston, "The Existential Reality of God: A Kierkegaardian Study," *Christian Scholar*, XLVIII (1965), pp. 224-235.

345. –, "The Function of Choice in Human Existence," *Journal of Religion*, XLV (1965), pp. 196-210.

346. Collidge, Mary L., "Ethics—Apollonian and Dionysian," *Journal of Philosophy*, XXXVIII (1941), pp. 449-465.

347. Collignon, Jean, "Kafka's Humor," *Yale French Studies*, XVI (1954), pp. 53-62.

348. Collins, James, "The Appeal of Existentialism," *Common-*

weal, LXI (1954), pp. 7-9.

349. —, "An Approach to Karl Jaspers," *Thought,* XX (1954), pp. 657-691.

350. —, "The Existentialism of Jean-Paul Sartre," *Thought,* XXII (1948), pp. 59-100.

351. —. *The Existentialists: A Critical Study* (Chicago: Henry Regnery Co., 1952).

352. —, "Faith and Reflection in Kierkegaard," *Journal of Religion,* XXXVII (1957), pp. 10-20.

353. —, "Gabriel Marcel and the Mystery of Being," *Thought,* XVIII (1943), pp. 665-693.

354. —, "The German Neoscholastic Approach to Heidegger," *The Modern Schoolman,* XXI (1943-1944), pp. 143-152.

355. —, "Jaspers on Science and Philosophy," in Paul Schilpp, ed., *The Philsoophy of Karl Jaspers* (New York: Tudor Publishing Co., 1957), pp. 115-140.

356. —, "Karl Jaspers' Philosophical Logic," *New Scholasticism,* XXIII (1943), pp. 414-420.

357. —, "Kierkegaard and Christian Philosophy," *The Thomist,* XIV (1951), pp. 441-465.

358. —, "Kierkegaard's Critique of Hegel," *Thought,* XVIII (1943), pp. 74-100.

359. —. *The Mind of Kierkegaard* (Chicago: Henry Regnery Co., 1953).

360. —, "The Mind of Kierkegaard: The Problem and the Personal Outlook," *The Modern Schoolman,* XXVI (1948-1949), pp. 1-22.

361. —, "Three Kierkegaardian Problems," *The New Scholasticism,* XXII (1948).

362. Colm, Hanna. *The Extentialist Approach to Psychotherapy with Adults and Chidlren* (New York: Grune and Stratton, 1966).

363. –, "Healing as Participation: Comments Based on Paul Tillich's Existential Philosophy," *Psychiatry,* XVI (1953), pp. 99-111.

364. –, "Psychotherapy and the Ground of Being," *Psychoanalysis and the Psychoanalytic Review,* XLVII (1960), p. 4.

365. Coltera, J. T., "Psychoanalysis and Existentialism," *American Psychoanalytic Association Journal,* X (1962), pp. 209-215.

366. Comerchero, Victor, ed. *Values in Conflict: Christianity, Marxism, Psychoanalysis, Existentialism* (New York: Appleton-Century-Crofts, 1970).

367. Comstock, W. R., "Aspects of Aesthetic Existence: Kierkegaard and Santayana," *International Philosophical Quarterly,* VI (1966), pp. 189-213.

368. Cook, Gladys C., "Jean-Paul Sartre's Doctrine of Human Freedom and Responsibility," *Bucknell Review,* I (June, 1949), pp. 12-21.

369. Coolidge, Mary L., "The Experimental Temper in European Philosophy," *Journal of Philosophy,* LII (1955), pp. 477-493.

370. Copleston, Frederick Charles, "Centenary of Friedrich Nietzsche," *Studies,* XXXIII (1944), pp. 465-474.

371. –, "Concerning Existentialism," *The Month* (January, 1949), pp. 46-54.

372. –. *Contemporary Philosophy: Studies of Logical Positivism and Existentialism* (Westminster, Maryland: Newman Press, 1956).

373. –, "Existence and Religion," *Dublin Review,* CCXX

(1947), pp. 50-63.

374. –, "Existentialism," *Philosophy,* I (1948), pp. 19-37.

375. –. *Existentialism and Modern Man: Aquinas Papers, No. 9* (London: Aquinas Society, 1948).

376. –, "Existentialism and Religion," *The Dublin Review* (Spring, 1947), pp. 50-63.

377. –, "Foreground and Background in Nietzsche," *Review of Metaphysics,* XXI (1968), pp. 506-523.

378. –, "Friedrich Nietzsche," *Philosophy,* XVII (1942), pp. 231-244.

379. –. *Friedrich Nietzsche: Philosopher of Culture* (London: Burns, Oats, 1942).

380. –, "Man Without God," *The Month,* CLXXXIV (1947), pp. 18-27.

381. –, "Nietzsche and National Socialism," *Dublin Review* (1941), pp. 225-243.

382. –, "The Philosophy of the Absurd," *Modern Churchman,* III (1947), pp. 157-164.

383. –. *St. Thomas and Nietzsche* (Oxford: Oxford University Press, 1944).

384. –, "What is Existentialism?" *The Month,* CLXXXIII (1947), pp. 13-21.

385. Cording, Richard Arnold. *Sartre's Theory of Freedom,* Ph.D. diss., University of Missouri (1969).

386. Coreth, E., "From Hermeneutics to Metaphysics," *International Philosophical Quarterly,* XI (1971), pp. 249-259.

387. Corngold, Stanley, "*Sein und Zeit:* Implications for Poetics," Special Heidegger and Literature issue, *bound-*

ary 2, IV, 2 (1976), pp. 439-454.

388. Couch, John Philip, "Camus and Faulkner: The Search for the Language of Modern Tragedy," *Yale French Studies,* XXV (1960), pp. 120-125.

389. Courtney, R., "Imagination and the Dramatic Act: Comments on Sartre, Ryle and Furlong," *Journal of Aesthetics and Art Criticism,* XXX (1971-1972), pp. 163-170.

390. Coutinho, Arno, "Nietzsche's Critique of Judaism," *Review of Religion,* III (1939), pp. 161-166.

391. Cox, Harvey. *The Secular City* (New York: Macmillan Co., 1965).

392. Craib, Ian. *Existentialism and Sociology: A Study of Jean-Paul Sartre* (New York: Cambridge University Press, 1976).

393. Cranston, Maurice. *Jean-Paul Sartre* (New York: Grove Press, 1962).

394. —, "The Later Thought of Jean-Paul Sartre," in Philip Rahv, ed., *Modern Occasions* (New York: Farrar, Straus and Giroux, 1966), pp. 181-201.

395. —. *The Quintessence of Sartrism* (New York: Harper Torchbooks, 1971).

A misleading and superficial study largely on Sartre's political thought and concept of *engagée.* Very short.

396. Cress, D. W., "Heidegger's Criticism of 'Entitative Metaphysics' in his Later Works," *International Philosophical Quarterly,* XII (1972), pp. 69-86.

397. Crites, Stephen. *In the Twilight of Christendom: Hegel vs. Kierkegaard on Faith and History,* Studies in Religion, No. 2. (Chambersburg, Pennsylvania: American Academy of Religion, 1971).

398. Crookshank, Francis. *Individual Psychology and Nietzsche* (London: 1933).

399. Croxall, Thomas H. *Glimpses and Impressions of Kierkegaard* (Welwyn: J. Nisbet, 1959).

400. –. *Kierkegaard Commentary* (London: J. Nisbet, 1959).

401. –. *Kierkegaard: Johannes Climacus* (London: Adam and Charles Black, 1958).

402. –, "Kierkegaard on 'Authority'," *Hibbert Journal,* XL (1950), pp. 145-152.

403. Cruickshank, John. *Albert Camus and the Literature of Revolt* (New York: Oxford University Press, 1959).

404. –, "Existentialism After Twelve Years: An Evaluation," *Dublin Review,* CCXXXI (1957), pp. 52-65.

405. –, ed., *French Literature and Its Background,* vol. VI (London: Oxford University Press, 1970), pp. 226-243.

406. Cumming, Robert Denoon, "Existentialist Psychology in Action," in Benjamin B. Wolman, ed., *Scientific Psychology* (New York: Basic Books, 1965).

407. –, "The Literature of Extreme Situations," in Morris Philipson, ed., *Aesthetics Today* (Cleveland: Meridian Books, 1961).

408. –, "Existence and Communication," *Ethics,* LXV, pp. 79-101.

409. Cunningham, G., "On Nietzsche's Doctrine of the Will to Power," *Philosophical Review,* XXVIII (1919), pp. 479-490.

410. Dailey, C., "Natural History and Phenomenology," *Journal of Individual Psychology,* XVI (1960), pp. 36-44.

411. Dallen, James, "Existentialism and the Catholic Thinker," *Catholic World,* CC (1965), pp. 294-299.

412. Daniels, Graham, "Sartre and Merleau-Ponty: An Existentialist Quarrel," *French Studies*, XXIV (October, 1970), pp. 379-392.

413. Danto, Arthur C., "The Eternal Recurrence," in Robert Solomon, ed., *Nietzsche: A Collection of Critical Essays* (New York: Anchor Books, 1973), pp. 316-321.

414. –. *Nietzsche as Philosopher* (New York: Macmillan, 1965).

415. –, "Nietzsche's Perspectivism," in Robert Solomon, ed., *Nietzsche: A Collection of Critical Essays* (New York: Anchor Books, 1973), pp. 29-57.

416. –. *Jean-Paul Sartre* (New York: Viking Press, 1967).

417. D'Arcy, M. C., "The Clown and the Philosopher," *Month* (January, 1949), pp. 7-16.

418. Dauenhauer, B. P., "An Approach to Heidegger's Way of Philosophizing," *Southern Journal of Philosophy*, IX (1971), pp. 265-275.

419. Davenport, Manuel M., "A Critique of Sartre's Concept of Freedom," *Philosophy Today*, XVII (Spring, 1973), pp. 22-27.

420. Davis, G. W. *Existentialism and Theology: An Investigation of the Contribution of Rudolph Bultmann to Theological Thought* (New York: Philosophical Library, 1957).

421. Deely, John N., "The Situation of Heidegger in the Tradition of Christian Philosophy," *The Thomist*, XXXI (1967), pp. 159-244.

422. –. *The Tradition via Heidegger: An Essay on the Meaning of Being in the Philosophy of Martin Heidegger* (The Hague: Martinus Nijhoff, 1971).

423. – and Joseph A. Novak, "The Idea of Phenomenology,"

New Scholasticism, XLIV, 3 (1970).

424. DeHuszar, George, "Nietzsche's Theory of Decadence and the Transvaluation of All Values," *Journal of the History of Ideas,* VI (1945), pp. 259-272.

425. Delius, Harald, "Descriptive Interpretation," *Philosophy and Phenomenological Research,* XIII (1953), pp. 305-323.

426. Delp, Alfred, "Modern German Existential Philosophy," *The Modern Schoolman,* XIII (1935-1936), pp. 62-66.

427. de Man, Paul. *Blindness and Insight: Essays in the Rhetoric of Contemporary Criticism* (New York: Oxford University Press, 1971).

Very good, if occasionally disjointed examination of the post-Heideggerian and phenomenological critics.

428. Demos, R., "Tillich's Philosophical Theology," *Philosophy and Phenomenological Research,* XIX (1958), pp. 74-85.

429. Dempsey, Peter J. *The Psychology of Sartre* (Westminster: Newman Press, 1950).

430. Demske, James M. *Being, Man, and Death: A Key to Heidegger* (Lexington: University Press of Kentucky, 1970).

431. –, "Heidegger's Quadrate and Revelation of Being," *Philosophy Today,* VIII (1964).

432. Demson, D., "Kierkegaard's Sociology," *Religion in Life,* XXVII (1958), pp. 257-266.

433. Denton, David E., ed. *Existentialism and Phenomenology in Education: Collected Essays* (New York: Teachers College Press, 1974).

434. Derrida, Jacques, "The Ends of Man," *Philosophy and Phenomenological Research,* XXX (1969), pp. 31-57.

435. –. *Of Grammatology,* tr. by Gayatri Chakravorty Spivak (Baltimore: The Johns Hopkins Press, 1976).

Spivak provides an 87-page introduction and notes (but no index, which is needed) to this work which is perhaps the single most important post-Heideggerian work (examining *écriture* in all its permutations), important for the study of literature and Saussurean linguistics as well as Existentialism.

436. –. *Speech and Phenomena and Other Essays on Husserl's Theory of Signs,* tr. with an introduction by David B. Allison (Evanston: Northwestern University Press, 1973).

Includes the important essay "Differance."

437. Desan, Wilfred. *The Tragic Finale: An Essay on the Philosophy of Jean-Paul Sartre* (Cambridge: Harvard University Press, 1954).

438. de Unamuno, Minguel. *Perplexities and Paradoxes* (New York: Philosophical Library, 1945).

439. –. *The Tragic Sense of Life,* tr. by J. E. C. Flitch (New York: Dover, 1957).

440. Dewey, Bradley R., "The Erotic-Demonic in Kierkegaard's 'Diary of the Seducer'," *Scandinavica,* X (1971), pp. 1-24.

441. Diamond, Malcolm L. *Martin Buber: Jewish Existentialist* (New York: Harper and Row, 1968).

442. –, "Faith and Its Tensions: A Criticism of Religious Existentialism," *Judaism,* XIII (1964), pp. 317-327.

443. –, "Kierkegaard and Apologetics," *Journal of Religion,* IV (1964), pp. 122-132.

444. Diaz, Janet Winecoff. *The Major Themes of Existentialism in the Work of José Ortega y Gasset* (Chapel Hill: University of North Carolina Press, 1970).

445. Dieckmann, Herbert, "French Existentialism before Sartre," *Yale French Studies,* I, 1 (1948), pp. 33-41.

446. Diem, Hermann. *Kierkegaard: An Introduction,* tr. David Green (Richmond: John Knox Press, 1966).

447. –. *Kierkegaard's Dialectic of Existence,* tr. by H. Knight (London: Oliver and Boyd, 1959).

448. Dinkler, E., "Existentialist Interpretation of the New Testament," *Journal of Religion,* XXXII (1952), pp. 87-96.

449. Doherty, Cyril Michael. *The Theme of Culpability in the Literary Works of Jean-Paul Sartre,* Ph.D. diss., University of Wisconsin (1973).

450. Domenach, J. M., "Camus-Sartre Debates: Rebellion vs. Revolution," *Nation,* CLVI (1953), pp. 202-203.

451. Dondeyne, A. *Contemporary European Thought and Christian Faith* (Pittsburgh: Duqesne University Press, 1958).

452. Doran, Robert M., "Sartre's Critique of the Husserlian Ego," *The Modern Schoolman,* XLIV (May, 1967), pp. 307-318.

453. Doubrovsky, Serge, " 'The Nine of Hearts'. Fragment of a Psychoreading of *La Nausée,*" tr. by Carol Bové, *boundary 2,* V, 2 (1977), pp. 411-420.

454. –, "Sartre and Camus: A Study in Incarceration," *Yale French Studies,* XXV (Spring, 1960), pp. 85-92.

455. Douglas, G. H., "Heidegger's Notion of Poetic Truth," *The Personalist,* XLVII (1966), pp. 500-508.

456. –, "Heidegger on the Education of Poets and Philosophers," *Educational Theory,* XXII (1972), pp. 443-449.

457. Douglas, Kenneth. *A Critical Bibliography of Existentialism*

(The Paris School), Yale French Studies, Special Monograph No. 1, 1950 (Kraus Reprint Corp., 1966).

An important, well organized, annotated early bibliography. Many materials discussed are in French.

458. Douglas, K. N., "The Nature of Sartre's Existentialism," *The Virginia Quarterly Review* (April, 1947), pp. 244-260.

459. Doyle, J. P., "Heidegger and Scholastic Metaphysics," *Modern Schoolman,* XLIX (1972), pp. 201-220.

460. Downs, Lynwood G. *Nietzschean Ideas in Modern German Literature* (Ithaca: Cornell University Press, 1915).

461. Drimmer, Melvin. *Nietzsche in American Thought: 1895-1925,* Ph.D. diss., University of Rochester (1965).

462. Driscoll, G., "Heidegger: A Response to Nihilism," *Philosophy Today,* XI (1967), pp. 17-38.

463. –, "Heidegger's Ethical Monism," *The New Scholasticism,* XLII (1968), pp. 497-510.

464. –, "Nietzsche and Eternal Recurrence," *The Personalist,* XLVII (1966), pp. 461-474.

465. Dru, Alexander, "What Existentialism Is: The Error of Sartre and Mounier," *The Tablet,* CLXXXVIII (November 2, 1946), pp. 225-226.

466. Drucker, P. F., "Unfashionable Kierkegaard," *Sewanee Review,* LVII (1949), pp. 587-602.

467. Dufrenne, Mikel, "Existentialism and Existentialisms," *Philosophy and Phenomenological Research,* XXVI, 1 (1965), pp. 51-62.

468. Duhrssen, Alfred, "Some French Hegelians," *Review of Metaphysics,* VII (1953), pp. 323-337.

469. Duncan, Elmer H., "Kierkegaard's Teleological Suspension

of the Ethical: A Study of Exception-Cases," *Southern Journal of Philosophy,* I (1963), pp. 9-18.

470. –, "Kierkegaard's Use of Paradox–Yet Once More," *Journal of Existentialism,* VII (1967), pp. 319-328.

471. Dupré, Louis K., "The Constitution of the Self in Kierkegaard's Philosophy," *International Philosophical Quarterly,* III (1963), pp. 506-526.

472. –. *Kierkegaard as Theologian* (London: Sheed and Ward, 1963).

473. Dupré, Wilhelm, "Phenomenology and Systematic Philosophy," *Philosophy Today,* XIII (1969), pp. 284-295.

474. Durfee, Harold, "Albert Camus and the Ethics of Rebellion," *Journal of Religion,* XXXVIII (1958), pp. 29-45.

475. –, "Camus' Challenge to Modern Art," *Journal of Aesthetics and Art Criticism,* XIV (1955), pp. 201-205.

476. Durkan, J., "Philosopher of Incarnation: A Study of G. Marcel," *Tablet,* CXC (1947), pp. 263-264.

477. Duroche, L. L. *Aspects of Criticism: Literary Study in Present-Day Germany,* Vol. IV of Stanford Studies in Germanics and Slavics, ed. by Edgar Lohner, C. H. Van Schoonerveld, and F. W. Strothmann (The Hague: Mouton, 1967).

478. Dutt, K. Guru. *Existentialism and Indian Thought* (New York: 1960).

479. Earle, William, "Being versus Tragedy," *Chicago Review,* XIV (1960), pp. 107-114.

480. –, "The Concept of Existence?" *Journal of Philosophy,* LVII (1960), pp. 734-744.

481. –, "Freedom and Existence," *Review of Metphysics,* IX (1955), pp. 46-56.

482. –, "Hegel and Some Contemporary Philosophers," *Philosophy and Phenomenological Research,* XX (1960), pp. 352-364.

483. –, "Jaspers and Existential Analysis," *Journal of Existential Psychiatry,* I (1960), pp. 166-176.

484. –, "Jaspers' Philosophical Anthropology," in Paul Schilpp, ed., *The Philosophy of Karl Jaspers* (New York: Tudor Publishing Co., 1957), pp. 523-538.

485. –, "The Life of the Transcendental Ego," *Review of Metaphysics,* XIII (1959), pp. 3-28.

486. –, "The Paradox and Death of God: Kierkegaard and Nietzsche," in C. W. Christian and Glenn R. Wittig, eds., *Radical Theology: Phase Two* (Philadelphia: Lippincott, 1967), pp. 27-42.

487. –, James M. Edie, and John Wild. *Christianity and Existentialism: Essays* (Evanston: Northwestern University Press, 1963).

488. –, "Phenomenology and Existentialism," *Journal of Philosophy,* LVII (1960), pp. 75-84.

489. –, "Wahl on Heidegger on Being," *Philosophical Review,* LXVII (1958), pp. 85-90.

Review-article of Wahl's book *Heidegger: Einführung in die Metaphysik* (Tubingen, 1953).

490. Edie, James M., ed. *An Invitation to Phenomenology: Studies in the Phenomenology of Experience* (Chicago: Quadrangle, 1965).

491. –, ed. *New Essays in Phenomenology: Studies in the Philosophy of Experience* (Chicago: Quadrangle, 1969).

492. –, *et al,* eds. *Paterns of the Life-World: Essays in Honor of John Wild* (Evanston: Northwestern University Press, 1970).

493. –, "Phenomenology as a Rigorous Science," *International Philosophical Quarterly,* XLVIII (1967), pp. 490-508.

494. –, ed. *Phenomenology in America: Studies in the Philosophy of Experience* (Chicago: Quadrangle, 1967).

495. –, "Transcendental Phenomenology and Existentialism," in Joseph J. Kockelmans, ed., *Phenomenology: The Philosophy of Edmund Husserl and its Interpretation* (New York: Anchor Press, 1967), pp. 237-251.

496. –, "Vico and Existential Philosophy," in Giorgio Tagliacozzo and Hayden V. White, eds., *Giambattisata Vico: An Internation Symposium* (Baltimore: The Johns Hopkins Press, 1969).

497. Edinborough, A., "Sartre and the Existentialist Novel," *Queen's Quarterly,* LVI (1949), pp. 105-112.

498. Edmondson, P. E. *Sartrean Freedom: A Changing Perspective,* Ph.D. diss., Duke University (1967).

499. Edwards, Brian F. M., "Kafka and Kierkegaard: A Reassesment," *German Life and Letters,* XX (1947), pp. 218-225.

500. Edwards, C. N., "Guilt in the Thought of Soren Kierkegaard," *Encounter,* XXVII (1966), pp. 141-157.

501. Ehman, Robert R., "Personal Love," *Personalist,* XLIX (1968), pp. 116-141.

On Sartre.

502. Ehrmann, Jacques, "Camus and the Existential Adventure," *Yale French Studies,* XXV, 1960, pp. 93-97.

503. Elkin, Henry, "Comment on Sartre from the Standpoint of Existential Psychotherapy," *Review of Existential Psychology and Psychiatry,* I (1961), pp. 189-195.

504. Ellenberger, H. F., "Phenomenology and Existential Analysis," *Canadian Psychiatric Association Journal,* II

(1957), pp. 137-146.

505. Eller, Vernard. *Kierkegaard and Radical Discipleship: A New Perspective* (Princeton: Princeton University Press, 1967).

506. Elliston, Frederick and Peter McCormick, eds. *Husserl: Expositions and Appraisals* (Notre Dame: Notre Dame University Press, 1976).

507. Ellmann, Richard. *The Identiy of Yeats* (London: Oxford University Press, 1954).

Pp. 91-98 on Yeats and Nietzsche.

508. Elveton, R. O., ed. and tr. *The Phenomenology of Husserl: Selected Critical Readings* (Chicago: Quadrangle Books, 1970).

509. Embree, Lester E., ed. *Life-World and Consciousness: Essays for Aron Gurwitsch* (Evanston: Northwestern University Press, 1972).

510. Erickson, Stephen A. *Language and Being: An Analytic Phenomenology* (New Haven: Yale University Press, 1970).

Largely on Heidegger's analysis of language.

511. –, "Martin Heidegger," *Review of Metaphysics,* XIX (1965-1966), pp. 462-492.

512. –, "Meaning and Language," *Man and World,* I (1968), pp. 563-586.

On Heidegger and Wittgenstein.

513. –, "Worlds and World Views," *Man and World,* II (1969), pp. 228-247.

514. Esslin, Martin, "The Absurdity of the Absurd," *Kenyon Review,* XXII (1960), pp. 670-673.

515. Estall, N. M., "Existentialism as a Philosophy," *Toronto Quarterly,* XXIX (1960), pp. 297-309.

516. Evans, Oliver, "The Rise of Existentialism," *South Atlantic Quarterly,* XLVII (1948), pp. 152-156.

517. Evans, Robert O., "Existentialism in Greene's 'The Quiet American,'' *Modern Fiction Studies,* III (1957), pp. 241-248.

518. Fairhurst, Stanley J., "Soren Kierkegaard: A Bibliography," *Modern Schoolman,* XXI (1953), pp. 19-22.

519. Fairly, Barker, "Friedrich Nietzsche and the Poetic Impulse," *Bulletin of the John Rylands Library,* XIX (1935), pp. 344-361.

520. Falk, Eugene H. *Types of Thematic Structure: The Nature and Function of Motifs in Gide, Camus, and Sartre* (Chicago: University of Chicago Press, 1967).

521. Fallico, Arturo B. *Art and Existentialism* (Englewood Cliffs: Prentice-Hall, 1962).

522. Farber, L., "The Therapeutic Despair," *Psychiatry,* XXI (1958), pp. 7-20.

523. Farber, M., ed. *Philosophic Thought in France and the United States* (Buffalo: University of Buffalo Press, 1950).

524. Farber, Marjorie, "Heidegger on the Essence of Truth," *Philosophy and Phenomenological Research,* XVIII (1957-1958), pp. 523-532.

525. –, "Subjectivity in Modern Fiction," *Kenyon Review,* VII (1945), pp. 645-652.

526. –, "What is Philosophy?" *Philosophy and Phenomenological Research,* XXI (1960-1961), pp. 255-259.

527. Farber, Marvin. *The Aims of Phenomenology: The Motives, Methods, and Impact of Husserl's Thought* (New

York: Harper and Row, 1966).

528. —, "Experience and Transcendence: A Chapter in Recent Phenomenology and Existentialism," *Philosophy and Phenomenological Research,* XII (1951), pp. 1-23.

529. —. *The Foundation of Phenomenology: Edmund Husserl and the Quest for a Rigorous Science of Philosophy* (Cambridge: Harvard University Press, 1943).

530. —, "Heidegger on the Essence of Truth," *Philosophy and Phenomenological Research,* XVIII (1958).

531. —, "The Ideal of a Presuppositionless Philosophy," in Joseph J. Kockelmans, ed., *Phenomenology: The Philosophy of Edmund Husserl and its Interpretation* (New York: Anchor Press, 1967), pp. 37-57.

532. —. *Naturalism and Subjectivism* (Springfield, Illinois: Thomas, 1959).

533. —. *Phenomenology as a Method and as a Philosophical Discipline* (Buffalo: University of Buffalo Press, 1928).

This is the earliest major study of Phenomenology in English, and still serves as an excellent point of departure for Phenomenological studies. Farber was the most important American proponent of study in the discipline.

534. —. *Philosophical Essays in Memory of Edmund Husserl* (Cambridge: Harvard University Press, 1940).

535. —, "A Review of Recent Phenomenological Literature," *Journal of Philosophy,* XXVII (1930), pp. 337-349.

536. Farrell, B. A., "The Logic of Existential Psychoanalysis," *New Society,* VI (October 1, 1965), pp. 9-11.

537. Farrelly, J., "Religious Reflections on Man's Transcendence," *The Thomist,* XXXVII (1973), pp. 284-301.

538. Fasel, Oscar. *Unamuno's Thought and German Philosophy,* Ph.D. diss., Columbia University (1957).

539. Fauconnier, R. L., "French Novelists in Revolt," *Queen's Quarterly,* LXIII (1957), pp. 609-619.

540. Fay, Thomas, "Early Heidegger and Wittgenstein on World," *Philosophical Studies,* XXI (1973), pp. 161-171.

541. –, "Heidegger on Logic: A Genetic Study of His Thought on Logic," *Journal of the History of Philosophy,* XII, 1 (1974).

542. –. *Heidegger on Logic: An Encounter of his Thought with Wittgenstein,* Ph.D. diss., New York (1971).

543. Feifel, Herman, ed. *The Meaning of Death* (New York: McGraw-Hill, 1959).

544. Fell, J. P., "Heidegger's Notion of Two Beginnings," *Review of Metaphysics,* XXV (1971), pp. 213-237.

545. –, "Sartre's Theory of Motivation: Some Clarifications," *Journal of the British Society for Phenomenology,* I (May, 1970), pp. 27-34.

546. –. *Sartre's Theory of the Passions* (New York: Columbia University Press, 1962).

547. Fenger, Henning, "Kierkegaard–A Literary Approach," *Scandinavica,* III (1964), pp. 1-16.

548. Ferm, Deane W., "Two Conflicting Trends in Protestant Theological Thinking," *Religion in Life,* XXV (1956), pp. 582-594.

549. Figgis, J. N. *The Will to Freedom* (New York: Scribners, 1917).

On Nietzsche.

550. Fingarette, Herbert. *Self-Deception* (New York: Humani-

ties Press, 1969).

551. Finklestein, Sidney Walter. *Existentialism and Alienation in American Literature* (New York: International Pub., 1965).

552. Fitch, R. E., "The Social Philosophy of Paul Tillich," *Religion in Life,* XXVII (1958), pp. 247-256.

553. Flake, Otto. *Nietzsche* (Baden-Baden: P. Keppler, 1947).

554. Flores, K., "Franz Kafka and the Nameless Guilt," *Quarterly Review of Literature,* III, pp. 382-405.

555. Foot, Philippa, "Nietzsche: The Revaluation of Values," in Robert Solomon, ed., *Nietzsche: A Collection of Critical Essays* (New York: Anchor Press, 1973), pp. 156-168.

556. Ford, Richard S., "Existentialism: Philosophy or Theology?" *Religion in Life,* XXVIII (1959), pp. 433-442.

557. Forster, George. *Friedrich Nietzsche* (New York: 1931).

558. Forster-Nietzsche. *The Life of Nietzsche* (New York: Sturgis, 1912).

559. –. *The Lonely Nietzsche* (London: W. Heinemann, 1915).

560. Foster, Grace, "The Natural History of the Will," *American Scholar,* XV (1946), pp. 277-287.

Comparison of Nietzsche and Emerson.

561. Foulk, Gary J., "Plantinga's Criticisms of Sartre's Ethics," *Ethics,* LXXXII (1972), pp. 330-333.

See article by Alvin Plantinga.

562. Foulquié, Paul. *Existentialism,* tr. by Kathleen Raine (New York: Roy Publishers, 1950).

563. Fowlie, Wallace. *Climate of Violence: The French Literary*

Tradition from Baudelaire to the Present (New York: Macmillan, 1967), esp. pp. 205-218.

564. Fowlie, Wallace, "Existentialist Hero: A Study of *L'Age de raison,*" *Yale French Studies,* I, 1 (1948), pp. 53-61.

565. Frank, Erich. *Philosophical Understanding and Religious Truth* (New York: Oxford University Press, 1945).

566. Frank, J., "Existentialist Ethics," *New Republic,* CXXIX (1953), pp. 18-20.

567. Frank, Joseph, "Existentialist in the Underworld," in R. Richman, ed., *Arts at Mid-Century* (New York: Horizon Press, 1954).

568. Frank, Rachel, "Unamuno: Existentialism and the Spanish Novel," *Accent,* IX (1949), pp. 80-88.

569. Frankl, Viktor, "Beyond Self-Actualization and Self-Expression," *Journal of Existential Psychiatry,* I (1960), pp. 5-21.

570. —. *The Doctor and the Soul: From Psychotherapy to Logotherapy,* tr. by Richard and Clara Winston (New York: Alfred Knopf, 1966).

571. —. *From Death-Camp to Existentialism* (Boston: Beacon Press, 1959).

572. —, "Logotherapy and the Challenge of Suffering," *Review of Existential Psychology and Psychiatry,* I (1961).

573. —, "Logos and Existence in Psychotherapy," *American Journal of Psychotherapy,* VII (1953), pp. 8-15.

574. —. *Man's Search for Meaning: An Introduction to Logotherapy* (New York: Washington Square Press, 1969).

575. Franquiz, J. A., "Appraisal of Heidegger's Epistemology as a Foundation for a Metaphysics of Religion," *Wesleyan Studies in Religion,* LVII (1964-1965), pp. 23-29.

576. Freehof, Solomon B., "Aspects of Existentialism," *Carnegie Magazine,* XXII (1949), pp, 292-294.

577. —, "Existentialism: World's Despair," *Carnegie Magazine,* XXXI (1957), pp. 120-125.

578. Frenzel, Ivo. *Friedrich Nietzsche* (New York: Bobbs-Merrill, 1967).

579. Friedman, Lawrence, "Psychoanalysis, Existentialism, and the Esthetic Universe," *Journal of Philosophy,* LV (1958), pp. 617-631.

580. Friedman, Maurice S., "Dialogue and the 'Essential We': The Basis of Values in the Philosophy of Martin Buber," *American Journal of Psychoanalysis,* XX (1960), pp. 26-34.

581. —, "Martin Buber and Christian Thought," *Review of Religion,* XVIII (1953), pp. 31-43.

582. —. *Martin Buber: Mystic, Existentialist, Social Prophet: A Study in the Redemption of Evil,* Doctoral Dissertation, University of Chicago (1950).

583. —. *Martin Buber: The Life of Dialogue* (London: Routledge and Kegan Paul, 1955).

Excellent exposition of Buber's Jewish Existentialism.

584. —, "Martin Buber's Theory of Knowledge," *Review of Metaphysics,* VIII (1954), pp. 264-281.

585. —, "Sex in Sartre and Buber," *Review of Existential Psychology and Psychiatry,* III (1963), pp. 113-124.

586. —, "Symbol, Myth, and History in the Thought of Martin Buber," *Journal of Religion,* XXXIV (1954), pp. 1-12.

587. —. *To Deny Our Nothingness: Contemporary Images of Man* (London: Gollancz, 1967).

588. Freund, E. H., "Man's Fall in Martin Heidegger's Philoso-

phy," *Journal of Religion,* XXIV (1944).

589. Frings, M. S., "Heidegger and Scheler," *Philosophy Today,* XII (1968), pp. 21-30.

590. –, "*Nietzsche* by Martin Heidegger," *Journal of Philosophy,* LIX (1962), pp. 830-835.

A review essay of the massive study.

591. Fritz, Helen M., "Joyce and Existentialism," *James Joyce Review,* II (Autumn, 1958), pp. 13-21.

592. Frizell, Bernard, "Existentialism: Postwar Paris Enthrones a Bleak Philosophy of Pessimism," *Life* (June 17, 1946), pp. 59-60.

593. Frohock, W. M., "Camus: Image, Influence, and Sensibility," *Yale French Studies,* II (1949), pp. 91-99.

594. –, "The Prolapsed World of Jean-Paul Sartre," *Accent,* VII (1946), pp. 3-13.

595. Fromm, Erich. *Man for Himself: An Inquiry into the Psychology of Ethics* (New York: Rinehart, 1947).

596. –. *Escape from Freedom* (New York: Rinehart, 1941).

597. –. *Psychoanalysis and Religion* (New Haven: Yale University Press, 1950).

598. –. *The Sane Society* (New York: Rinehart, 1955).

599. Fromm-Reichman, F. and J. L. Moreno, eds. *Progress in Psychotherapy* (New York: Grune and Stratton, 1956).

600. Fulton, Street, "Husserl's Significance for the Theory of Truth," *The Monist,* XLV (1935), pp. 264-306.

601. Gadamer, Hans-Georg, "Concerning Empty and Ful-filled Time," in Edward G. Ballard and Charles E. Scott, eds., *Martin Heidegger in Europe and America* (The

Hague: Martinus Nijhoff, 1973), pp. 77-90.

602. –. *Truth and Method* (New York: Seabury Press, 1975).

Though a very poor translation, this book is an important statement by a student of Heidegger's; a major examination of language.

603. Gajdenko, P. P., "The 'Fundamental Ontology' of Heidegger as a Basis of Philosophical Irrationalism," *Soviet Studies in Philosophy,* IV (1965-1966), pp. 44-55.

604. Galdston, I., "Ethos, Existentialism, and Psychotherapy," *Mental Hygiene,* XLIV (1960), pp. 529-534.

605. –, "Existentialism as a Perenniel Philosophy of Life and Being," *Journal of Existential Psychiatry,* I (1960), pp. 379-397.

606. Gallagher, Kenneth T. *The Philosophy of Gabriel Marcel* (New York: Fordham University Press, 1962).

607. Gans, S. L. *An Analysis of the Philosophical Methodology of Martin Heidegger,* Ph.D. diss., Pennsylvania State University (1967).

608. –, "Ethics or Ontology: Levinas and Heidegger," *Philosophy Today,* XVI (1972), pp. 117-121.

609. Garelick, H. M. *The Anti-Christianity of Kierkegaard* (New York: Humanities Press, 1966).

610. –, "The Irrationality and Supra-Rationality of Kierkegaard's Paradox," *Southern Journal of Philosophy,* II (1964), pp. 75-86.

611. Gates, J. A. *The Life and Thought of Kierkegaard for Everyman* (London: Westminster Press, 1960).

612. Geiger, M., "An Introduction to Existential Philosophy," *Philosophy and Phenomenological Research,* III (1943), pp. 255-278.

613. Geismar, Edward. *Lectures on the Religious Thought of Soren Kierkegaard* (Minneapolis: Augsburg Pub. House, 1938).

614. Gelblum, Tuvia, "Classical Samkhya and the Phenomenology of Sartre," *Philosophy East and West,* XIX (1969), pp. 45-58.

615. –, "Samkhya and Sartre," *Journal of Indian Philosophy,* I, 1 (1970), pp. 75-82.

616. Gelley, A. de, "Staiger, Heidegger, and the Task of Criticism," *Modern Language Quarterly,* XXIII (1962), pp. 195-216.

617. Gelven, Michael. *A Commentary on Heidegger's "Being and Time"* (New York: Harper and Row, 1970).

Gelven displays an unfortunate tendency to oversimplify or use seemingly frivolous examples (i.e., references to a Paul Simon song to illustrate Heidegger's notion of *Gerede*), but this book is an extremely valuable guide to the difficult passages of Heidegger's text. The book is set up to give a running commentary, section by section, keyed to *Being and Time.*

618. –, "Guilt and Human Meaning," *Humanitas,* IX (1972), pp. 69-81.

619. –, "Heidegger and Tragedy," Special Heidegger and Literature issue, *boundary 2,* IV, 2 (1976), pp. 555-570.

620. Georgiades, Niki, "What is Existentialism?" *World Review* (October, 1945), pp. 14-19.

621. Gerber, R. J., "Focal Points in Recent Heidegger Scholarship," *New Scholasticism,* XLII (1968), pp. 561-577.

622. –, "Heidegger: Thinking and Thanking Being," *Modern Schoolman,* XLIV (1966-1967), pp. 205-222.

623. –, "Kierkegaard, Reason, and Faith," *Thought,* XLIV (1969), pp. 29-52.

624. Gershman, Herbert S., "The Structure of Revolt in Malraux, Camus and Sartre," *Symposium,* XXIV (1970), pp. 27-35.

625. Gibson, A., "Existentialism: An Interim Report," *The Meanjin Quarterly,* VII (Autumn, 1948), pp. 41-52.

626. Gier, N. F. *Heidegger and the Ontological Difference: A Historical-Philosophical Analysis,* Ph.D. diss., Claremont Graduate School (1972).

627. Gill, J. H., ed. *Essays on Kierkegaard* (Minneapolis: Burgess Pub. Co., 1969).

628. Gillan, Garth. *The Horizons of the Flesh: Critical Perspectives on the Thought of Merleau-Ponty* (Carbondale: Southern Illinois University Press, 1973).

629. Gillon, Adam, "The Absurd and 'Les valeurs ideales' in Conrad, Kafka, and Camus," *Polish Review,* VI (1961), pp. 3-10.

630. –, "Conrad and Sartre," *The Dalhousie Review,* XL, 1 (1960), pp. 61-71.

631. Gilson, Etienne. *Being and Some Philosophers* (Toronto: 1949).

632. –, "Existence and Philosophy," *Proceedings of the American Catholic Association,* XXI (1946), pp. 4-16.

633. –. *The Terrors of the Year Two Thousand* (Toronto: 1949).

On Nietzsche.

634. Ginsberg, Mitchell, "Nietzschean Psychiatry," in Robert Solomon, ed., *Nietzsche: A Collection of Critical Essays* (New York: Anchor Press, 1973), pp. 293-315.

635. Girard, René, "Existentialism and Literary Criticism," *Yale French Studies,* XVI (1954), pp. 45-52.

636. Gleiman, Lubomir, "The Challenge of Nietzsche," *Thought,* XLII (1967), pp. 52-68.

637. Glicksberg, C. I., "Aesthetics of Nihilism," *University of Kansas City Review,* XXVII (1960), pp. 127-130.

638. –, "Existentialism in Extremis," *The University of Kansas City Review,* XXVII (1960), pp. 31-36.

639. –, "Existentialism versus Marxism," *Nineteenth Century* (May, 1950), pp. 335-341.

640. –. *The Ironic Vision in Modern Literature* (The Hague: Martinus Nijhoff, 1969).

641. –, "Literary Existentialism," *Art Quarterly,* IX (1949), pp. 24-39.

642. –, "The Literary Struggle for Selfhood," *The Personalist,* XLII (1961), pp. 52-65.

643. –, "The Literature of Absurdity," *Western Humanities Review,* XII (1958), pp. 29-38.

644. –, "Sartre: Existentialism in Fiction," *Prairie Schooner,* XXIII (Spring, 1949), pp. 12-18.

645. –. *The Tragic Vision in Twentieth Century* (Carbondale: Southern Illinois University Press, 1963). See especially pp. 97-109.

646. Glicksman, M., "A Note on the Philosophy of Heidegger," *The Journal of Philosophy,* XXXV (1938), pp. 93-104.

647. Goff, Robert, "On Sartre's Language," *Man and World,* III (September-November, 1970), pp. 370-374.

648. –, "Saying and Being with Heidegger and Parmenides," *Man and World,* V (1972), pp. 62-78.

649. –, "Wittgenstein's Tools and Heidegger's Implements," *Man and World,* I (1968), pp. 447-462.

650. Goldstein,Julius, "The Key-Note to the Work of Nietzsche," *Mind,* XI (1902), pp. 216-226.

651. Goldthrope, Rhiannon, "The Presentation of Consciousness in Sartre's *La Nuasée* and Its Theoretical Basis: Reflection and Facticity," *French Studies,* XXII, 2 (1968), pp. 114-132.

652. Gordy, Michael, "The Transcendent Ego and the Emptiness of Consciousness," *Journal of Phenomenological Psychology,* II, 2 (1972), pp. 175-194.

653. Gōtlind, Erik Johan Anders. *Three Theories of Emotion: Some Views on Philosophical Method* (Lund: Gleerup; Copengagen: Munsgaard, 1958).

654. Gould, C. C. *Authenticity and Being-With-Others: A Critique of Heidegger's Sein und Zeit,* Ph.D. diss., Yale University (1971).

655. Gould, James A. and Willis H. Truitt, eds. *Existentialist Philosophy* (Encino, California: Dickenson Pub., 1973).

656. Graaf, W. L., "Rilke in the Light of Heidegger," *Laval Théologique et Philosophique,* XVII (1961), pp. 165-172.

657. Graef, H. C. *Modern Gloom and Christian Hope* (Chicago: Henry Regnery Co., 1959).

658. –, "Prophets of Gloom," *Catholic World,* CLXXXIII (1956), pp. 202-206.

659. Gras, Vernon W., ed. *European Literary Theory and Practice: From Existential Phenomenology to Structuralism* (New York: Dell Publishing Co., 1973).

A collection of essays by Heidegger, Binswanger, Barthes, Poulet, and others.

660. Gray, J. Glenn, "Heidegger 'Evaluates' Nietzsche," *Journal of the History of Ideas,* XIV (1953), pp. 304-309.

661. —, "Heidegger's 'Being'," *Journal of Philosophy,* XLIX (1952), pp. 415-422.

662. —, "Heidegger's Course: From Human Existence to Nature," *Journal of Philosophy,* LIV (1957), pp. 8, 197-207.

663. —, "The Idea of Death in Existentialism," *The Journal of Philosophy,* XLVIII (1951), pp. 113-127.

664. —, "Martin Heidegger: On Anticipating My Own Death," *The Personalist,* XLVI (1965), pp. 439-458.

665. —, "Salvation on the Campus: Why Existentialism is Capturing the Students," *Harper's Magazine* (May, 1965), pp. 53-59.

666. —, "The Splendour of the Simple," *Philosophy East and West,* XX, 3 (1970).

On Heidegger.

667. —. *The Warriors: Reflections on Men in Battle* (New York: Harcourt, Brace, Inc., 1959).

668. de Greef, J., "Philosophy and Its 'Other'," *International Philosophical Quarterly,* X (1970), pp. 252ff.

669. Greene, Norman Nathaniel. *Jean-Paul Sartre: The Existentialist Ethic* (Ann Arbor: University of Michigan Press, 1960).

670. Greene, Theodore M., "Anxiety and the Search for Meaning," *Texas Quarterly,* I, 3 (1958), pp. 172-191.

671. Greening, T., "Existential Fiction and the Paradox of Ethics," *Antioch Review,* XXIII (1963), pp. 93-107.

672. Greenlee, Douglas, "Sartre: Presuppositions of Freedom," *Philosophy Today,* XII (1968), pp. 176-183.

673. Greenman, M. A., "Existence and the Limits of Analysis," *Philosophy and Phenomenological Research,* XV

(1955), pp. 551-557.

674. Greenwood, E. B., "Literature and Philosophy," *Essays in Criticism,* XX (1970), pp. 5-18.

675. Gregory, J. C., "Sartre's Existentialism," *Contemporary Review* (September, 1949), pp. 163-168.

676. Grene, Marjorie, "The Aesthetic Dialogue of Sartre and Merleau-Ponty," *Journal of the British Society for Phenomenology,* I (1970), pp. 59-72.

677. –, "Authenticity: An Existential Virtue," *Ethics,* LXII (1952), pp. 266-274.

678. –. *Dreadful Freedom: A Critique of Existentialism* (Chicago: University of Chicago Press, 1948). Republished as *Introduction to Existentialism,* 1959.

679. –, "Heidegger: Philosopher and Prophet," *The Twentieth Century,* CLXIV (1958), pp. 545-555.

680. –, "Kierkegaard: The Philosophy," *Kenyon Review,* IX (1947), pp. 48-69.

681. –. *Martin Heidegger* (New York: Hilary, 1957).

682. –. *Sartre* (New York: New Viewpoints, 1973).

683. –, "Sartre's Theory of Emotions," *Yale French Studies,* I, 1 (1948), pp. 97-101.

684. –, "Two More Existentialists–Karl Jaspers and Gabriel Marcel," *Kenyon Review,* IX (1947), pp. 382-399.

685. Griffith, G. O., "Kierkegaard on Faith: A Study of Fear and Trembling," *Hibbert Journal,* XLIII (1943), pp. 58-63.

686. Grimsley, Ronald, "An Aspect of Sartre and the Unconscious," *Philosophy,* XXX (1955), pp. 33-44.

687. –, " 'Dread' as a Philosophical Concept," *Philosophical*

Quarterly, VI (1956), pp. 245-256.

688. –. *Existentialist Thought* (Cardiff: University of Wales Press, 1955).

689. –, "Kierkegaard and Descartes," *Journal of the History of Philosophy*, IV (1966), pp. 31-41.

690. –, "Kierkegaard and Leibniz," *Journal of the History of Ideas*, XXVI (1965), pp. 383-396.

691. –, "Kierkegaard, Vigny and 'the Poet'," *Revue de Littérature Comparée* (1960), pp. 52-80.

692. –, "Sartre and the Phenomenology of the Imagination," *Journal of the British Society for Phenomenology*, III (January, 1972), pp. 58-72.

693. –. *Soren Kierkegaard and French Literature: Eight Comparative Studies* (Cardiff: University of Wales Press, 1966).

694. –, "Two Philosophical Views of the Literary Imagination," *Comparative Literature Studies*, VIII (March, 1971), pp. 42-57.

695. Grossman, Morris, "How Sartre Must be Read: An Examination of a Philosophic Method," *Bucknell Review*, XVI (March, 1968), pp. 18-29.

696. Groves, J. L. *The Influence of Heidegger in Latin American Philosophy*, Ph.D. diss., Boston University (1960).

697. Grugan, A. A. *Thought and Poetry: Language as Man's Homecoming: A Study of Martin Heidegger's Question of Being and Its Ties to Friedrich Hölderlin's Experience of the Holy*, Ph.D. diss., Duquesne University (1972).

698. Guicharnaud, Jacques, "Those Years: Existentialism 1943-1945," *Yale French Studies*, XVI (1954), pp. 127ff.

699. Gupta, R. W., "What is Heidegger's Notion of Time?" *Revue*

Internationale de Philosophie, XIV (1960), pp. 163-193.

700. Gurwitsch, Aron. *Field of Consciousness* (Pittsburgh: Duquesne University Press, 1964).

701. –, "A Non Egological Conception of Consciousness," *Philosophy and Phenomenological Research,* I (March, 1941), pp. 325-338.

702. –, "On the Intentionality of Consciousness," in Joseph J. Kockelmans, ed., *Phenomenology: The Philosophy of Edmund Husserl and Its Interpretation* (New York: Anchor Press, 1967), pp. 118-136.

703. –. *Studies in Phenomenology and Psychology* (Evanston: Northwestern University Press, 1966).

704. Guthrie, George P., "The Importance of Sartre's Phenomenology for Christian Theology," *Journal of Religion,* XLVII (January, 1967), pp. 10-26.

705. Gutmann, James, "Confidence and the 'Will to Power' from Nietzsche," *Review of Religion,* XIX (1955), pp. 131-135.

706. –, "The Tremendous Moment," *Journal of Philosophy,* LI (1954), pp. 837-842.

On Nietzsche's concept of the eternal recurrence.

707. Haas, W. S. *The Destiny of the Mind: East and West* (London: Faber and Faber, 1956).

708. Haecker, T. *Soren Kierkegaard,* tr. by H. Dru (New York: Oxford University Press, 1937).

709. Hakim, Eleanor, "Jean-Paul Sartre: The Dialectics of Myth," *Salmagundi,* I, 2 (1966), pp. 59-94.

710. Halevi, Jacob L., "Kierkegaard and the Midrash," *Judaism,* IV (1955), pp. 13-28.

711. –, "Kierkegaard's Suspension of the Ethical: Is it Jewish?" *Judaism,* VIII (1959), pp. 292-302.

712. Halévy, Daniel. *The Life of Friedrich Nietzsche* (London: 1911).

713. Hall, E. W., "Existential Normatives," *Journal of Philosophy,* LV (1958), pp. 75-77.

714. Hamblen, Emily. *Friedrich Nietzsche and His New Gospel* (Boston: 1911, 1940).

715. –. *A Guide to Nietzsche* (Girard, Kansas: 1923).

716. Hamburg, C. H., "A Cassirer-Heidegger Seminar," *Philosophy and Phenomenological Research,* XXV (1964-1965), pp. 208-222.

717. Hamilton, Kenneth, "Life in the House that Angst Built," *Hibbert Journal,* LVII (1958), pp. 46-55.

718. –. *The Promise of Kierkegaard* (Philadelphia: Lippincott, 1969).

719. Hamrick, W. S., "Heidegger and the Objectivity of Aesthetic Truth," *The Journal of Value Inquiry,* V (1970-1971), pp. 120-130.

720. Hanly, C. M. T., "Phenomenology, Consciousness and Freedom," *Dialogue,* V (March, 1966), pp. 323-345.

721. Hanna, Thomas, "Albert Camus and the Christian Faith," *Journal of Religion,* XXXVI (1956), pp. 224-233.

722. –. *The Lyrical Existentialists* (New York: Atheneum, 1962).

Deals solely with Kierkegaard, Nietzsche, and Camus.

723. –. *The Thought and Art of Albert Camus* (Chicago: Henry Regnery Co., 1958).

724. Hanneborg, Knut. *The Study of Literature: A Contribution*

to the Phenomenology of the Human Sciences (Oslo: Universitetsforlagert, 1967).

725. Hanselmann, J. F. S. *Martin Heidegger's fundamental Ontology and Its Theological Implications,* Ph.D. diss., University of Hartford (1952).

726. Hardré, Jacques, "The Existentialism of Jean-Paul Sartre," *The Carolina Quarterly,* I (March, 1949), pp. 49-55.

727. –, "Sartre's Existentialism and Humanism," *Studies in Philology,* XLVIII (1952), pp. 534-537.

728. Hare, Peter H., *et al. Studies on Exisatentialist Themes* (Buffalo: State University of New York at Buffalo, 1968).

729. Harper, Ralph. *The Existential Experience* (Baltimore: The Johns Hopkins University Press, 1972).

730. –. *Existentialism: A Theory of Man* (Cambridge: Harvard University Press, 1948).

731. –. *Nostalgia: An Existential Exploration of Longing and Fulfillment in the Modern Age,* foreword by Richard A. Macksey (Cleveland: Press of Case Western Reserve University, 1966).

732. –. *The Seventh Solitude: Man's Isolation in Kierkegaard, Dostoyevsky, and Nietzsche* (Baltimore: Johns Hopkins University Press, 1965).

733. –, "Two Existential Interpretations," *Philosophy and Phenomenological Research,* V (1944-1945), pp. 392-397.

734. Harries, Karsten, "Heidegger and Hölderlin: The Limits of Language," *The Personalist,* XLIV (1963), pp. 5-23.

735. –, "Heidegger's Conception of the Holy," *The Personalist,* XLVII (1966), pp. 169-184.

736. –, "Language and Silence: Heidegger's Dialogue with

Georg Trakl," Special Heidegger and Literature issue, *boundary 2,* IV, 2 (1976), pp. 495-512.

737. Hartman, Geoffrey H., "The Fulness and Nothingness of Literature," *Yale French Studies,* XVI (1954), pp. 63-78.

738. Hartmann, Klaus. *Sartre's Ontology: A Study of Being and Nothingness in the Light of Hegel's Logic* (Evanston: Northwestern University Press, 1966).

739. – and R. E. Santoni, "Sartre's Ontology," *International Philosophical Quarterly,* VIII (1968), pp. 303 ff.

740. Hartt, J. N., "Beyond Existentialism," *Yale Review,* XLV (1956), pp. 444-451.

741. –, "God, Transcendance and Freedom in the Philosophy of Karl Jaspers," *Review of Metaphysics,* IV (1950-1951), pp. 247-258.

742. –, "On the Possibility of an Existentialist Philosophy," *Review of Metaphysics,* III (1949), pp. 94-106.

743. Hassett, J. D., "Heidegger, Being, and a World in Turmoil," *Thought,* XXXVI (1961), pp. 537-554.

744. Hayes, D. G., "Nietzsche's Eternal Recurrence: A Prelude to Heidegger," *The Journal of Existentialism,* VI (1965-1966), pp. 189-196.

745. Hazleton, Roger, "Marcel on Mystery," *Journal of Religion,* XXXVIII (1958), pp. 155-167.

746. –, "Was Nietzsche an Anti-Christian?" *Journal of Religion,* XII (1942), pp. 63-88.

747. Heaton, J. M., "Saying and Showing in Heidegger and Wittgenstein," *Journal of the British Society for Phenomenology,* III (1972), pp. 42-45.

748. Heidegger, Martin, "The Age of the World View," tr. by Marjorie Grene, *Measure* (1951), pp. 269-284.

749. –, "Art and Space," tr. by Charles H. Siebert, *Man and World*, VI, 1 (1973).

750. –. *Being and Time*, tr. by John Macquarrie and Edward Robinson (New York: Harper and Row, 1962).

This is perhaps the single most important primary work of twentieth century Existentialism, and supplies most of the themes and much of the vocabulary for all of the philosophers of existence who would follow. Though massive in its present form, *Sein und Zeit* is only one third of the work Heidegger projected but later abandoned. Heidegger begins by "destructing" (what the Derrideans prefer to call "deconstructing") the entire Western ontotheological tradition. Heidegger's thesis, in this introductory section, is that certain pre-Socratic thinkers (principally Heraclitus) were close to the primordial question of "How does it stand with Being?" or "What does it mean to Be?" (the *Seinsfrage*). All philosophers after Heraclitus (except, most notably, Kierkegaard and Nietzsche) got away from this primordial question and, in moving from the *Seinsfrage*, covered up the truth (for which Heidegger goes back to the Greek word for truth, *aletheia*, which he interprets etymologically as meaning "uncovering that which has been covered over"). Part One extrapolates on Heidegger's notion of the *Dasein*, the Being who is also a Being-there, a Being-in-the World. Part Two explores the necessity of Being to be in-the-World, and Part Three explains what the "Worldhood of the World" is, and Heidegger takes advantage of his discussion of spatiality to bludgeon his double-headed *bete-noir* of Hegel and Descartes. Part Four contrasts the *Dasein* with the *Das Man*, the they-self. Sartre will develop and simplify this in his analysis of *les'Autres* in *Being and Nothingness*. Part Five explores the pervasive themes of Fear and *Angst*, understanding (*Verstehen*), assertion, authenticity, authentic and inauthentic discourse (*Rede* and *Gerede*), curiosity, ambiguity, falling and throwness (*Verfallen* and *Geworfenheit*). The second section of the volume deals with a radical awareness of temporality, and the Dasein's relation with time, concentrating on the force of every moment as a Being which is always moving towards Death (*Sein-zum-Tode*). *Being and Time* is extremely difficult, at first, and the neophyte might be best approaching it with Michael Gelven's *A Commentary on Heidegger's Being and Time* (item 617 of this Bibliography) in hand.

751. —. *Discourse on Thinking: A Translation of Gelassenheit,* tr. by John M. Anderson and E. Hans Freund (New York: Harper and Row, 1966).

752. —. *Early Greek Thinking,* tr. by David Farrell Krell and Frank A. Capuzzi (New York: Harper and Row, 1975).

753. —. *The End of Philosophy,* tr. by Joan Stambaugh (New York: Harper and Row, 1973).

754. —. *The Essence of Reasons,* tr. by Terence Malick (Evanston: Northwestern University Press, 1969).

755. —. *Existence and Being,* with an introduction and analysis by Werner Brock (Chicago: Henry Regnery Co., 1949).

See note for item 240 of this Bibliography.

756. —. *Hegel's Concept of Experience,* tr. by Kenley Royce Dove (New York: Harper and Row, 1970).

757. —, "The Idea of Phenomenology," tr. by John N. Deely *et al, New Scholasticism,* XLIV (1970), pp. 325-344.

758. —. *Identity and Difference,* tr. by Joan Stambaugh (New York: Harper and Row, 1969).

Bilingual text. This work is valuable as a representation of the later Heidegger, the socalled post-*Kehre* (after the Turn) Heidegger, in which some claim Heidegger turned against much that he had written in *Being and Time.* Most interesting in the two sections ("The Principle of Identity," and "The Onto-Theo-Logical Constitution of Metaphysics") is the almost mystically religious treatment the *Logos* concept, and a pointing toward the directions that will be taken in the late sixties and early seventies by the *Tel Quel* Group and Jacques Derrida.

759. —. *Introduction to Metaphysics,* tr. by Ralph Manheim (New Haven: Yale University Press, 1959). *An Introduction to Metaphysics* (New York: Anchor Press, 1961).

760. —. *Kant and the Problem of Metaphysics,* tr. by James S. Churchill (Bloomington: Indiana University Press, 1962).

761. —, "Nietzsche as Metaphysician," tr. by Joan Stambaugh, in Robert Solomon, ed., *Nietzsche: A Collection of Critical Essays* (Anchor Press, 1973), pp. 105-113.

762. —. *On the Question of Being,* tr. by William Kluback and Jean T. Wilde (New York: Twayne, 1958).

763. —. *On the Way to Language,* tr. by Peter D. Hertz (New York: Harper and Row, 1971).

764. —, "The Origin of the Work of Art," in Albert Hofstadter and Richard Kuhns, eds., *Philosophies of Art and Beauty* (New York: Random House, Modern Library, 1964), pp. 649-701.

765. —, "Plato's Doctrine of Truth," tr. by John Barlow, and "Letter on Humanism," tr. by Edgar Lohner, both in William Barrett and Henry D. Aiken, eds., *Philosophy in the Twentieth Century* (New York: Random House, 1962).

766. —. *Poetry, Language, Thought,* tr. by Alfred Hofstadter (New York: Harper and Row, 1971).

767. —, "The Problem of Non-Objectifying Thinking and Speaking," in Jerry Gill, ed., *Philosophy and Religion* (Minneapolis: Burgess Publishing Co., 1968).

768. —, "The Problem of Reality in Modern Philosophy," tr. by

Philip J. Bossert, *Journal of the British Society for Phenomenology,* IV, 1 (1973).

769. –, "A Recollection," tr. by Hans Siegfried, *Man and World,* III, 1 (1970).

770. –. *What is Philosophy?* tr. by William Kluback and Jean T. Wilde (New York: Twayne, 1958).

771. –. *What is a Thing?* tr. by W. B. Barton and Vera Deutsch (Chicago: Henry Regnery, 1968).

772. –. *What is Called Thinking?* tr. by Fred D. Wieck and J. Glenn Gray (New York: Harper and Row, 1968).

773. –, "Who is Nietzsche's Zarathustra?" *Review of Metaphysics,* XX (1967), pp. 411-431.

774. Heinecken, Martin L., "Kierkegaard as Christian," *Journal of Religion,* XXXVII (1957), pp. 20-31.

775. –. *The Moment Before God* (Philadelphia: Muhlenburg Press, 1956).

Primarily on Kierkegaard.

776. Heinemann, Frederick Henry. *Existentialism and the Modern Predicament* (New York: Harper and Row, 1953).

777. –, "Theologia Diaboli," *The Hibbert Journal,* LII (October, 1953), pp. 65-72.

778. –, "What is Alive and What is Dead in Existentialism?" *Revue internationale de Philosophie,* III (1949), pp. 306-310.

779. Held, M., "The Historical Kierkegaard: Faith or Gnosis," *Journal of Religion,* XXXVII (1957), pp. 260-267.

780. Heller, Erich. *The Artist's Journey into the Interior and Other Essays* (New York: Random House, 1965).

781. –, "Burckhardt and Nietzsche," *Cambridge Journal,* II (1948-1949), pp. 387-401.

782. –. *The Disinherited Mind* (New York: Farrar, Straus and Cudahy, 1957).

783. –, "The Importance of Nietzsche," *Encounter,* XXII (1964), pp. 59-66.

784. –, "Nietzsche and Goethe," *Cambridge Journal,* IV (1950-1951), pp. 579-598.

785. Heller, Otto. *Prophets of Dissent* (New York: 1918).

Pp. 109-157 on Nietzsche.

786. Hellerich, G. *An Investigation into the Educational Implications of Sartre's Notion of 'Being With' and the Reaction of Martin Buber,* Ph.D. diss., University of Kansas (1967).

787. –, "What is Often Overlooked in Existentialist Situation-Ethics," *Journal of Thought,* V (1970), pp. 46-54.

788. Hellmann, Anton, "Hauptmann and the Nietzschean Philosophy," *Poet Lore,* XXIV (1913), pp. 341-347.

789. Helstrom, K. L., "Sartre's Notion of Freedom," *The Southern Journal of Philosophy,* III, 3 (1972), pp. 111-120.

790. Hems, John M., "Husserl and/or Wittgenstein," *International Philosophical Quarterly,* VIII (1968), pp. 547-578.

791. Henle, Robert J., "Existentialism and the Judgement," *Proceedings of the American Catholic Philosophical Association,* XXI (1946), pp. 40-53.

792. Hennig, John, "Karl Jaspers' Attitude Toward History," in Paul Schilpp, ed., *The Philosophy of Karl Jaspers* (New York: The Tudor Pub. Co., 1957), pp. 565-592.

793. –, "Nietzsche, Jaspers and Christianity," *Blackfriars,* XXIX (1948), pp. 476-480.

794. Henriksen, Aage. *Methods and Results of Kierkegaard Studies in Scandinavia* (Copenhagen, 1951).

795. Heppenstall, Rayner, "Jean-Paul Sartre," *Quarterly Review of Literature,* IV, 4 (1946), pp. 416-427.

796. –, "Poetry and Existenz," *Humanitas,* II (1948), pp. 19-24.

On the works of Friedrich Hölderlin.

797. Herberg, W. *Four Existentialist Theologians* (New York: Doubleday, 1958).

798. Hering, Jean, "Concerning Image, Idea and Dream: Phenomenological Notes in Connection with Jean-Paul Sartre's book *L'Imaginaire,*" tr. by A. S. Limouze and Helmut Kuhn, *Philosophy and Phenomenological Research,* VIII (1947), pp. 188-205.

799. Heringman, Bernard, "The Poetry of Synthesis," *Perspective,* VII (Autumn, 1954), pp. 167-175.

Largely on Wallace Stevens and philosophy: since superceded by the Thomas J. Hines book.

800. Hersch, Jeanne, "Jaspers' Conception of Tradition," in Paul Schilpp, ed., *The Philosophy of Karl Jaspers* (New York: Tudor Pub. Co., 1957), pp. 593-610.

801. Hertz, P. D. *Martin Heidegger: Language and the Foundations of Interpretation,* Ph.D. diss., Stanford University (1967).

802. Heschel, Abraham Joshua. *God in Search of Man: A Philosophy of Judaism* (New York: Farrar, Straus, and Giroux, 1955).

803. –. *Man is Not Alone: A Philosophy of Religion* (New York: Farrar, Straus and Giroux, 1951; Noonday, 1976).

804. –. *A Passion for Truth* (New York: Farrar, Straus, and

Giroux, 1974).

A fascinating comparison of the teachings of the *tzaddik* Reb Manahem Mendl of Kotzk and Soren Kierkegaard.

805. –. *Who is Man?* (Stanford: Stanford University Press, 1965).

806. Hesse, Hermann, "Zarathustra's Return," in Robert Solomon, ed., *Nietzsche: A Collection of Critical Essays* (New York: Anchor Press, 1973), pp. 375-385.

807. Higgins, D. J. *Possibility in Pierce and Heidegger: A Propaedeutic for Synthesis,* Ph.D. diss., Columbia University (1968).

808. Hillesheim, James W., "Nietzsche on Education," *Education,* LXXXIV (1963), pp. 226-230.

809. –. *Nietzsche's Philosophy of Education: A Critical Exposition,* Ph.D. diss., University of Southern California (1967).

810. Hillman, James. *Emotions: A Comprehensive Phenomenology of Theories and their Meanings for Therapy* (London: Routledge and Kegan Paul, 1960).

811. Himmelstrup, Jens. *Soren Kierkegaard: International Bibliografi* (Copenhagen: Nyt Nordisk Forlag, 1962).

Most complete on European sources on Kierkegaard.

812. Hinchcliffe, Arnold P. *The Absurd* (London: Methuen, 1969).

813. Hines, Thomas J. *The Later Poetry of Wallace Stevens: Phenomenological Parallels with Husserl and Heidegger* (Lewisburg: Bucknell University Press, 1976).

814. Hinners, R. C. and Q. Lauer, "Being and God in Heidegger's Philosophy," *Proceedings of the American Catholic Philosophical Association,* XXXI (1957), pp. 157-165.

815. Hinners, R., "The Freedom and Finiteness of Existence in Heidegger," *The New Scholasticism,* XXXIII (1959), pp. 32-48.

816. Hintikka, K., "Cogito Ergo Sum: Inference or Performance," *Philosophical Review,* LXXI (1962), pp. 3-32.

817. –, "Existential Presuppositions and Existential Commitments," *Journal of Philosophy,* LVI (1959), pp. 125-137.

818. Hirsch, E. D., Jr. *Validity in Interpretation* (New Haven: Yale University Press, 1967).

819. Hirsch, Elisabeth Feist, "Martin Heidegger and the East," *Philosophy East and West,* XX, 3 (1970), pp. 247-264.

820. Hochland, Jamina, "A Theme in Sartre's Literary Work." *Journal of the British Society for Phenomenology,* I (1970), pp. 93-99.

821. Hocking, W. E., "Marcel and the Ground Issues of Metaphysics," *Philosophy and Phenomenological Research,* XIV (1954), pp. 439-469.

822. Hodgson, P. C., "Heidegger, Revelation, and the Word of God," *Journal of Religion,* XLIX (1969), pp. 228-252.

823. Hodin, J. P., "Modern Art and the Philosopher: A Conversation with Karl Jaspers," *Quandrum,* III, p. 5-14.

824. Hoffman, Frederick J. *The Mortal No: Death and the Modern Imagination* (Princeton: Princeton University Press, 1964).

See especially pp. 436-452.

825. Hoffman, Kurt, "The Basic Concepts of Karl Jaspers' Philosophy," in Paul Schilpp, ed., *The Philosophy of Karl Jaspers* (New York: Tudor Pub. Co., 1957), pp. 95-114.

826. –. *Existential Philosophy: A Study of Its Past and Present*

Forms, Ph.D. diss., Harvard University (1949).

827. Hofstadter, Albert, "Enownment," Special Heidegger and Literature issue, *boundary 2,* IV, 2 (1976), pp. 357-378.

828. – and Richard Francis Kuhns, eds. *Philosophies of Art and Beauty: Selected Readings in Aesthetics from Plato to Heidegger* (New York: Modern Library, 1964).

829. Hohlenberg, Johannes. *Soren Kierkegaard,* tr. by T. H. Croxall (London: 1954).

830. Holdheim, William. *Gide and Nietzsche,* Ph.D. diss., Yale University (1955).

831. –, "Young Gide's Reaction to Nietzsche," *PMLA,* LXXII (1957), pp. 534-544.

832. Hollingdale, R. J. *Nietzsche: The Man and His Philosophy* (Baton Rouge: Louisiana State University Press, 1965).

833. Holm, Søren, "Jaspers' Philosophy of Religion," in Paul Schilpp, ed., *The Philosophy of Karl Jaspers* (New York: Tudor Pub. Co., 1957), pp. 667-692.

834. Holmer, P. L., "Kierkegaard and Religious Propositions," *Journal of Religion,* XXV (1955), pp. 135-146.

835. –, "Kierkegaard and the Sermon," *Journal of Religion,* XXXVII (1957), pp. 1-10.

836. Hook, S., "Pragmatism and Existentialism," *Antioch Review* (1959), pp. 151-168.

837. –, "The Quest for Being," *Journal of Philosophy,* L (1953), pp. 709-731.

838. –, "Two Types of Existentialist Religion and Ethics," *Partisan Review,* XXVI (1959), pp. 58-63.

839. Hooper, S., ed. *Spiritual Problems in Contemporary Litera-*

ture (New York: Harper Torchbooks, 1957).

840. Hopkins, Jasper, "Theological Language and the Nature of Man in Jean-Paul Sartre's Philosophy," *Harvard Theological Review,* LXI (1968), pp. 27-38.

841. Hora, Thomas, "Epistemological Aspects of Existence and Psychotherapy," *Journal of Individual Psychology,* XV (1959), pp. 166-173.

842. –, "Existential Communication and Psychotherapy," *Psychoanalysis,* V (1957), pp. 38-45.

843. –, "Existential Group Psychotherapy," *American Journal of Psychotherapy,* XIII (1959), pp. 83-92.

844. –, "Existential Psychiatry and Group Psychotherapy," *American Journal of Psychoanalysis,* XXI (1961), pp. 58-74.

845. –, "Ontic Perspectives in Psychoanalysis," *American Journal of Psychoanalysis,* XIX (1959), pp. 134-142.

846. –, "The Process of Existential Psychotherapy," *Psychiatry Quarterly,* XXXIV (1960), pp. 495-504.

847. –, "Tao, Zen and Existential Psychotherapy," *Psychologia,* II (1959), pp. 236-242.

848. Horgby, I., "The Double Awareness in Heidegger and Wittgenstein," *Inquiry,* II (1959), pp. 235-264.

849. Houston, Mona T., "The Sartre of Madame de Beauvoir," *Yale French Studies,* XXX (December, 1963), pp. 23-29.

850. Howey, R. L. *A Critical Examination of Heidegger's and Jaspers' Interpretation of Nietzsche,* Ph.D. diss., University of Southern California (1969).

851. Hoy, David Couzens, "The Poet and the Owl: Heidegger's Critique of Hegel," Special Heidegger and Literature issue, *boundary 2,* IV, 2 (1976), pp. 393-410.

852. Hoy, Peter C. *Camus in English: An Annotated Bibliography of Albert Camus's Contributions to English and American Periodicals and Newspapers* (1945-1968), revised and enlarged edition (Paris: Lettres modernes, 1971).

853. Hubben, William. *Dostoyevsky, Kierkegaard, Nietzsche, and Kafka: Four Prophets of Our Destiny* (New York: Collier Books, 1952).

854. Huertas-Jourda, José. *The Existentialism of Miguel de Unamuno* (Gainesville: University of Florida Press, 1963).

855. Hummel, Herman, "Emerson and Nietzsche," *New England Quarterly,* XIX (19546), pp. 63-84.

856. Husserl, Edmund. *Cartesian Meditations: An Introduction to Phenomenology,* tr. by Dorion Cairns (The Hague: Martinus Nijhoff, 1960).

857. —. *The Crisis of European Sciences and Transcendental Phenomenology: An Introduction to Phenomenology,* tr. by David Carr (Evanston: Northwestern University Press, 1970).

858. —. *Experience and Judgment,* tr. by James Spencer Churchill and Karl Ameriks (Evanston: Northwestern University Press, 1973).

859. —. *Formal and Transcendental Logic,* tr. by Dorion Cairns (The Hague: Martinus Nijhoff, 1969).

860. —. *The Idea of Phenomenology,* tr. by William P. Alston and George Nakhnikian (The Hague: Martinus Nijhoff, 1964).

861. —. *Ideas: General Introduction to Pure Phenomenology,* tr. by W. r. Boyce Gibson (New York: Humanities Press, 1931; Collier, 1962).

862. —. *Logical Investigations,* tr. by J. N. Findlay (New York: Humanities Press, 1970).

863. —. *The Paris Lectures,* tr. by Peter Koestenbaum (The Hague: Martinus Nijhoff, 1964).

864. —, "Phenomenology," in *Encyclopaedia Britannica,* 14th ed. (1927), vol. XVII, pp. 699-702.

865. —. *Phenomenology and the Crisis of Philosophy, Philosophy as a Rigorous Science, and Philosophy and the Crisis of European Man,* tr. by Quentin Lauer (New York: Harper and Row, 1965).

866. —. *The Phenomenology of Internal Time-Consciousness,* ed. by Martin Heidegger and tr. by James S. Churchill (Bloomington: Indiana University Press, 1964).

867. —, "A Reply to a Critic of My Refutation of Logical Positivism," tr. by Dallas Willard, *The Personalist,* LIII (1972), pp. 5-13.

868. —, "Syllabus of a Course of Four Lectures on Pheneomenological Method and Phenomenological Philosophy," *Journal of the British Society for Pehnomenology,* I (1970), pp. 38-45.

869. de Huszar, George, "The Essence of Nietzsche," *South Atlantic Quarterly,* XLIII (1944), pp. 368-374.

870. Hutchinson, J. A. *Faith, Reason, and Existence: An Introduction to Contemporary Philosophy of Religion* (New York: Oxford University Press, 1956).

871. Hyland, D. A., "Art and the Happening of Truth: Reflections on the End of Philosophy," *Journal of Aesthetics and Art Criticism,* XXX (1971), pp. 177-187.

872. Hymen, Frieda Clark, "Kierkegaard and the Hebraic Mind," *Journal of Ecumenical Studies,* IV (1967), pp. 554-556.

873. Hyppolite, Jean, "A Chronology of French Existentialism," *Yale French Studies,* XVI (1954), pp. 100-102.

874. Ihde, Don. *Hermeneutic Phenomenology: The Philosophy*

of Paul Ricoeur (Evanston: Northwestern University Press, 1971).

875. —, "Language and Two Phenomenologies," in Edward G. Ballard and Charles E. Scott, eds., *Martin Heidegger in Europe and America* (The Hague: Martinus Nijhoff, 1973), pp. 147-156.

876. —. *Sense and Significance* (Pittsburgh: Duquesne University Press, 1973).

Particularly important, from the point of view of Heidegger studies, is Ihde's study of the phenomenology of the audible, and the meaning of the Word.

877. Ilie, P., "Nietzsche in Spain: 1890-1910," *PMLA,* LXXIX (1964), pp. 80-96.

878. Irving, John A., "Thoughts on Existentialism," *Queen's Quarterly,* LVII (1950), pp. 298-303.

879. Jacobi, Joseph, "The Nietzschean Idea and the Christian Ideal: Superman and Saint," *American Catholic Quarterly,* XLI (1916), pp. 463-491.

880. Jaeger, H., "Heidegger and the Work of Art," *Journal of Aesthetics and Art Criticism,* XVII (1958-1959), pp. 58-71.

881. —, "Heidegger's Existential Philosophy and Modern German Literature," *Publication of the Modern Language Association,* LXVII (1952), pp. 655-683.

882. Jaffe, Adrian H., "Emerson and Sartre: Two Parallel Theories of Responsibility," *Comparative Literature Studies,* I (1964), pp. 113-117.

883. Jameson, Frederic, "The Laughter on Nausea," *Yale French Studies,* XXIII (1959), pp. 26-32.

884. —. *Sartre: The Origins of a Style* (New Haven: Yale University Press, 1961).

885. Jaquette, W. A. *Value, Nothingness and Sartre,* Ph.D. diss., University of Missouri (1969).

886. Jarrett-Kerr, Martin, "The Dramatic Philosophy of Jean-Paul Sartre," *Tulane Drama Review,* I (June, 1957), pp. 41-48.

887. –, "Gabriel Marcel on Faith and Unbelief," *Hibbert Journal,* XLV (1947), pp. 321-326.

888. Jaspers, Karl. *The European Spirit,* tr. by R. G. Smith (London: SCM Press, 1948).

889. –. *Existentialism and Humanism,* tr. by E. B. Ashton (New York: Moore, 1952).

890. –. *The Future of Mankind,* tr. by E. B. Ashton (Chicago: University of Chicago Press, 1961).

891. –. *General Psychopathology,* tr. by J. Hoenig and M. W. Hamilton (Chicago: University of Chicago Press, 1963).

892. –. *The Great Philosophers: The Foundations, The Paradigmatic Individuals: Socrates, Buddha, Confucius, Jesus; The Seminal Founders of Philosophical Thought: Plato, Augustine, Kant,* tr. by Ralph Manheim (New York: Harcourt, Brace, 1962).

893. –. *The Great Philosophers: The Original Thinkers: Anaximander, Heraclitus, Parmenides, Plotinus, Anselm, Nicholas of Cuda, Spinoza, Lao-Tzu, Nagarjuna,* tr. by Ralph Manheim (New York: Harcourt, Brace & World, 1966).

894. –. *The Idea of the University,* tr. by H. A. T. Reiche and H. F. Vanderschmidt (Boston: Beacon Press, 1959).

895. –, "Importance of Nietzsche, Marx, and Kierkegaard in the History of Philosophy," tr. by S. Godman, *Hibbert Journal,* XLIX (1951), pp. 226-234.

896. –, "Man as His Own Creator," in Robert Solomon, ed.,

Nietzsche: A Collection of Critical Essays (New York: Anchor Press, 1973), pp. 131-155.

897. –. *Man in the Modern Age,* tr. by Eden and Cedar Paul (New York: Humanities Press, 1933; London: Routledge and Kegan Paul, 1933; Garden City, New York: Doubleday, 1956).

898. –. *Myth and Christianity* (New York: Noonday Press, 1958).

899. –. *Nietzsche and Christianity,* tr. by E. B. Ashton (Chicago: Regnery-Gateway, 1961).

900. –, "Nietzsche and the Present," tr. by Ralph Manheim, *Partisan Review,* XIX (1952), pp. 19-30.

901. –. *Nietzsche: An Introduction to the Understanding of His Philosophical Activity,* tr. by Charles F. Wallraff and Frederick Schmitz (Tucson: University of Arizona Press, 1965).

902. –. *The Origin and Goal of History,* tr. by Michael Bullock (New Haven: Yale University Press, 1953).

903. –. *The Perenniel Scope of Philosophy,* tr. by Ralph Manheim (New Haven: Yale University Press, 1950).

904. –, "Philosophical Autobiography," in Paul Schilpp, ed., *The Philosophy of Karl Jaspers* (New York: Tudor Pub. Co., 1957), pp. 3-94.

905. –. *Philosophical Faith and Revelation,* tr. by E. B. Ashton (New York: Harper and Row, 1967).

906. –. *Philosophy,* tr. by E. B. Ashton, 3 vols. (Chicago: University of Chicago Press, 1969-1971).

907. –. *Philosophy and the World: Selected Essays and Lectures,* tr. by E. B. Ashton (Chicago: Henry Regnery Co., 1963).

908. –. *Philosophy is for Every Man,* tr. by R. F. C. Hull and G.

Wels (London: Hutchinson, 1969).

909. —. *Philosophy of Existence,* tr. and with an introduction by Richard F. Grabau (Philadelphia: University of Pennsylvania Press, 1971).

910. —. *The Question of German Guilt,* tr. by E. B. Ashton (New York: Dial Press, 1947).

911. —. *Reason and Anti-Reason in Our Time,* tr. by Stanley Godman (New Haven: Yale University Press, 1952).

912. —. *Reason and Existenz: Five Lectures,* tr. and with an introduction by William Earle (New York: Noonday Press, 1955).

913. —. *Three Essays: Leonardo, Descartes, Max Weber,* tr. by Ralph Manheim (New York: Harcourt, Brace & World, 1964).

914. —. *Tragedy is Not Enough,* tr. by H. A. T. Reiche, H. T. Moore, and K. W. Deutsch (Boston: Beacon Press, 1952; London: V. Gollancz, 1953).

915. —. *Truth and Symbol,* tr. by Jean T. Wilde *et al* (New Haven: Yale University Press, 1959).

916. —. *The Way to Wisdom,* tr. by Eden and Cedar Paul (New Haven: Yale University Press; London: Routledge and Kegan Paul, 1951).

917. Javet, P., "Sartre: From *Being and Nothingness* to *A Critique of Dialectical Reasoning,*" *Philosophy Today,* V (1965), pp. 176-183.

918. Jersild, Paul T., "Nietzsche's Attack on Christendom," *Lutheran Quarterly,* XVI (1964), pp. 231-238.

919. Johannesson, E. O., "Isak Dinesen, Soren Kierkegaard, and the Present Age," *Books Abroad,* XXXVI (1962), pp. 20-24.

920. John, S., "Sacrilege and Metamorphosis: Two Aspects of

Sartre's Imagery," *Modern Language Quarterly,* XX, 1 (1959), pp. 57-66.

921. John, Sister H. J., "Variations on a Theme: Sartre, Buber, and Marcel," *Commonweal,* LXIV (1961), pp. 100-102.

922. Johnson, H. A., "On Sartre and Kierkegaard," *American Scandinavian Review* (September, 1947), pp. 220-225.

923. — and Niels Thulstrup, eds. *A Kierkegaard Critique* (New York: Harper and Bros., 1962).

924. Jolivet, Régis. *Französische Existenzphilosophie. Aus dem Französischen übers, von Ernst Scheider. Bibliographische Einführungen in das Studium der Philosophie, 9* (Bern: A. Francke, 1948).

Useful bibliography for European sources on Existentialism.

925. —. *Introduction to Kierkegaard,* tr. by W. H. Barber (London: 1950).

926. —. *Sartre: The Theology of the Absurd,* tr. by Wesley C. Piersol (Westminster, Maryland: Newman Press, 1967).

927. Jonas, H., "Heidegger and Theology," *Review of Metaphysics,* XVIII (1964-1965), pp. 207-233.

928. Jones, W. A. *The Development of the Social Philosophy of Sartre,* Ph.D. diss., Notre Dame University (1970).

929. Jørgensen, Aage. *Søren Kierkegaard-litteratur 1961-1970: En foreløbig bibliografi* (Aarhus: Akademisk Boghandel, 1971).

930. Jung, H. Y., "Confucianism and Existentialism as the Way of Man," *Philosophy and Phenomenological Research,* XXX (1969-1970), pp. 186-202.

931. Kaam, A. van, "Clinical Implications of Heidegger's Concepts of Will, Decision, and Responsibility," *Review of*

Existential Psychology and Psychiatry, I (1961), pp. 205-216.

932. Kaelin, Eugene Francis. *Art and Existence: A Phenomenological Aesthetics* (Lewisburg: Bucknell University Press, 1970).

933. –. *An Existentialist Aesthetic: The Theories of Sartre and Merleau-Ponty* (Madison: University of Wisconsin Press, 1962).

934. Kahn, E., "Becoming and Being in Time and Space," *Psychiatry Quarterly,* XXXIII (1960), pp. 548-559.

935. Kahn, Ernest, "Sartre, The Philosopher and Writer," *Contemporary Review,* CXCVI (November, 1959), pp. 243-245.

936. Kainz, Howard P., "Ambiguities and Paradoxes in Kierkegaard's Existential Categories," *Philosophy Today,* XII (1969), pp. 138-145.

937. –, "The Relationship of Dread to Spirit in Man and Woman, According to Kierkegaard," *The Modern Schoolman,* XLVII (1969), pp. 1-13.

938. Kallagher, K. T., "Being in a Situation," *Review of Metaphysics,* XIII (1959), pp. 320-340.

939. Kaplan, Abraham. *The New World of Philosophy* (New York: Vintage Books, 1963).

940. Kaplan, Mordecai M., "Martin Buber: Theologian, Philosopher and Prophet," *The Reconstructionist* (May 2, 1952).

941. Karl, Frederick Robert and Leo Hamalian, eds. *The Existentialist Mind: Documents and Fictions* (Greenwich: Connecticut: Fawcett Publishers, 1974).

A small, popular anthology.

942. Kates, C. A., "Heidegger and the Myth of the Cave," *The*

Personalist, L (1969), pp. 532-548.

943. Kaufmann, F., "Discussion: Concerning Kraft's Philosophy of Existence," *Philosophy and Phenomenological Research,* I (1940), pp. 359-364.

944. –, "The Value of Heidegger's Analysis of Existence for Literary Criticism," *Modern Language Notes,* XLVIII (1933), pp. 487-491.

945. Kaufmann, Fritz, "Karl Jaspers and a Philosophy of Communication," in Paul Schilpp, ed., *The Philosophy of Karl Jaspers* (New York: Tudor Pub. Co., 1957), pp. 210-296.

946. Kaufmann, LeRoy C. *The Influence of Friedrich Nietzsche on American Literature,* Ph.D. diss., University of Pennsylvania (1963).

947. Kaufmann, Walter, "Art, Tradition, and Truth," *Partisan Review,* XVII, pp. 9-28.

948. –. *Critique of Religion and Philosophy* (New York: Harper and Bros., 1958).

949. –, "The Death of God and the Revaluation," in Robert Solomon, ed., *Nietzsche: A Collection of Critical Essays* (New York: Anchor Press, 1973), pp. 9-28.

950. –, "The Discovery of the Will to Power," *Ibid.,* pp. 226-242.

951. –, "Existentialism and Death," *Chicago Review,* XIII (1959), pp. 73-93.

952. –, ed. *Existentialism from Dostoyevsky to Sartre* (New York: Meridian Books, 1956).

953. –. *The Faith of a Heretic* (New York: Doubleday, 1961).

954. –. *From Shakespeare to Existentialism* (Boston: Beacon Press, 1959; New York: Doubleday, 1960).

955. –, "A Hundred Years After Kierkegaard," *Kenyon Review*, XVIII, pp. 182-211.

956. –, "Jaspers' Relation to Nietzsche," in Paul Schilpps, ed., *The Philosophy of Karl Jaspers* (New York: Tudor Pub. Co., 1957), pp. 407-436.

957. –, "Nietzsche and Rilke," *Kenyon Review*, XVII (1955), pp. 1-23.

958. –, "Nietzsche Between Homer and Sartre: Five Treatments of the Orestes Story," *Revue internationale de Philosophie*, XVIII (1964), pp. 50-73.

959. –, "Nietzsche in the Light of his Suppressed Manuscripts," *Journal of the History of Philosophy*," II (1964), pp. 205-225.

960. –. *Nietzsche: Philosopher, Psychologist, Antichrist* (Princeton: Princeton University Press, 1950; revised edition, 1969, with excellent bibliography).

961. –. *Nietzsche's Theory of Values*, Ph.D. diss., Harvard University (1947).

962. –, "Some Typical Misconceptions of Nietzsche's Critique of Christianity," *Philosophical Review*, LXI (1952), pp. 595-599.

963. –. *Tragedy and Philosophy* (New York: Doubleday, 1968).

964. Kean, C. *The Meaning of Existence* (New York: Harper and Bros., 1947).

965. Kecskemeti, Paul, "Existentialism: A New Trend in Philosophy," *New Directions 10* (New York: New Directions, 1948), pp. 290-308.

966. Keen, Sam. *Gabriel Marcel* (Richmond, Virginia: John Knox Press, 1967).

967. Kegley, C. W., "Paul Tillich and the Philosophy of Art,"

Journal of Aesthetics and Art Criticism, XIX (1960), pp. 175-185.

968. Kelley, D. A., "The Earth as Home," *Religious Humanism,* VI (1972), pp. 178 ff.

On Heidegger's philosophy.

969. Kelman, Harold, "Communing and Relating," *American Journal of Psychotherapy,* XIV (1960), pp. 70-96.

Continued in serial form in the *American Journal of Psychoanalysis.*

970. –, "Existentialism: A Phenomenon of the West," *International Journal of Psychiatry,* V (1960), pp. 299-302.

971. Kenevan, P. B. *Time, Consciousness, and the Ego in the Philosophy of Sartre,* Ph.D. diss., Northwestern University (1969).

972. Kennard, Jean Elizabeth. *Towards a Novel of the Absurd: A Study of the Relationship Between the Concept of the Absurd as Defined in the Works of Sartre and Camus and Ideas and Form in the Fiction of John Barth, Samuel Beckett, Nigel Dennis, Joseph Heller and James Purdy,* Ph.D. diss., Berkeley (1969).

973. Kern, Edith G. *Existential Thought and Fictional Technique: Kierkegaard, Sartre, Beckett* (New Haven: Yale University Press, 1970).

974. –, ed. *Sartre: A Collection of Critical Essays* (Englewood Cliffs: Prentice-Hall, 1962).

975. –, "The Self and the Other: A Dilemma of Existential Fiction," *Comparative Literature Studies,* V, 3 (1968), pp. 329-337.

976. Kerr, Jarrett. "Dramatic Philosophy of Gabriel Marcel," *Dublin Review,* CCXXII (1949), pp. 43-55.

977. –, "Gabriel Marcel on Faith and Unbelief," *Hibbert*

Journal, XLV (1947), pp. 321-326.

978. Keyes, C. D., "An Evaluation of Levinas' Critique of Heidegger," *Research in Phenomenology*, II (1972), pp. 121-142.

979. –, "Truth as Art: An Interpretation of Heidegger's *Zein und Zeit* (sec. 44) and *Der Ursprung des Kunstwerkes*," in John Sallis, ed., *Heidegger and the Path of Thinking* (Pittsburgh: Duquesne University Press, 1970), pp. 65-84.

980. Kierkegaard, Søren. *Attack Upon Christendom* (Princeton: Princeton University Press, 1944).

981. –. *Christian Discourses*, tr. by Walter Lowrie (New York: Oxford University Press, 1939).

982. –. *The Concept of Dread*, tr. by Walter Lowrie (Princeton: Princeton University Press, 1944).

983. –. *The Concept of Irony, with Constant Reference to Socrates*, tr. by Lee M. Capel (New York: Harper & Row, 1966).

984. –. *Concluding Unscientific Postscript*, tr. by D. F. Swenson (Princeton: Princeton University Press, 1941).

985. –. *Edifying discourses: A Selection* (New York: Harper & Bros., 1959).

986. –. *Either/Or: A Fragment of Life*, tr. by D. F. and L. M. Swenson (vol. 1) and Walter Lowrie (vol. 2) (Princeton: Princeton University Press, 1944).

987. –. *Fear and Trembling and The Sickness Unto Death*, tr. by Walter Lowrie (Garden City, New York: Doubleday, 1954).

988. –. *For Self-Examination and Judge for Yourselves!* (New York: Oxford University Press, 1941).

989. –. *The Gospel of Suffering and Lilies of the Field* (Minne-

apolis: Augsburg, 1949).

990. —. *The Journals of Soren Kierkegaard,* tr. by Alexander Dru (New York: Oxford University Press, 1938).

991. —. *The Last Years: Journals 1853-1855,* tr. and ed. by R. Gregor Smith (New York: Harper and Row, 1965).

992. —. *Philosophical Fragments, or a Fragment of Philosophy,* tr. by D. F. Swenson (Princeton: Princeton University Press, 1936).

993. —. *The Point of View for My Work as an Author* (New York: Oxford University Press, 1939).

994. —. *The Present Age* (New York: Oxford University Press, 1940.

995. —. *Purity of Heart,* tr. by Douglas V. Steere (New York: Harper & Bros., 1938).

996. —. *Repetition: An Essay in Experimental Psychology* (New York: Harper and Row, 1941).

997. —. *Stages on Life's Way,* tr. by Walter Lowrie (Princeton: Princeton University Press, 1940).

998. —. *Thoughts on Crucial Situations in Human Life* (Minneapolis: Augsburg, 1941).

999. —. *Three Discourses on Imagined Occasions* (Minneapolis: Augsburg, 1941).

1000. —. *Training in Christianity,* tr. by Walter Lowrie (Princeton: Princeton University Press, 1944).

1001. —. *The Works of Love,* tr. by H. and E. Hong (New York: Harper and Row, 1962).

1002. Killinger, John, "Existentialism and Human Freedom," *English Journal,* L (1961), pp. 303-313.

1003. —. *Hemingway and the Dead Gods: A Study in Existen-*

tialism (Lexington: University of Kentucky Press, 1960).

A superficial and coercive study, often misleading.

1004. Kilzer, E., "The Modes of Existence," *Proceedings of the American Philosophical Association,* XXI (1946), pp. 66 ff.

1005. King, Joe M., "Kierkegaard as an Existentialist," *Furman Studies,* XV, pp. 35-44.

1006. King, M. Y., "Truth and Technology," *Human Context,* V (1973), pp. 1-34.

1007. King-Farlow, John, "Self Deceivers and Sartrean Seducers," *Analysis,* XXIII (June, 1963), pp. 131-136.

1008. Kingston, Frederick Temple. *A Comparison of Christian and Non-Christian Existentialism as Exemplified by the Works of Contemporary French Writers,* Ph.D. diss., Oxford University, Christ College (1954).

1009. –, "Freedom and Being Free," *Anglican Theological Review,* XXXVIII (1956), pp. 153-160.

1010. –. *French Existentialism: A Christian Critique* (Toronto: University of Toronto Press, 1961).

1011. –, "An Introduction to Existentialist Thought," *Dalhousie Review,* XL (Summer, 1960), pp. 181-188.

1012. Kisiel, Theodore, "The Happening of Tradition: The Hermeneutics of Gadamer and Heidegger," *Man and World,* II (1969), pp. 358-385.

1013. –, "The Mathematical and the Hermeneutical: On Heidegger's Notion of the Apriori," in Edward G. Ballard and Charles E. Scott, eds., *Martin Heidegger in Europe and America* (The Hague: Martinus Nijhoff, 1973), pp. 109-120.

1014. –, "On the Dimensions of a Phenomenology of Science

in Husserl and the Young Dr. Heidegger," *Journal of the British Society for Phenomenology,* IV (1973), pp. 217-234.

1015. Klaf, Franklin S., " 'Night Song'–Nietzsche's Poetic Insight into the Psychotic Process," *Psychoanalytic Review,* XLVI (1959), pp. 80-89.

1016. Klein, M. *After Alienation* (New York: World Publishing Co., 1962).

1017. Klemke, E. D., "Some Misinterpretations of Kierkegaard," *Hibbert Journal,* LVII (1958-1959), pp. 259-270.

1018. Kleppner, Amy M., "Philosophy and the Literary Medium: The Existentialist Predicament," *Journal of Aesthetics and Art Criticism,* XXIII (1964), pp. 207-217.

1019. Knauss, Gerhard, "The Concept of 'Encompassing' in Jaspers' Philosophy," in Paul Schilpp, ed., *The Philosophy of Karl Jaspers* (New York: Tudor Pub. Co., 1957), pp. 141-176.

1020. Kneller, George Frederick. *Existentialism and Education* (New York: Wiley and Sons, 1958).

Good introductory survey to this relatively new field.

1021. Knight, Arthur H., "Nietzsche and Epicurean Philosophy," *Philosophy,* VIII (1933), pp. 431-445.

1022. –. *Some Aspects of the Life and the Work of Nietzsche* (New York: Russell and Russell, 1967).

1023. Knight, Everett W. *Literature Considered a Philosophy: The French Example* (New York: Collier Books, 1957).

1024. Koch, Adrianne D. *Philosophy for a Time of Crisis* (New York: Dutton, 1959).

1025. Kockelmans, Joseph J. *Edmund Husserl's Phenomenological Psychology: A Historico-Critical Study*

(Pittsburgh: Duquesne University Press, 1967).

1026. —. *A First Introduction to Husserl's Phenomenology* (Pittsburgh: Duquesne University Press, 1967).

1027. —, "Heidegger on Time and Being," in Edward G. Ballard and Charles E. Scott, eds., *Martin Heidegger in Europe and America* (The Hague: Martinus Nijhoff, 1973), pp. 55-76.

1028. —. *Martin Heidegger: A First Introduction to His Philosophy* (Pittsburgh: Duquesne University Press, 1965).

1029. —, ed. *On Heidegger and Language* (Evanston: Northwestern University Press, 1972).

Includes Kockelmans' essays, "Language, Meaning, and Eksistence," pp. 3-32, and "Ontological Difference, Hermeneutics, and Language," pp. 195-234.

1030. —. *Phenomenology and Physical Science: An Introduction to the Philosophy of Physical Science* (Pittsburgh: Duquesne University Press, 1966).

1031. —, ed. *Phenomenology: The Philosophy of Edmund Husserl and Its Interpretation* (New York: Doubleday/Anchor, 1967).

Includes essays by Heidegger, Husserl, and many other major figures. Kockelmans' own essays are "Some Fundamental Themes of Husserl's Phenomenology," pp. 24-36; "Intentional and Constitutive Analyses," pp. 137-146; "Husserl's Transcendental Idealism," pp. 183-193; "Husserl's Phenomenological Philosophy in the Light of Contemporary Criticism," pp. 221-236; "Husserl's Original View on Phenomenological Psychology," pp. 418-449; and "Towards a Descriptive Science of Man," pp. 533-555.

1032. —, "World-Constitution: Reflections on Husserl's Transcendental Idealism," *Analecta Husserliana*, I (1971), pp. 11-35.

1033. – and Theodore Kisiel, eds. *Phenomenology and the Natural Sciences* (Evanston: Northwestern University Press, 1970).

1034. Koestenbaum, Peter, "Existential Psychiatry, Logical Positivism and Phenomenology," *Journal of Existential Psychiatry,* I (1961), pp. 399-425.

1035. –. *The Vitality of Death: Essays in Existential Psychology and Philosophy* (Westport, Connecticut: Greenwood, 1971).

1036. Kohak, Erazim V., "Existence and the Phenomenological Epokhe," *Journal of Existentialism,* VIII (Fall, 1967), pp. 19-47.

1037. Kolle, Kurt, "Jaspers and Psychopathologist," in Paul Schilpp, ed., *The Philosophy of Karl Jaspers* (New York: Tudor Pub. Co., 1957), pp. 437-466.

1038. Korg, J., "Cult of Absurdity," *Nation,* CLXXXI (1955), pp. 517-518.

1039. Kotchen, T., "Existential Mental Health: An Empirical Approach," *Journal of Individual Psychology,* XVI (1960), pp. 174-181.

1040. Kraft, J., "In Reply to Kaufmann's Critical Remarks About My 'Philosophy of Existence'," *Philosophy and Phenomenological Research,* I (1940), pp. 364-365.

See item 943 of this Bibliography.

1041. –, "The Philosophy of Existence," *Philosophy and Phenomenological Research,* I (1940), pp. 339-358.

See items 943 and 1040 of this Bibliography.

1042. Kreeft, P., "Zen in Heidegger's Gelassenheit," *International Philosophical Quarterly* (1971), pp. 521-545.

1043. Krell, David Farrell, "Art and Truth in Raging Discord:

Heidegger and Nietzsche on the Will to Power," Special Heidegger and Literature issue, *boundary 2*, IV, 2 (1976), pp. 379-392.

1044. —. *Nietzsche and the Task of Thinking: Martin Heidegger's Reading of Nietzsche*, Ph.D. diss., Duquesne University (1971).

1045. —, "Towards an Ontology of the Play," *Research in Phenomenology*, II (1972), pp. 63-93.

1046. Krieger, Leonard, "History and Existentialism in Sartre," in Kurt Wolff and Barrington Moore, eds., *The Critical Spirit: Essays in Honor of Herbert Marcuse* (Boston: Beacon Press, 1967), pp. 239-266.

1047. Kritzeek, J., "Philosophy of Anxiety," *Commonweal*, LXIII (1956), pp. 572-574.

1048. Kroner, Richard J., "Existentialism and Christianity," *Encounter*, XVII (1956), pp. 219-244.

1049. —, "Heidegger's Private Religion," *Union Seminary Quarterly Review*, XL (1956), pp. 23-37.

1050. Kuale, Steinar and Carl E. Guenness, "Skinner and Sartre: Towards a Radical Phenomenology of Behavior?" *Review of Existential Psychology and Psychiatry*, VII (Spring, 1967), pp. 128-150.

1051. Kuhn, Helmut. *Encounter with Nothingness: An Essay on Existentialism* (London: Methuen, 1951).

1052. —, "Existentialism," in V. Ferm, ed., *A History of Philosophical Systems* (London: Rider, 1958).

1053. —, "Existentialism and Metaphysics," *The Review of Metaphysics*, I (1947), pp. 37-60.

1054. —, "Existentialism: Christian versus Anti-Christian," *Theology Today*, VI (October, 1949), pp. 311-323.

1055. —, "The Phenomenological Concept of 'Horizon'," in

Marvin Faber, ed., *Philosophical Essays in Memory of Edmund Husserl* (Cambridge: Harvard University Press, 1960).

1056. Kuhn, Reinhard, "Proust and Sartre: The Heritage of Romanticism," *Symposium,* XVIII (1964), pp. 293-306.

1057. Kunz, Hans, "Critique of Jaspers' Concept of 'Transcendence'," in Paul Schilpp, ed., *The Philosophy of Karl Jaspers* (New York: Tudor Pub. Co., 1957), pp. 499-522.

1058. Kurtz, P. W., "Kierkegaard, Existentialism, and the Contemporary Scene," *Antioch Review,* XXI (1961-1962), pp. 471-489.

1059. Kuspit, Donald B., "Nietzsche's Conception of Monumental History," *Archiv für Philosophie,* XIII (1965), pp. 95-115.

1060. Kwant, Remy C. *Encounter* (Pittsburgh: Duquesne University Press, 1961).

1061. —. *From Phenomenology to Metaphysics: An Inquiry into the Last Period of Merleau-Ponty's Philosophy* (Pittsburgh: Duquesne University Press, 1966).

1062. —, "Merleau-Ponty and Phenomenology," in Joseph J. Kockelmans, ed., *Phenomenology: The Philosophy of Edmund Husserl and Its Interpretation* (New York: Anchor Press, 1967), pp. 375-396. Also, "Merleau-Ponty's Criticism of Husserl's Eidetic Reduction," pp. 393-410 in the same volume.

1063. —. *The Phenomenological Philosophy of Merleau-Ponty* (Pittsburgh: Duquesne University Press, 1963).

1064. —. *Phenomenology of Expression,* tr. by Henry J. Koren (Pittsburgh: Duquesne University Press, 1969).

1065. Lafarge, René. *Jean-Paul Sartre: His Philosophy,* tr. by Marina Smyth-Kok (Dublin: Gill and Macmillan,

1970).

1066. Laing, R. D. *The Divided Self: An Existential Study in Sanity and Madness* (New York: Tavistock, 1960).

1067. –, "An Examination of Tillich's Theory of Anxiety and Neurosis," *British Journal of Medical Psychology,* XXX (1957), pp. 88-91.

1068. –. *The Self and Others* (London: Tavistock Pub., 1961).

1069. – and D. G. Cooper. *Reason and Violence: A Decade of Sartre's Philosophy, 1950-1960* (London: Tavistock Pub., 1964; New York: Pantheon Books, 1971).

1070. Lakich, John J., "Metaphysical, Ethical and Political Quest in Expressionism and the Literature of Commitment," *Kentucky Romance Quarterly,* XV, 1 (1968), pp. 37-56.

1071. Landgrebe, Ludwig. *Problems in Contemporary European Philosophy,* tr. by Kurt F. Reinhardt (New York: Frederick Ungar, 1966).

1072. Landor, A., "Nietzsche: An Artist Philosopher," *German Life and Letters* (1948), pp. 204-208.

1073. Landor, A. C., "Nietzsche: A Re-Appraisal," *Modern Languages,* XLIII, 4 (1962), pp. 132-135.

1074. –, "The Philosophy of Friedrich Nietzsche," *German Life and Letters,* III (1950), pp. 134-138.

1075. Langan, Thomas, "Heidegger and the Possibility of Authentic Christianity," *Proceedings of the American Catholic Philosophical Association* (1972), pp. 101-112.

1076. –, "Heidegger in France," *Modern Schoolman,* XXXIII (1955-1956), pp. 114-118.

1077. –, "Heidegger: The Problem of the Thing," in John Sallis, ed., *Heidegger and the Path of Thinking*

(Pittsburgh: Duquesne University Press, 1970), pp. 105-115.

1078. –, "Is Heidegger a Nihilist?" *The Thomist,* XXI (1958), pp. 302-319.

1079. –. *The Meaning of Heidegger: A Critical Study of an Existentialist Phenomenology* (New York: Columbia University Press, 1959).

A useful study for specialists, but beginners will find the constant use of German words and phrases overwhelming (many of the footnotes are also in German). Specialists might find Langan's totally uncritical discipleship to Heidegger especially annoying.

1080. –. *Merleau-Ponty's Critique of Reason* (New Haven: Yale University Press, 1966).

1081. –, "A Note in Response to Rukavina's Comment," *New Scholasticism,* XXXIII (1959), pp. 358-359.

1082. –, "Transcendance in the Philosophy of Heidegger," *New Scholasticism,* XXXII (1958), pp. 45-60.

1083. Langman, L., "The Estrangement from Being: An Existential Analysis of Otto Rank's Psychology," *Journal of Existential Psychiatry,* I (1961), pp. 455-477.

1084. Lanigan, Richard L., "Maurice Merleau-Ponty Bibliography," *Man and World,* III (1970), pp. 289-319.

1085. Lansner, K., "Albert Camus," *The Kenyon Review,* XIV (1952), pp. 562-578.

1086. Lanz, Henry, "The New Phenomenology," *The Monist,* XXXIV (1924), pp. 511-527.

1087. Lapointe, Francois H., "Bibliography of Gabriel Marcel," *Modern Scholasticism,* XLIX (1971), pp. 23-49.

1088. –, "A Bibliography of Maurice Merleau-Ponty," *Human Inquiries,* XI (1971), pp. 63-78.

1089. –, "A Bibliography on Paul Ricoeur," *Philosophy Today,* XVII (1973), pp. 176-182.

1090. –, "Phenomenology, Psychoanalysis and the Unconscious," *Journal of Phenomenological Psychology,* II, 1 (1971), pp. 5-25.

1091. Larrabee, Harold A., "Existentialism is Not Humanism," *The Humanist,* VIII, 1 (1948), pp. 7-11.

1092. Larsen, Robert E., "Kierkegaard's Absolute Paradox," *Journal of Religion,* XLII, pp. 34-43.

1093. Larson, C. W. R., "Kierkegaard and Sartre," *Personalist,* XXXV (1954), pp. 128-137.

1094. Larson, G. T., "Classical Samkhya and the Phenomenological Ontology of Jean-Paul Sartre," *Philosophy East and West,* XIX (1969), pp. 45-58.

1095. Latzel, Edwin, "The Concept of 'Ultimate Situation' in Jaspers' Philosophy," in Paul Schilpp, ed., *The Philosophy of Karl Jaspers* (New York: Tudor Pub. Co., 1957), pp. 177-209.

1096. Lauer, Quentin. *Edmund Husserl: Phenomenology and the Crisis of Philosophy* (New York: Harper and Row, 1965).

1097. –, "Four Phenomenologists," *Thought,* XXXIII (1958), pp. 183-204.

On Scheler, Heidegger, Sartre, and Merleau-Ponty.

1098. –, "On Evidence," in Joseph J. Kockelmans, ed. *Phenomenology: The Philosophy of Edmund Husserl and Its Interpretation* (New York: Anchor Press, 1967), pp. 150-157.

Also, "The Other Explained Intentionally," pp. 167-182 in the same volume.

1099. –. *The Triumph of Subjectivity* (New York: Fordham

University Press, 1958). Reprinted as *Phenomenology: Its Genesis and Prospect* (New York: Harper Torchbooks, 1958).

1100. Lavrin, Janko. *Nietzsche: An Approach* (London: 1948).

1101. –. *Nietzsche and Modern Consciousness: A Psycho-Critical Study* (London: 1922).

1102. –, "Tolstoi and Nietzsche," *Slavonic Review,* IV (1925), pp. 67-82.

1103. Lawall, Sarah N. *Critics of Consciousness: The Existential Structures of Literature* (Cambridge: Harvard University Press, 1968).

1104. Lawrence, Nathaniel and Daniel O'Connor, eds. *Readings in Existential Phenomenology* (Englewood Cliffs, New Jersey: Prentice-Hall, 1967).

1105. Lawson, Lewis. *Kierkegaard's Presence in Contemporary American Life: Essays from Various Disciplines* (Metuchen, New Jersey: The Scarecrow Press, 1970).

1106. –, "Walker Percy's Indirect Communications," *Texas Studies in Literature and Languages,* XI (1969), pp. 867-900.

1107. Lea, F. A. *The Tragic Philosopher: A Study of Friedrich Nietzsche* (London: Methuen, 1957).

1108. Lee, Edward N. and Maurice Mandelbaum, eds. *Phenomenology and Existentialism* (Baltimore: Johns Hopkins Press, 1967).

A major collection with a good selection of source material from Husserl, Heidegger, Sartre, etc.

1109. Lee, R. F., "Emerson Through Kierkegaard: Toward a Definition of Emerson's Theory of Communication," *Journal of English Literary History,* XXIV (1957), pp. 229-248.

1110. Lees, F. N., "T. S. Eliot and Nietzsche," *Notes and Queries,* XI (1964), pp. 386-387.

1111. Lefebre, L. *The Psychology of Karl Jaspers* (New York: Tudor Pub. Co., 1957).

1112. Lefevre, Perry, ed. *The Prayers of Kierkegaard* (Chicago: University of Chicago Press, 1956).

1113. LeGrand, A., "Albert Camus: From Absurdity to Revolt," *Culture* (December, 1953), pp. 406-522.

1114. Lehan, Richard Daniel. *A Dangerous Crossing: French Literary Existentialism and the Modern French Novel* (Carbondale: Southern Illinois University Press, 1973).

1115. Lehan, Richard, "Existentialism in Recent American Fiction: The Demonic Quest," *Texas Studies in Literature and Language,* I (1959), pp. 181-202.

1116. –, "French and American Philosophical and Literary Existentialism: A Selected Checklist," *Wisconsin Studies in Contemporary Literature,* I, 3 (1960), pp. 74-88.

1117. Leon, P., "Existentialism and Objectivity," *Hibbert Journal,* L (1951), pp. 342-347.

1118. –, "An Existentialist 'Proof of the Existence of God'," *Hibbert Journal,* LI (1952), pp. 24-28.

1119. Leonard, L., "Towards an Ontological Analysis of Detachment," *Philosophy Today,* XVI (1972), pp. 268-280.

1120. Lessing, Arthur, "Hegel and Existentialism: On Unhappiness," *Personalist,* XLIX (1968), pp. 67-77.

1121. –. *'Man is Freedom': A Critical Study of the Conception of Human Freedom in the Philosophies of Martin Heidegger and Jean-Paul Sartre,* Ph.D. diss., Tulane University (1967).

1122. –, "Marxist Existentialism," *Review of Metaphysics,* XX (1970), pp. 461-484.

1123. Levin, David M., "Induction and Husserl's Theory of Eidetic Variation," *Philosophy and Phenomenological Research,* XXIX (1969), pp. 1-15.

1124. –. *Reason and Evidence in Husserl's Phenomenology* (Evanston: Northwestern University Press, 1971).

1125. Levinas, Emmanuel, "Intuition of Essences," in Joseph J. Kockelmans, ed., *Phenomenology: The Philosophy of Edmund Husserl and Its Interpretation* (New York: Anchor Press, 1967), pp. 83-104.

1126. –. *Totality and Infinity* (Pittsburgh: Duquesne University Press, 1969).

1127. Levine, Stephen K. *Art and Being in the Philosophy of Martin Heidegger: An Interpretation and Critique of "Der Ursprung des Kunstwerks,* Ph.D. diss. (1968).

1128. von Leyden, W., "Two Aspects of Existentialism," *Durham University Journal* (June, 1948), pp. 84-96.

1129. Lewis, Wyndham. *The Writer and the Absolute* (London: Methuen, 1952), esp. pp. 77-150.

1130. Lichtigfeld, A., "The God-Concept in Jaspers' Philosophy," in Paul Schilpp, ed., *The Philosophy of Karl Jaspers* (New York: Tudor Pub. Co., 1957), pp. 693-702.

1131. –. *Jasper's Metaphysics* (London: Colibri Press, Ltd., 1955).

1132. Lindbeck, G., "Philosophy and Existenz in Early Christianity," *Review of Metaphysics,* X (1957), pp. 428-441.

1133. Lingis, A., "Truth and Art: Heidegger and the Temples of Constantinople," *Philosophy Today,* XVI (1972), pp. 122-134.

1134. Little, Arthur, "Existentialism and the New Literature," *Studies,* XXXV (1946), pp. 459-467.

1135. Lockridge, Ernest H., "A View of the Sentimental Absurd: Sterne and Camus," *Sewanee Review,* LXXII (1964), pp. 652-667.

1136. Lohmann, Johannes, " 'Ontological Difference' and Language," in Joseph J. Kockelmans, ed., *On Heidegger and Language* (Evanston: Northwestern University Press, 1972), pp. 303-364.

1137. Long, E. T., "Being and Thinking," *Southern Journal of Philosophy,* IX (1971), pp. 131-140.

1138. –. *Jaspers and Bultmann: A Dialogue Between Philosophy and Theology in the Existentialist Tradition* (Durham: Duke University Press, 1968).

1139. –, "Jasper's Philosophy of Existence as a Model for Theological Reflection," *International Journal for Philosophy of Religion,* I (1972), pp. 35-43.

1140. Long, Madeliene. *Sartrean Themes in Contemporary American Literature,* Ph.D. diss., Columbia University (1967).

1141. Long, Wilbur, "Existentialism, Christianity, and Logos," *The Personalist,* XLVII (1966), pp. 149-168.

1142. Lönning, Per. *The Dilemma of Contemporary Theology Prefigured in Luther, Pascal, Kierkegaard, Nietzsche* (Oslo: 1962; New York: 1964).

1143. Loose, J., "Christian as Camus's Absurd Man," *Journal of Religion,* XLII, pp. 203-214.

1144. Love, Frederick. *The Young Nietzsche and the Wagnerian Experience* (Chapel Hill: University of North Carolina Press, 1963).

1145. Löwenstein, Julius, "Judaism in Jaspers' Thought," in Paul Schilpp, ed., *The Philosophy of Karl Jaspers*

(New York: Tudor Pub. Co., 1957), pp. 643-666.

1146. Lõwith, Karl. *From Hegel to Nietzsche,* tr. by David E. Green (New York: Doubleday, 1967).

1147. –. *From Hegel to Nietzsche: The Revolution in 19th Century Thought* (New York: 1964).

1148. –, "M. Heidegger and F. Rosenzweig or Temporality and Eternity," *Philosophy and Phenomenological Research,* III (1942-1943).

1149. –. *Nature, History, and Existentialism, and Other Essays in the Philosophy of History,* with a critical introduction by Arnold Levison (Evanston: Northwestern University Press, 1966).

1150. –, "The Nature of Man and the World of Nature," in Edward G. Ballard and Charles E. Scott, ed., *Martin Heidegger in Europe and America* (The Hague: Martinus Nijhoff, 1973), pp. 37-46.

1151. –, "Problem and Background of Existentialism," *Social Research,* XV (1948), pp. 345-369.

1152. Lowrie, David, tr. and ed. *Christian Existentialism: A Berdyaev Anthology* (London: George Allen and Unwin, Ltd., 1965).

1153. Lowrie, Walter, "Existence as Understood by Kierkegaard and/or Sartre," *Sewanee Review,* LVIII (1950), pp. 379-401.

1154. –. *Kierkegaard* (New York: Oxford University Press, 1938).

1155. –. *A Short Life of Kierkegaard* (Princeton: Princeton University Press, 1942).

1156. de Lubac, Henri, "The Mystique of Nietzsche," *Month,* III (1950), pp. 18-37.

1157. Lübbe, H., "Bibliographie der Heidegger-Litteratur 1917-

1955," *Zeitschrift für Philosophische Forschung,* XI (1957), pp. 401-452.

1158. Ludovici, A. *Nietzsche and Art* (London: Constable, 1911).

1159. Ludovici, A. M. *Nietzsche: His Life and Works* (London: 1910).

1160. Luijpen, Wilhelmus Antonius Maria. *Existential Phenomenology* (Pittsburgh: Duquesne University Press, 1969).

1161. – and Henry J. Koren. *A First Introduction to Existential Phenomenology* (Pittsburgh: Duquesne University Press, 1969).

1162. –. *Phenomenology and Atheism,* tr. by Walter van de Putte (Pittsburgh: Duquesne University Press, 1964).

On Marx, Nietzsche, Sartre, and Merleau-Ponty.

1163. –. *Phenomenology and Humanism: A Primer in Existential Phenomenology* (Pittsburgh: Duquesne University Press, 1966).

1164. –. *Phenomenology and Metaphysics,* tr. by Henry Koren (Pittsburgh: Duquesne University Press, 1965).

1165. Lund, Margaret, "The Single Ones," *The Personalist,* XLI (1960), pp. 15-24.

On Nietzsche and Kierkegaard.

1166. Lund, Mary Graham, "The Existentialism of Ibsen," *Personalist,* XLI (1960), pp. 310-317.

1167. Lynch, L. E., "Past and Being in Jean-Paul Sartre," *American Catholic Philosophical Association Proceedings,* XXII (1947), pp. 212-220.

1168. McCormick, P., "Heidegger's Meditation on the Word," *Philosophical Studies,* XVIII (1969), pp. 76-99.

1169. –, "Interpretating the Later Heidegger," *Philosophical Studies,* XIX (1970), pp. 83-101.

1170. –, "Saying and Showing in Heidegger and Wittgenstein," *Journal of the British Society for Phenomenology,* III (1972), pp. 27-35.

1171. McEachran, F. *Existentialism and Modern Literature* (New York: Citadel Press, 1963).

1172. –, "The Existential Philosophy," *Hibbert Journal* (April 1948), pp. 232-238.

1173. –, "Literature of Existentialism," *Contemporary Review,* CCIII (1963), pp. 257-264.

1174. –, "Nietzsche, Spinoza and Human Pity," *Contemporary Review,* CLIV (1938), pp. 707-715.

1175. –, "The Significance of Soren Kierkegaard," *The Hibbert Journal,* XLIV (1945-1946), pp. 135-141.

1176. McElroy, Davis Dunbar. *Existentialism and Modern Literature: An Essay in Existentialist Criticism* (New York: Citadel Press, 1963).

1177. McEvilly, W., "Kant, Heidegger, and the Upanishads," *Philosophy East and West,* XII (1963), pp. 311-317.

1178. McGill, V. J., "Sartre's Doctrine of Freedom," *Revue internationale de philosophie,* III (1949), pp. 329-342.

1179. McGinley, J., "The Essential Thrust of Heidegger's Thought," *Philosophy Today,* XV (1971), pp. 242-249.

1180. –, "Heidegger's Concern for the Lived-World in his Dasein-Analysis," *Philosophy Today,* XVI (1972), pp. 92-116.

1181. –. *The Question of Life in Heidegger's Being and Time,* Ph.D. diss., Boston College (1971).

1182. McInerny, Ralph, "The Ambiguity of Existential Metaphysics," *Laval Théologique et Philosophique,* XII (1956), pp. 120-124.

1183. –, "Ethics and Persuasion: Kierkegaard's Existential Dialectic," *Modern Schoolman,* XXXIII (1956), pp. 219-239.

1184. –, "The Teleological Suspension of the Ethical," *The Thomist,* XX (1957), pp. 295-310.

1185. McKinnon, Alastair, "Believing the Paradox: A Contradiction in Kierkegaard?" *Harvard Theological Review,* LXI (1968), pp. 63-66.

1186. –, "Kierkegaard: 'Paradox' and Irrationalism," *Journal of Philosophy,* LXII (1965), pp. 651-652. Reprinted in *Journal of Existentialism,* VII (1967), pp. 401-416.

1187. McMahan, Knight. *The Ethical Development of Friedrich Nietzsche,* Ph.D. diss., Harvard University (1937).

1188. McMahon, Joseph. *Humans Being: The World of Jean-Paul Sartre* (Chicago: University of Chicago Press, 1971).

1189. MacGregor, G., "Jean-Paul Sartre and Existentialism," *Modern Churchman* (March, 1948), pp. 34-44.

1190. –, "What is Existentialism?" *Modern Churchman* (July, 1947), pp. 106-114.

1191. MacIntyre, Alasdair, "Existentialism," in D. J. O'Connor, ed., *A Critical History of Western Philosophy* (London: Collier-Macmillan, 1964), pp. 509-529.

1192. Mackey, David, "Sartre and the Problem of Evil," *Journal of the British Society for Phenomenology,* I (1970), pp. 80-82.

1193. Mackey, Louis. *Kierkegaard: A Kind of Poet* (Philadelphia: University of Pennsylvania Press, 1971).

1194. –, "Kierkegaard and the Problem of Existential Philosophy," *Review of Metaphysics,* IX (1956), pp. 404-419.

1195. –, "Kierkegaard's Lyric of Faith: A Look at *Fear and Trembling,*" *Rice University Institute Pamphlets,* XLVII (1960), pp. 30-47.

1196. –, "Philosophy and Poetry in Kierkegaard," *Review of Metaphysics,* XXIII (1969), pp. 316-332.

1197. –, "Some Versions of the Aesthetic: Kierkegaard's *Either/Or,*" *Rice University Studies,* L (1964), pp. 39-54.

1198. Macksey, Richard, "The Artist in the Labyrinth: Design or Dasein," *Modern Language Notes,* LXXVII (1962), pp. 239-256.

1199. MacNiven, C. D., "Analytic and Existential Ethics," *Dialogue,* IX (June, 1970), pp. 1-19.

1200. Macomber, William B. *The Anatomy of Disillusion: Martin Heidegger's Notion of Truth* (Evanston: Northwestern University Press, 1967).

1201. Macquarrie, John. *An Existentialist Theology: A Comparison of Heidegger and Bultmann* (London: Student Christian Movement Press, 1955).

1202. –, "Existentialism and Christian Thought," in Perry Lefevre, ed., *Philosophical Resources for Christian Thought* (Nashville: Abingdon Press, 1968), pp. 123-140.

1203. –. *An Existentialist theology: A Comparison of Heidegger and Bultmann,* with a foreword by Rudolf Bultmann (London: Student Christian Movement Press, 1965).

1204. –. *Existentialism* (Philadelphia: Westminster, 1972).

1205. –. *Martin Heidegger* (Richmond: John Knox Press, 1968).

1206. —. *Studies in Christian Existentialism* (Philadelphia: Westminster, 1966).

1207. MacRae, D. G. *Ideology and Society* (London: Heinemann, 1962), pp. 198-207.

1208. Madison, M. M., "Primacy of Existence: The Existential Protest against the Logos," *The Personalist,* XLVI (1965), pp. 5-16.

1209. Magalaner, Marvin, "Joyce, Nietzsche and Hauptmann in James Joyce's *A Painful Case,*" *PMLA,* LXVIII (1953), pp. 95-102.

1210. Magmer, J., "Why Do Protestant Theologians Use Existentialism?" *Catholic World,* CLXXXI (1955), pp. 19-24.

1211. Magnan, Henri, ". . .Said Jean-Paul Sartre," *Yale French Studies,* XVI (1954), pp. 3-7.

1212. Magnus, B. *Heidegger and Nietzsche's Doctrine of the Eternal Recurrence,* Ph.D. diss., Columbia University (1967).

1213. —, "Heidegger and the Truth of Being," *International Philosophical Quarterly,* IV (1964), pp. 245-264.

1214. Magnus, Bernd. *Heidegger's Metahistory of Philosophy: Amor Fati, Being and Truth* (The Hague: Martinus Nijhoff, 1970).

1215. Main, W. W., "The Meaning of Meaninglessness," *World Humanities Review,* XII, pp. 241-249.

1216. Malantschuk, Gregor. *Kierkegaard's Thought,* ed. and tr. by Howard V. and Edna H. Hong (Princeton: Princeton University Press, 1971).

One of the clearest and best-organized books on Kierkegaard; a good introduction.

1217. —. *Kierkegaard's Way to the Truth* (Minneapolis: Augsberg Publishing House, 1963).

1218. Malik, Charles H. *The Metaphysics of Time in the Philosophies of A. N. Whitehead and M. Heidegger,* Ph.D. diss., Harvard University (1937).

1219. Malmquist, C. P., "A Comparison of Orthodox and Existential Psychoanalytic Concepts of Anxiety," *Journal of the Nervous and Mental Diseases,* CXXXI (1960), pp. 371-382.

1220. Manasse, Ernst Moritz, "Max Weber's Influence on Jaspers," in Paul Schilpp, ed., *The Philosophy of Karl Jaspers* (New York: Tudor Pub. Co., 1957), pp. 369-392.

1221. Mandel, Oscar, "Artists Without Masters," *The Virginia Quarterly Review,* XXXIX (1963), pp. 401-419.

1222. Manger; Philip, "Kierkegaard in Max Frisch's Novel *Stiller,*" *German Life and Letters,* XX (1967), pp. 119-131.

1223. Mann, Golo, "Freedom and the Social Sciences in Jasper's Thought," in Paul Schilpp, ed., *The Philosophy of Karl Jaspers* (New York: Tudor Pub. Co., 1957), pp. 551-564.

1224. Mann, Thomas, "Nietzsche's Philosophy in the Light of Contemporary Events," see Robert Solomon, ed., *Nietzsche: A Collection of Critical Essays* (New York: Anchor Press, 1973).

1225. Manser, Anthony R. *Sartre: A Philosophic Study* (London: Athlone Press; New York: Oxford University Press, 1966).

1226. Mansfield, Lester, "Existentialism: A Philosophy of Hope and Despair," *Rice Institute Pamphlets,* XLI (1954), pp. 1-25.

1227. Manthey-Zorn, Otto. *Dionysus: The Tragedy of Nietzsche* (Amherst: University of Massachusetts Press,

1956).

1228. Maquet, A. *Albert Camus: The Invincible Summer* (New York: George Braziller, 1958).

1229. Marantz, Enid, "The Theme of Alienation in the Literary Works of Jean-Paul Sartre," *Mosaic*, II (1968), pp. 29-44.

1230. Marcel, Gabriel. *Being and Having*, tr. by Katherine Farrer (Westminster: Dacre Press, 1949).

1231. —. *The Decline of Wisdom*, tr. by Manya Harari (London: Harvill Press, 1954).

1232. —. *The Existential Background of Human Dignity* (Cambridge: Harvard University Press, 1963).

1233. —. *Homo Viator: Introduction to a Metaphysic of Hope*, tr. by E. Craufurd (New York: Harper and Bros., 1951).

Collected essays from the 1940's.

1234. —. *Man Against Mass Society*, tr. by G. S. Fraser (Chicago: Henry Regnery Co., 1962).

1235. —. *Metaphysical Journal*, tr. by Bernard Wall (Chicago: Henry Regnery Co., 1952).

1236. —. *The Mystery of Being*, tr. by G. S. Fraser and R. Hague, 2 vols. (Chicago: Henry Regnery Co., 1950-1951).

1237. —. *Philosophical Fragments 1909-1914 and The Philosopher and Peace*, tr. by Lionel A. Blair (Notre Dame: University of Notre Dame Press, 1965).

1238. —. *The Philosophy of Existence*, tr. by Manya Harari (New York: Philosophical Library, 1949). Republished as *The Philosophy of Existentialism* (New York: Citadel Press, 1956).

1239. –. *Presence and Immortality,* tr. by Michael A. Machado (Pittsburgh: Duquesne University Press, 1967).

1240. –. *Problematic Man,* tr. by Brian Thompson (New York: Herder and Herder, 1967).

1241. –, "Sartre's Concept of Liberty," *Thought,* XXII (1947), pp. 15-18.

1242. –. *Searchings* (New York: Newman, 1967).

1243. –, "Some Reflections on Existentialism," *Philosophy Today,* VIII (1964), pp. 248-257.

1244. Marcuse, Herbert, "Existentialism: Remarks on Jean-Paul Sartre's *L'Etre et Le Néant,*" *Philosophy and Phenomenological Research,* VIII (1947-1948), pp. 309-336.

1245. Margolis, J., "Existentialism Reclaimed," *Personalist,* XLII (1961), pp. 14-21.

1246. –, "The Mode of Existence of a Work of Art," *Philosophical Studies,* IX, pp. 88-94.

1247. Marias, J., "Presence and Absence of Existentialism in Spain," *Philosophy and Phenomenological Research,* XV (1954), pp. 180-191.

1248. Marias, Julian, "Metaphysics: Existence and Human Life," *Yale French Studies,* XVI (1954), pp. 118-126.

1249. Maritain, Jacques. *Existence and the Existent,* tr. by Lewis Galantiere and Gerald B. Phelan (New York: Image Books, 1948).

1250. –, "From Existential Existentialism to Academic Existentialism," *Sewanee Review,* LXVI (1948), pp. 210-229.

1251. Markus, R. J., "Existentialism and the Person," *Humanitas,* II (1947), pp. 20-23.

1252. –, "Metaphysics of Love: A Study of Gabirel Marcel," *Tablet*, CXCIX (1950), pp. 401-402.

1253. Marsak, Leonard M. *French Philosophers from Descartes to Sartre* (New York: World, 1961).

1254. Marson, M. J., "The Atheism of Jean-Paul Sartre," *Modern Churchman*, XLIV (1954), pp. 49-54.

1255. Martin, Bernard. *The Existentialist Theology of Paul Tillich* (New York: Bookman Associates, 1963).

1256. Martin, Vincent. *Existentialism: Kierkegaard, Sartre and Camus* (Washington, D.C.: Thomist Press, 1962).

1257. Marx, Werner. *Heidegger and the Tradition*, tr. by Theodore Kisiel and Murray Greene (Evanston: Northwestern University Press, 1971).

1258. –, "Heidegger's New Conception of Philosophy: The Second Phase of Existentialism," *Social Research*, XXII (1955), pp. 455-474.

1259. –, "The World in Another Beginning: Poetic Dwelling and the Role of the Poet," in Joseph J. Kockelmans, ed. *On Heidegger and Language* (Evanston: Northwestern University Press, 1972), pp. 235-259.

1260. Maslow, A., "Cognition of Being in the Peak Experience," *Journal of Genetic Psychology*, XCIV (1959), pp. 43-66.

1261. –, "Remarks on Existentialism and Psychology," *Existential Inquiry*, I (1960), p. 1.

1262. Mason, H. A., "Existentialism and Literature: A Letter from Switzerland," *Scrutiny*, XIII (1945), pp. 82-98.

1263. Masserman, J. H. and J. L. Moreno, eds. *Progress in Psychotherapy*, Vol. II (New York: Grune and Stratton, 1957).

1264. Masters, Brian. *A Student's Guide to Sartre* (London:

Heinemann, 1970).

1265. Matthews, Honor. *The Hard Journey: The Myth of Man's Rebirth* (London: Chatto and Windus, 1968).

See especially pp. 97-113.

1266. Maurer, R., "From Heidegger to Practical Philosophy," *Idealistic Studies,* III (1973), pp. 133-162.

1267. Maurois, André. *From Proust to Camus: Profiles of Modern French Writers* (New York: Doubleday, 1966).

1268. May, Rollo, "Anxiety and Values," *Progressive Psychotherapy,* II (1957), pp. 82-97.

1269. –. *The Divided Self* (London: Tavistock, 1960).

1270. –, "The Existential Approach," in *The American Handbook of Psychiatry, vol. 2,* ed. by Silvano Arietti (New York: Basic Books, 1959), pp. 1348-1361.

1271. –. *Existential Psychology* (New York: Random House, 1961).

1272. –. *Love and Will* (New York: Norton, 1967).

1273. –. *Man's Search for Himself* (New York: Norton, 1953).

1274. –. *The Meaning of Anxiety* (New York: Ronald, 1950).

1275. –, Ernest Angel, and Henry F. Ellenberger, eds. *Existence: A New Dimension in Psychiatry and Psychology* (New York: Basic Books, 1958).

1276. Mayer, Frederick. *New Perspectives for Education* (Washington: Public Affairs Press, 1962).

1277. Mayerhodd, Milton, "Sartre on Man's Incompleteness: A Critique and Counter-Proposal," *International Philosophical Quarterly,* III (December, 1963), pp. 600-609.

1278. Mays, Wolfe and S. C. Brown. *Linguistic Analyses and Phenomenology* (Lewisburg: Bucknell University Press, 1972).

1279. Medina, Angel, "Husserl on the Nature of the 'Subject'," *New Scholasticism,* XLV (1971), pp. 547-572.

1280. Mehta, Jarava Lal, "Heidegger and the Comparison of Indian and Western Philosophy," *Philosophy East and West,* XX, 3 (1970).

1281. –. *Martin Heidegger: The Way and the Vision* (Honolulu: University Press of Hawaii, 1976).

One of the most recent books on Heidegger, this is also one of the most complete and learned. Mehta's style is often more convoluted and involved than any other Heidegger exegetes, but it does not quite overcome the delineation of Heidegger's thinking.

1282. –. *The Philosophy of Martin Heidegger* (Varanasi, India: Banaras Hindu University Press, 1967). Abridged version (New York: Harper and Row, 1971).

1283. Mellor, Stanley. *Individualism in German Thought, with Special Reference to Nietzsche and Schopenhauer,* Ph.D. diss., Harvard University (1909).

1284. Mencken, K. L. *The Philosophy of Friedrich Nietzsche* (Port Washington: Kennikat Press, 1913, 1967).

1285. Merlan, Philip, "Time Consciousness in Husserl and Heidegger," *Philosophy and Phenomenological Research,* VIII (1948), pp. 23-53.

1286. Merleau-Ponty, Maurice. *Adventures of the Dialectic,* tr. by Joseph Bien (Evanston: Northwestern University Press, 1973).

1287. –, "Cezanne's Doubt," *Partisan Review,* XIII (1946), pp. 464-478.

1288. –. *In Praise of Philosophy,* tr. by John Wild and James

M. Edie (Evanston: Northwestern University Press, 1963).

1289. –, "Marxism and Philosophy," *Politics,* IV (July-August, 1947), pp. 173-175.

1290. –. *Phenomenology of Perception,* tr. by Colin Smith (London: Routledge and Kegan Paul, 1962).

1291. –. *The Primacy of Perception and Other Essays,* ed. and introduced by James M. Edie (Evanston: Northwestern University Press, 1964).

1292. –. *The Prose of the World,* tr. by John O'Neill (Evanston: Northwestern University Press, 1970).

1293. –. *Sense and Non-Sense,* tr. by Hubert L. Dreyfus and Patricia Allen Dreyfus (Evanston: Northwestern University Press, 1964).

1294. –. *Signs,* tr. by Richard C. McCleary (Evanston: Northwestern University Press, 1964).

1295. –. *The Structure of Behavior,* tr. by Alden L. Fisher (Boston: Beacon Press, 1963).

1296. –. *The Visible and the Invisible,* tr. by Alphonso Lingis (Evanston: Northwestern University Press, 1968).

1297. Merleau-Ponty, Maurice, "What is Phenomenology," *Cross Currents,* IV (1956).

"What is Phenomenology?" reprinted in Joseph J. Kockelmans, ed., *Phenomenology: The Philosophy of Edmund Husserl and Its Interpretation* (New York: Anchor Press, 1967), pp. 356-374.

1298. Merritt, Richard N., "God, Sartre, and the New Theologians," *Journal of General Education,* XVII (1965), pp. 125-134.

1299. Meyer, Henrietta Hilda. *Reflections Upon the Life and Thought of Soren Kierkegaard* (London: Guild of

Pastoral Theology, 1966).

1300. Meyerhoff, Hans, "Emotive Existentialist Theories of Ethics," *Journal of Philosophy,* XLVIII (1951), pp. 769-783.

1301. –, "On Existence and Enlightenment," *Partisan Review,* XXVI (1959), pp. 290-299.

1302. –, "The Return to the Concrete," *Chicago Review,* XIII, 2 (1959), pp. 27-38.

1303. Michaelson, C., "Kierkegaard's Theology of Faith," *Religion in Life,* XXXII (1963), pp. 225-237.

1304. Michalson, Carl, ed. *Christianity and the Existentialists* (New York: Charles Scribner's Sons, 1956).

1305. –, "Existence is a Mysticism," *Theology Today,* XII (1955), pp. 155-168.

1306. Miedzianogora, Myriam. *Gilbert Ryle and Jean-Paul Sartre: A Comparative Study of Two Theories of Mind,* Ph.D. diss., Columbia University (1966).

1307. Mihalich, Joseph C. *Existentialism and Thomism* (New York: Philosophical Library, 1960).

1308. –. *The Notion of Value in the Existentialism of Jean-Paul Sartre,* Ph.D. diss., Georgetown University (1965).

1309. –, "Some Aspects of Freedom in Sartre's Existentialism," *Four Quarters,* VIII (1959), pp. 10-25.

1310. Miller, A., "A Reflection on Some Attitudes toward Death in Contemporary Non-Christian Writing," *Encounter,* XXII (1961), pp. 84-92.

1311. Miller, Albert J. *Selective Bibliography of Existentialism in Education and Related Topics* (Jericho, New York: Exposition Press, 1969).

1312. Miller, J. Hillis, "Wallace Stevens' Poetry of Being," *Jour-*

nal of English Literary History, XXXI (1964), pp. 86-105.

1313. Miller, L. L. *In Search of the Self* (Philadelphia: Muhlenberg Press, 1962).

1314. Miller, M. and J. Chotlos, "Obsessive and Hysterical Syndromes in the Light of Existential Considerations," *Journal of Existential Psychiatry*, I (1960), pp. 315-330.

1315. Millholland, D., "Albert Camus and Existentialism," *Religious Humanism*, II (1968), pp. 162-166.

1316. Millikan, J. D. *Heidegger, Time, and Self-Transcendence*, Ph.D. diss., Yale University (1966).

1317. Minkowski, Eugène. *Lived Time: Phenomenological and Psychopathological Studies*, tr. by Nancy Metzel (Evanston: Northwestern University Press, 1933).

1318. Mitchell, Charles, "*The Lord of the Flies* and the Escape from Freedom," *Arizona Quarterly*, XXII (1966), pp. 27-40.

1319. Moehling, Karl A. *Martin Heidegger and the Nazi Party: An Examination*, Ph.D. diss., Northern Illinois University Press (1972).

1320. Moeller, Charles, "Albert Camus: The Question of Hope," *Cross Currents*, VIII (1958), pp. 172-184.

1321. Moeller, J., " 'Nietzsche and Metaphysics': Heidegger's Interpretation of Nietzsche," *Philosophy Today*, VIII (1964), pp. 118-132.

1322. Mohrt, M., "Ethic and Poetry in the Work of Camus," *Yale French Studies*, I (1948), pp. 113-118.

1323. Molina, Fernando. *Existentialism as Philosophy* (Englewood Cliffs, New Jersey: Prentice-Hall, 1962).

1324. –, ed. *The Sources of Existentialism as Philosophy*

(Englewood Cliffs, New Jersey: Prentice-Hall, 1969).

1325. Molnar, Thomas, "Albert Camus: Guide of a Generation," *Catholic World,* CLXXXVI (1958), pp. 272-277.

1326. –. *Sartre: Ideologue of Our Time* (New York: Funk and Wagnall's, 1968).

1327. Mood, J. J., "Leadbelly on Angst. Heidegger on the Blues," *Philosophy Today,* XIV (1970), pp. 161-167.

1328. –, "Poetic Languaging and Primal Thinking: A Study of Barfield, Wittgenstein, and Heidegger," *Encounter,* XXVI (1965), pp. 417-435.

1329. Moore, A., "Existential Phenomenology," *Philosophy and Phenomenological Research,* XXVII (1966-1967), pp. 408-414.

1330. Moore, Henry T. *Twentieth Century French Literature Since World War II* (Carbondale: Southern Illinois University Press, 1966), pp. 34-73.

1331. Moore, W. G., "Kierkegaard and His Century," *Hibbert Journal,* XXXVI (1936), pp. 568-582.

1332. More, P. E. *Nietzsche* (Boston: Houghton, Mifflin, 1912).

1333. Moreno, J. L., "Concept of the Encounter," *Journal of Existential Psychiatry,* I (1960), pp. 144-154.

1334. Morgan, George A., Jr. *What Nietzsche Means* (Cambridge: Harvard University Press, 1941; New York: Harper and Row, 1965).

1335. Morris, Charles, "Nietzsche—An Evaluation," *Journal of the History of Ideas,* IV, 3 (1945), pp. 285-293.

1336. Morris, Edward, "Intimacy," *Yale French Studies,* I, 1 (1948), pp. 73-79.

1337. Morris, Phyllis S., "The Laughing Lion: Nietzsche's Vision of the Overman," *Western Humanities Review,* XV

(1961), pp. 353-357.

1338. —, "Sartre and the Existence of Other Minds," *Journal of the British Society for Phenomenology,* I (1970), pp. 17-22.

1339. —. *Sartre's Concept of a Person,* Ph.D. diss., University of Chicago (1969).

1340. Morris, Van Cleve. *Existentialism in Education: What it Means* (New York: Harper and Row, 1966).

1341. Morrison, James C., "Heidegger's Criticism of Wittgenstein's Conception of Truth," *Man and World,* II (1969), pp. 551-573.

1342. —, "Husserl and Brentano on Intentionality," *Philosophy and Phenomenological Research,* XXXI (1970), pp. 121-138.

1343. Morrison, J. J., "Existential Import and Aristotelian Logic," *Philosophy and Phenomenological Research,* XV (1955), pp. 386-393.

1344. Morrissette, Bruce, "Oedipus and Existentialism: *Les Gommes* of Robbe-Grillet," *Wisconsin Studies in Contemporary Literature,* I, 3 (1960), pp. 43-73.

1345. Morriston, W., "Heidegger on the World," *Man and World,* V (1972), pp. 452-466.

1346. Moss, B. S., "This Existentialism," *Church Quarterly Review,* III (1948), pp. 191-198.

1347. Mougin, Henri, "The French Origins of Existentialism," *Science and Society,* II (1947), pp. 127-143.

1348. Mounier, Emmanuel. *Existentialist Philosophies: An Introduction,* tr. by Eric Blow (London: Rockliff, 1948).

1349. Mourant, John A., "The Limitations of Religious Existentialism," *International Philosophical Quarterly,* I

(1961), pp. 437-452.

1350. Mow, Joseph B., "Jean-Paul Sartre: Christian Theist?" *Christian Century,* LXXXIII (November 23, 1966), pp. 1437-1439.

1351. Mueller, G. E., "Existence and Existentialism," *Personalist,* XXXIV (1953), pp. 25-33.

1352. –, "Experiential and Existential Time," *Philosophy and Phenomenological Research,* VI (1946), pp. 424-435.

1353. Mueller, William R., "A Note on American-European Fiction," *Theology Today,* XXI (1964), pp. 221-223.

1354. Mügge, M. A. *Friedrich Nietzsche in His Life and Work* (New York: Brentano, 1915).

1355. Mullan, Hugh, "The Discovery of Existential Components Inherent in Contemporary Psychotherapy," *Journal of Existential Psychiatry,* I (1960), pp. 330-346.

1356. Munford, Clarence J., "Sartrean Existentialism and the Philosophy of History," *Cahiers d'Histoire mondiale,* XI (1968), pp. 392-404.

1357. Munitz, Milton Karl. *Existence and Logic* (New York: New York University Press, 1974).

1358. –. *The Mystery of Existence* (New York: Delta, 1965).

1359. Munson, T. N., "Heidegger's Recent Thought on Language," *Philosophy and Phenomenological Research,* XXI (1960-1961), pp. 361-372.

1360. Munz, P., "Sum Qui Sum," *Hibbert Journal,* L (1952), pp. 143-152.

1361. Murdoch, Iris, "The Existentialist Hero," *The Listener* (March 23, 1950), pp. 523-524.

1362. –, "The Novelist as Metaphysician," *The Listener* (March

16, 1950), pp. 473, 476.

1363. –. *Sartre, Romantic Rationalist* (Cambridge: Bowes and Bowes, and New Haven: Yale University Press, 1951).

1364. Murphy, Richard T., "Consciousness in Brentano and Husserl," *Modern Scholasticism,* XLV (1968), pp. 227-241.

1365. Muus, Rolf, "Existentialism and Psychology," *Educational Theory* (July, 1956), pp. 135-153.

1366. Naesev, Vincent. *The Sampler: The Danish Existentialist on the Morals of the Press* (Privately printed, 1952).

1367. Naess, Arne. *Four Modern Philosophers: Carnap, Wittgenstein, Heidegger, Sartre,* tr. by Alastair Hannay (Chicago: University of Chicago Press, 1968).

1368. Nakagawa, N., "On 'Analogical Characteristics' in Heidegger's Philosophy," *Journal of Religious Studies,* XXXIII (1960), pp. 55-56.

1369. Natanson, Maurice, "Albert Camus: Death at the Meridain," *Carolina Quarterly,* XI (1960), pp. 21-26, 65-69.

1370. –, "Being-in-Reality," *Philosophy and Phenomenological Research,* XX (1959), pp. 231-238.

1371. –, "Causation as a Structure of the *Lebenswelt,*" *Journal of Existential Psychiatry,* I (1960), pp. 346-366.

1372. –. *A Critique of Jean-Paul Sartre's Ontology, University of Nebraska Studies* (March, 1951), New Series, No. 6.

1373. –, "Death and Situation," *American Imago,* XVI (1959), pp. 447-457.

1374. –, ed. *Essays in Phenomenology* (The Hague: Martinus Nijhoff, 1966).

1375. —, "Existential Categories in Contemporary Literature," *Carolina Quarterly,* X (1958), pp. 17-30.

1376. —, "An Introduction to Existentialism," *University of Kansas City Review* (Winter, 1960), pp. 130-139.

1377. —, "Jean-Paul Sartre's Philosophy of Freedom," *Social Research,* XIX (1952), pp. 364-380.

1378. —. *Literature, Philosophy, and the Social Sciences: Essays in Existentialism and Phenomenology* (The Hague: Martinus Nijhoff, 1962).

1379. —, "Phenomenology and Existentialism: Husserl and Sartre on Intentionality," *Modern Schoolman,* XXXVII (1959), pp. 1-10.

1380. —, ed. *Phenomenology and Social Reality: Essays in Memory of Alfred Schutz* (The Hague: Martinus Nijhoff, 1970).

1381. —, "Phenomenology and Social Rôle," *Journal of the British Society for Phenomenology,* III, 3 (1972), pp. 218-230.

1382. —, "Phenomenology as a Rigorous Science," *International Philosophical Quarterly,* VII (1967), pp. 5-20.

1383. —, "Sartre and Literature," *University of Houston Forum* (Fall, 1959), pp. 4-11.

1384. —, "Sartre's Fetishism: A Reply to Van Meter Ames," *Journal of Philosophy,* XLVIII (1950), pp. 95-99.

See item 52 of this Bibliography.

1385. Nauman, St. Elmo. *The New Dictionary of Existentialism* (New York: Philosophical Library, 1971).

Spotty and simplistic with many of the most important terms not included. Much biographical information.

1386. Nelson, B., "The Balcony and Parisian Existentialism," *Tulane Drama Review,* VII (1963), pp. 60-79.

1387. Newman, Francis, "Origins of Sartre's Existentialism," *Ethics,* LXXXVI (1966), pp. 178-191.

1388. Niblett, W. R., "On Existentialism and Education," *British Journal of Educational Studies,* II (1954), pp. 101-111.

1389. Nicholls, Roger A., "Heinrich Mann and Nietzsche," *Modern Language Quarterly,* XXI (1960), pp. 165-178.

1390. –, "Nietzsche in the Early Work of Thomas Mann," *Publications in Modern Philology,* XLV (1955), p. 119 ff.

1391. Nicholson, G., "Camus and Heidegger: Anarchists," *University of Toronto Quarterly,* XLI (1971), pp. 14-23.

1392. Nicol, E. *The Theory and History of Existentialism: The Temporality of Being and Reason* (Mexico City: El Colegio de Mexico, 1950).

1393. Nielson, Niels C., "Demythologizing and the Philosophia Perennis: Bultmann, Jaspers, and Heidegger," *Rice University Studies,* L (1964), pp. 55-67.

1394. Nietzsche, Friedrich. *The Basic Works of Friedrich Nietzsche,* tr. and ed. by Walter Kaufmann (New York: Modern Library, Basic Books, 1968). Republished as *The Viking Portable Nietzsche* (New York: Viking Press, 1954, 1968).

1395. –. *Birth of Tragedy,* tr. by Walter Kaufmann (New York: Random House, 1967).

1396. –. *The Birth of Tragedy and The Geneology of Morals,* tr. by Francine Golffing (New York: Doubleday/Anchor Press, 1956).

1397. –. *Complete Works of Friedrich Nietzsche,* ed. by Oscar

Levy, 18 vols. (New York: Macmillan, 1909-1911). Reissued (New York: Russell and Russell, 1964).

The definitive edition of Nietzsche.

1398. –. *Early Greek Philosophy and Other Essays,* tr. by M. A. Mügge (London: Foulis, 1911; New York: Macmillan, 1924).

1399. –. *Thus Spake Zarathustra,* tr. by Walter Kaufmann (New York: Viking Press, 1956). Tr. by Marianne Cowan (Chicago: Regnery-Gateway, 1957). Tr. by R. J. Hollingdale (Baltimore: Penguin Books, 1961).

1400. –. *The Will to Power,* tr. by Walter Kaufmann and R. J. Hollingdale (New York: Random House, 1967, Vintage Books, 1968).

1401. Norburn, R., "Strange Prophet: Nietzsche and the Meaning of History," *Church Quarterly Review,* CXXXIX (1945), pp. 177-203.

1402. Nott, Kathleen, "German Influence on Modern French Thought," *The Listener* (January 13, 1955), pp. 73-75.

1403. Noxon, James, "Kierkegaard's Stages and *A Burnt-Out Case,*" *Review of English Literature,* III (1962), pp. 90-101.

1404. O'Brien, Conor Cruise, "The Gentle Nietzscheans," *New York Review of Books,* XV, 8 (November 5, 1970), pp. 12-16.

1405. Odajnyk, Walter. *Marxism and Existentialism* (New York: Anchor Books, 1965).

1406. O'Donnell, William G., "Kierkegaard: The Literary Manner," *Kenyon Review,* IX (1947), pp. 35-47.

1407. O'Faolain, Sean. *The Vanishing Hero: Studies in Novelists of the Forties* (London: Eyre and Spottiswoode, 1956).

1408. Olafson, Frederick A., "Consciousness and Intentionality in Heidegger's Thought," *American Philosophical Quarterly*, XII (1975), pp. 91-103.

1409. –, "Existential Psychoanalysis," *Ethics*, LXIV, 4 (1954).

1410. –, "Interpretation and the Dialectic of Action," *Journal of Philosophy*, LXIX (1972), pp. 718-734.

1411. –, "Nietzsche, Kant, and Existentialism," in Robert Solomon, ed., *Nietzsche: A Collection of Critical Essays* (New York: Anchor Press, 1973), pp. 194-201.

1412. –. *Principles and Persons: An Ethical Interpretation of Existentialism* (Baltimore: The Johns Hopkins Press, 1967).

1413. Olson, Esther. *An Analysis of the Nietzschean Elements in the Plays of Eugene O'Neill*, Ph.D. diss., University of Minnesota (1956).

1414. Olson, Robert G. *An Introduction to Existentialism* (London: Constable; New York: Dover Publications, 1962).

1415. –, "Three Theories of Motivation in the Philosophy of Jean-Paul Sartre," *Ethics*, LXVI (April, 1956), pp. 176-187.

1416. O'Mahony, B. E., "Martin Heidegger's Existential Analysis of Death," *Philosophical Studies*, XVIII (1969), pp. 58-75.

1417. O'Malley, John B. *The Fellowship of Being: An Essay on the Concept of Person in the Philosophy of Gabriel Marcel* (The Hague: Martinus Nijhoff, 1966).

1418. O'Mara, J., "Death and the Existentialist," *Studies* (December, 1950), pp. 427-437.

1419. –, "Kierkegaard Revealed," *Studies*, XXXVIII (1949), pp. 447-456.

1420. —, "The Meaning and Value of Existentialism," *Studies,* XL (1951), pp. 11-22.

1421. O'Meara, Thomas F., "Tillich and Heidegger: A Structural Relationship," *Harvard Theological Review,* LXI (1968), pp. 249-261.

1422. O'Neil, Charles, ed. *Etienne Gilson Tribute Presented by his North American Students with a Response by Etienne Gilson* (Milwaukee: Marquette University Press, 1959).

See particularly L. Lynch's essay, "Martin Heidegger: Language and Being," pp. 135-147.

1423. O'Neill, John. *Perception, Expression and History: The Social Phenomenology of Maurice Merleau-Ponty* (Evanston: Northwestern University Press, 1970).

1424. Ortega y Gasset, José. *Man in Crisis,* tr. by M. Adams (New York: Norton, 1959).

1425. Osborn, Andrew D. *Edmund Husserl and His Logical Investigations* (Cambridge: Harvard University Press, 1949).

1426. —. *The Philosophy of Edmund Husserl in its Development from his Mathematical Interest to his First Conception of Phenomenology in Logical Investigations* (New York: International Press, 1934).

1427. Oshima, S., "Barth's Analogia Relatinis and Heidegger's Ontological Difference," *The Journal of Religion,* LIII (1973), pp. 176-194.

1428. Ostermann, R., "An Introduction to Gabriel Marcel," *Catholic World,* CLXXVII (1953), pp. 187-193.

1429. Otani, Masaru, "Self-Manifestation of Freedom in 'Anxiety' by Kierkegaard," *Orbis Litterarum,* XXII, pp. 393-398.

1430. Ott, Heinrich, "Hermeneutic and Personal Structure of

Language," in Joseph J. Kockelmans, ed., *On Heidegger and Language* (Evanston: Northwestern University Press, 1972), pp. 169-194.

1431. Owen, P. O., "Existentialism and Ascetical Theology," *Church Quarterly Review*, CLS (1959), pp. 226-231.

1432. Owens, Thomas J. *Phenomenology and Intersubjectivity: Contemporary Interpretations of the Interpersonal Situation* (The Hague: Martinus Nijhoff, 1970).

1433. Owens, T. T., "Absolute Aloneness as Man's Existential Structure: A Study of Sartrean Ontology," *The New Scholasticism*, XL (July, 1966), pp. 341-360.

1434. Oxenhandler, Neal, "The Metaphor of Metaphor in *La Nausée*," *Chicago Review*, XV (1962), pp. 47-54.

1435. Pacifici, Sergio J., "Existentialism and Italian Literature," *Yale French Studies*, XVI (1954), pp. 79-88.

1436. Pageler, J. C. *The Soul and Time: First Principles of Modern Metaphysical Speculation as Represented in the Thought of Martin Heidegger*, Ph.D. diss., Claremont Graduate School (1967).

1437. Pait, James A., "Kierkegaard and the Problem of Choice," *Emory University Quarterly*, II (1946), pp. 237-245.

1438. Palmer, Donald D., "Unamuno's Don quixote and Kierkegaard's Abraham," *Revista de Estudios Hispanicos*, III (1969), pp. 295-312.

1439. Palmer, Richard. *Hermeneutics: Interpretation Theory in Schleiermacher, Dilthey, Heidegger, and Gadamer* (Evanston: Northwestern University Press, 1969).

Virtually the only book on post-Biblical Hermeneutics. Palmer studied under Gadamer, knows the field well, and is able to explain the many complexities of hermeneutics so that the average reader can comprehend it.

1440. –, "Postmodernity and Hermeneutics," *boundary 2,* V, 2 (1977), pp. 363-394.

1441. –, "The Postmodernity of Heidegger," Special Heidegger and Literature issue, *boundary 2,* IV, 2 (1976), pp. 411-432.

1442. Parkes, Henry B., "Nietzsche," *Scrutiny* (June, 1941), pp. 51-60.

1443. Parsons, Kathryn Pyne, "Nietzsche and Moral Change," in Robert Solomon, ed., *Nietzsche: A Collection of Critical Essays* (New York: Anchor Press, 1973), pp. 169-193.

1444. Passmore, John A. *A Hundred Years of Philosophy* (Harmondsworth: Penguin, 1968).

See especially "Existentialism and Phenomenology," pp. 476-516.

1445. Patka, Frederick, ed. *Existentialist Thinkers and Thought* (New York: Citadel Press, 1962).

1446. Patte, John, "Literature and Freedom: The Crisis of the Bourgeois Intellectual in France," *University of Denver Quarterly,* V, 2 (Summer, 1970), pp. 19-55.

1447. Patterson, Yolanda. *Solitude and Communication in the Works of Jean-Paul Sartre and Albert Camus,* Ph.D. diss., Standford University (1965).

1448. Paul, L. *The Meaning of Human Existence* (London: Faber and Faber, 1949).

1449. Paul, W. W., "Faith and Reason in Kierkegaard and Modern Existentialism," *Review of Religion,* XX (1956), pp. 149-163.

1450. Pelikan, Jaroslav. *Human Culture and the Holy; Essays on the True, the Good, and the Beautiful: Kierkegaard, Paul, Dostoyevski, Luther, Nietzsche, and Bach* (London: Student Christian Movement Press, 1959).

1451. Percy, Walker, "Man on the Train: Three Existential Modes," *Partisan Review,* XXIII (1956), pp. 478-494.

1452. Pereboom, M. Dirk, "Heidegger-Bibliographie, 1917-1966," *Freiburger Zeitschrift für Philosophie und Theologie,* XVI (1969).

1453. Perkins, Robert L. *Soren Kierkegaard* (Richmond: John Knox Press, 1969).

1454. Perotti, James L. *Heidegger on the Divine: The Thinker, the Poet and God* (Columbus: Ohio University Press, 1974).

1455. Perry, E., "Was Kierkegaard a Biblical Existentialist?" *Journal of Religion,* XXXVI (1956), pp. 17-23.

1456. Pervin, L., "Existentialism, Psychology, and Psychotherapy," *American Psychology,* XV (1960), pp. 305-309.

1457. Peters, Charles, "Friedrich Nietzsche and His Doctrine of Will to Power," *The Monist,* XXI (1911), pp. 357-375.

1458. Petras, John W., "God, Man, and Society: The Perspectives of Buber and Kierkegaard," *Journal of Religious Thought,* XXIII (1966-1967), pp. 119-128.

1459. Pettit, Philip. *On the Idea of Phenomenology* (Dublin: Scepter, 1969).

1460. –, "Parmenides and Sartre," *Philosophical Studies,* XVII (1968), pp. 161-184.

1461. Peyre, Henri, "Albert Camus: An Anti-Christian Moralist," *Proceedings of the American Philosophical Society,* CII (1958), pp. 477-482.

1462. –, "American Literature through French Eyes," *The Virginia Quarterly Review,* XXIII (1947).

1463. –. *The Contemporary French Novel* (New York: Oxford University Press, 1955).

1464. –, "Existentialism–A Literature of Despair?" *Yale French Studies,* I, 1 (1948), pp. 21-32.

1465. –. *French Novelists of Today* (New York: 1967).

See especially the chapter on Sartre, pp. 244-274.

1466. –. *Jean-Paul Sartre* (New York: Columbia University Press, 1968).

1467. –. *Literature and Sincerity* (New Haven: Yale University Press, 1963).

1468. Pfeffer, R., "Eternal Recurrence in Nietzsche's Moral Philosophy," *Review of Metaphysics,* XIX (1965), pp. 276-300.

1469. Pfeffer, Rose, "The Problem of Truth in Nietzsche's Philosophy," *The Personalist,* XLVIII (1967), pp. 5-24.

1470. Pfeiffer, Johannes, "On Karl Jaspers' Interpretation of Art," in Paul Schilpp, ed., *The Philosophy of Karl Jaspers* (New York: Tudor Pub. Co., 1957), pp. 703-718.

1471. Pfeil, Hans, "The Modern Denial of God: Its Origin and Tragedy," *Philosophy Today,* III (1959), pp. 19-27.

1472. Pfeutze, Paul E. *The Social Self in the Writing of George Herbert Mead and Martin Buber* (New York: Bookman Associates, 1954).

1473. Phelan, Gerald B., "The Existentialism of St. Thomas Aquinas," *Proceedings of the American Catholic Philosophical Association,* XXI (1946), pp. 25-40.

1474. Piorkowski, Henry, "The Path of Phenomenology: Husserl, Heidegger, Sartre, Merleau-Ponty," *Duns Scotus Philosophical Association,* XXX (1966), pp. 177-221.

1475. Pitte, F. P. van de, "The Role of Hölderlin in the Philosophy of Heidegger," *The Personalist,* XLII (1962), pp. 168-179.

1476. Pivcevic, Edo. *Husserl and Phenomenology* (London: Hutchinson, 1970).

1477. Plank, William Gene. *Sartre and Surrealism,* Ph.D. diss., University of Washington (1972).

1478. Plantinga, Alvin, "An Existentialist's Ethics," *Review of Metaphysics,* XII (1958), pp. 235-256.

1479. Pleydell-Pearce, A. G., "Freedom, Emotion and Choice in the Philosophy of Sartre," *Journal of the British Society for Phenomenology,* I (1970), pp. 35-46.

1480. Pöggeler, Otto, "Heidegger Today," in Edward G. Ballard and Charles E. Scott, eds., *Martin Heidegger in Europe and America* (The Hague: Martinus Nijhoff, 1973), pp. 1-36.

1481. –, "Heidegger's Topology of Being," in Joseph J. Kockelmans, ed., *On Heidegger and Language* (Evanston: Northwestern University Press, 1972), pp. 107-146.

1482. Pollman, Leo. *Sartre and Camus: Literature of Existence,* tr. by Helen Gregor Sebba (New York: Felix Ungar, 1970).

1483. Pomedli, M. M. *Heidegger and Freud: The Power of Death,* Ph.D. diss., Duquesne University (1972).

1484. Pondrom, Cyrena Norman, "Two Demonic Figures: Kierkegaard's Merman and Dostoyevsky's Underground Man," *Orbis Litterarum,* XXIII (1968), pp. 161-177.

1485. Poole, Roger C., "Hegel, Kierkegaard, and Sartre," *New Blackfriar's,* XLVII (1966), pp. 532-541.

1486. Popkin, R. H., "Hume and Kierkegaard," *Journal of Religion,* XXXI (1951), pp. 274-281.

1487. Porter, Dennis, "Sartre, Robbe-Grillet and the Psychotic Hero," *Modern Fiction Studies,* XVI, 1 (1970), pp. 13-25.

1488. Porterfield, Allen, "Auerbach and Nietzsche," *Modern Philology* (February, 1918), pp. 155-171.

1489. Poster, Mark. *Existential Marxism: A Study of French Social Theory Since World War II* (Princeton: Princeton University Press, 1975).

1490. Poteat, W. H., " 'I Will Die:' An Analysis of the Concept of Death in Existentialist Thought," *Philosophical Quarterly,* I (1959), pp. 46-58.

1491. Powell, Ralp, "The Late Heidegger's Omission of the Ontic-Ontological Structure of Dasein," in John Sallis, ed., *Heidegger and the Path of Thinking* (Pittsburgh: Duquesne University Press, 1970), pp. 116-137.

1492. Prenter, R., "The Concept of Freedom in Sartre Against a Kierkegaardian Background," tr. by H. Kaasa, *Dialog,* VII (1968), pp. 132-137.

1493. Price, G. *The Narrow Pass: A Study of Kierkegaard's Concept of Man* (New York: McGraw-Hill, 1963).

1494. Querido, R. M., "A Philosophy of Despair," *The National Review,* CXXIX (September, 1947), pp. 237-241.

1495. Quinn, B. J. *Sartre on Violence: A Political, Philosophical and Literary Study,* Ph.D. diss., Louisiana State University (1970).

1496. Rabil, Albert, Jr. *Merleau-Ponty: Existentialist of the Social World* (New York: Columbia University Press, 1967).

1497. Rahner, K., "The Concept of Existential Philosophy in Heidegger," *Philosophy Today,* XIII (1969), pp. 127-137.

1498. Rahv, Betty T. *From Sartre to the New Novel* (Port Washington: Kennikat Press, 1974).

1499. Ramsey, P., "Existenz and the Existence of God: A Study of Kierkegaard and Hegel," *Journal of Religion,* XXVIII (1948), pp. 157-176.

1500. Ranly, Ernest W. *Scheler's Phenomenology of Community* (The Hague: Martinus Nijhoff, 1966).

1501. Rasmussen, David M. *Mythic-Symbolic Language and Philosophical Anthropology: A Constructive Interpretation of the Thought of Paul Ricoeur* (The Hague: Martinus Nijhoff, 1971).

1502. Rather, L. J., "Existential Experience in Whitehead and Heidegger," *Review of Existential Psychology and Psychiatry,* I (1961), pp. 113-119.

1503. Rau, Catherine, "Aesthetic Views of Jean-Paul Sartre," *Journal of Aesthetics and Art Criticism,* IX (1950), pp. 139-147.

1504. –, "The Ethical Theory of Jean-Paul Sartre," *Journal of Philosophy,* XLVI (1949), pp. 536-545.

1505. Rauch, Leo. *Intentionality and its Development in the Phenomenological Psychology of Edmund Husserl,* Ph.D. diss., New York University (1968).

1506. –, "Sartre, Merleau-Ponty and the 'Hole' in Being," *Philosophical Studies,* XVIII (1969), pp. 119-132.

1507. Read, Herbert. *Existentialism, Marxism and Anarchism: Chains of Freedom* (London: Freedom Press, 1949).

1508. Reck, Rima Drell. *Literature and Responsibility: The French Novelist in the Twentieth Century* (Baton Rouge: Louisiana State University Press, 1969).

1509. Rehder, Helmut, "Literary Criticism and the Existentialism of Jaspers'," in Paul Schilpp, ed., *The Philosophy of Karl Jaspers* (New York: Tudor Pub. Co., 1957), pp. 719-747.

1510. Reichert, Herbert W., "Nietzschean Influence in Musil's *Der Mann ohne Eigenschaften,*" *The German Quarter-*

ly, XXXIX (1966), pp. 12-28.

1511. – and Karl Schlecta, eds. *International Nietzsche Bibliography* (Chapel Hill: University of North Carolina Press, 1960), revised and expanded, 1969.

1512. Reinhardt, Kurt F., "A Thomist Answers Sartre," *The Commonweal,* XLIX, 22 (March 11, 1949), pp. 545-546.

1513. –. *The Existentialist Revolt: The Main Themes and Phases of Existentialism: Kierkegaard, Nietzsche, Heidegger, Jaspers, Sartre, Marcel,* 2nd edition, with an *Appendix on Existentialist Psychotherapy* (New York: F. Ungar, Publishers, 1960).

1514. –, "The Problem of Human Existence," *Commonweal,* XLIX (1949), pp. 632-635.

1515. Renard, Henri, "Essence and Existence," *Proceedings of the American Catholic Philosophical Association,* XXI (1946), pp. 53-66.

1516. Replogle, Justin, "Auden's Religious Leap," *Wisconsin Studies in Contemporary Literature,* VII (1966), pp. 47-75.

1517. Reulet, A. S., "Being, Value, and Existence," *Philosophy and Phenomenological Research,* IX (1949), pp. 448-457.

1518. Reyburn, H. A., in collaboration with H. E. Hinderks and J. G. Taylor. *Nietzsche: The Story of a Human Philosopher* (London: 1948).

1519. Rhoades, Donald H., "Essential Varieties of Existentialism," *The Personalist,* XXXV (1954), pp. 32-40.

1520. Rice, Philip Blair, "Existentialism and the Self," *The Kenyon Review,* XII, 2 (Spring, 1950), pp. 304-320.

1521. Richards, George W., "Karl Marx and Friedrich Nietzsche: A Study of Ways of Salvation," *Religion in Life,* IV

(1935), pp. 176-193.

1522. Richardson, David Bonner. *Berdyaev's Philosophy of History: An Existentialist Theory of Social Creativity and Eschatology* (The Hague: Martinus Nijhoff, 1968).

1523. Richardson, W. J., "Heidegger and the Quest of Freedom," *Theological Studies,* XXVIII (1967), pp. 286-307.

1524. –, "Heidegger and Aristotle," *Heythrop Journal,* V (1964), pp. 58-64.

1525. –, "Heidegger and God–And Professor Jonas," *Thought,* XL (1965), pp. 13-40.

1526. –, "Heidegger and Plato," *The Heythorp Journal,* IV (1963), pp. 273-279.

1527. –, "Heidegger and Theology," *Theological Studies,* XXVI (1965), pp. 86-100.

1528. –, "Heidegger and the Origin of Language," *International Philosophical Quarterly,* II (1962), pp. 404-416.

1529. –, "Heidegger and the Problem of Thought," *Revue philosophique de Louvain,* LX (1962), pp. 58-78.

1530. –, "Heidegger's Critique of Science," *The New Scholasticism,* XLII, 4 (1968).

1531. –. *Heidegger: Through Phenomenology to Thought,* with a Preface by Martin Heidegger (The Hague: Mouton, 1963).

1532. –, "The Place of the Unconscious in Heidegger," *Review of Existential Psychology and Psychiatry,* V (1965), pp. 265-290.

1533. Richey, Clarence W., "On the Intentional Ambiguity of Heidegger's Metaphysics," *Journal of Philosophy,* LX (1958), pp. 1144-1148.

1534. Richter, Liselotte. *Jean-Paul Sartre,* tr. by Fred D. Wieck (New York: Frederick Ungar, 1970).

1535. Ricoeur, Paul. *Fallible Man,* tr. by C. Kelbley (Chicago: Regnery Co., 1965).

1536. —. *Freedom and Nature: The Voluntary and The Involuntary,* tr. by Erazim V. Kohak (Evanston: Northwestern University Press, 1966).

1537. —. *Freud and Philosophy: On Interpretation,* tr. by Dens Savage (New Haven: Yale University Press, 1970).

A phenomenological critique of Freudian analysis.

1538. —. *History and Truth,* tr. by Charles A. Kelbley (Evanston: Northwestern University Press, 1965).

1539. —. *Husserl: An Examination of His Philosophy,* tr. by Edward Ballard and Lester Embree (Evanston: Northwestern University Press, 1967).

1540. —, "The Relation of Jaspers' Philosophy to Religion," in Paul Schilpp, ed., *The Philosophy of Karl Jaspers* (New York: Tudor Pub. Co., 1957), pp. 611-642.

1541. —. *The Symbolism of Evil,* tr. by E. Buchanan (New York: Harper and Row, 1967).

1542. Riddel, Joseph N., "From Heidegger to Derrida to Chance: Doubling and (Poetic) Language," Special Heidegger and Literature issue, *boundary 2,* IV, 2 (1976), pp. 571-592.

1543. —. *The Clarivoyant Eye: The Poetry and Poetics of Wallace Stevens* (Baton Rouge: Louisiana State University Press, 1965).

1544. von Rintelen, Fritz Joachim. *Beyond Existentialism,* tr. by Hilda Graef (London: Allen and Unwin, 1961).

1545. —. *Contemporary German Philosophy and its Background* (Bonn: H. Bouvier u. Co. Verlag, 1970).

1546. –, "The Existentialism of Martin Heidegger," *The Personalist*, XXXVIII (1957), pp. 238-247, 376-382.

1547. Robbins, Leonard, "Zarathustra and the Magician or, Nietzsche contra Nietzsche: Some Difficulties in the Concept of the Overman," *Man and World*, IX, 2 (1976), pp. 175-195.

1548. Roberts, David Everett. *Existentialism and Religious Belief* (New York: Oxford University Press, 1957).

1549. –, "Faith and Freedom in Existentialism: A Study of Kierkegaard and Sartre," *Theology Today*, VIII (1952), pp. 469-482.

1550. Robinson, D. S., "Tillich and Marcel: Theistic Existentialists," *The Personalist*, XXXIV (1953), pp. 237-251.

1551. Robinson, J. M. and J. B. Cobb, Jr., eds. *The Later Heidegger and Theology* (New York: 1963).

1552. –. *The New Hermeneutic* (New York: Harper and Row, 1964).

1553. Rodriguez-Alcala, Hug, "José Ortega y Gasset and Jean-Paul Sartre on Existence and Human Destiny," *Research Studies of the State College of Washington*, XXIV (September, 1956), pp. 193-211.

1554. Roeming, Robert F., ed. *Camus: A Bibliography* (Madison: University of Wisconsin Press, 1968).

1555. Rogers, Robert, "The Moral Philosophy of Nietzsche," *The Personalist*, XLVI (1965), pp. 18-38.

1556. Rohde, H. P., ed. *The Auctioneer's Sales Record of the Library of Soren Kierkegaard* (Copenhagen: The Royal Library, 1967).

1557. Rhode, Peter P. *Soren Aabye Kierkegaard 1813-1855* (London: George Allen and Unwin, 1963).

1558. –. *Soren Kierkegaard: The Father of Existentialism,* tr. by Reginald Spink (Copenhagen: Undenrigministeriets Pressebureau, 1963).

1559. Rollin, B. E., "Heidegger's Philosophy of History in 'Being and Time'," *Modern Schoolman,* XLIX (1971-1972), pp. 97-112.

1560. Rombach, H., "Reflections on Heidegger's Lecture 'Time and Being'," *Philosophy Today,* X (1966), pp. 19-29.

1561. Rosen, S., "Heidegger's Interpretation of Plato," *Journal of Existentialism,* VII (1966-1967), pp. 477-504.

1562. Rosen, S. H., "Curiosity, Anxiety, Wonder," *Giornale di Metafisica,* XIV (1959), pp. 465-474.

1563. Rosenberg, Harold, "Does the Jew Exist?" *Commentary,* VII (January, 1949), pp. 8-18.

1564. Rosenfeld, Alvin H., " 'The Being of Language and the Language of Being': Heidegger and Modern Poetics," Special Heidegger and Literature issue, *boundary 2,* IV, 2 (1976), pp. 535-554.

1565. Ross, Joan and David Freed. *The Existentialism of Alberto Moravia* (Carbondale: Southern Illinois University Press, 1972).

1566. Rossi, L. R., "Albert Camus: The Plague of Absurdity," *Kenyon Review,* XX (1958), pp. 399-422.

1567. Rossman, Kurt, comp., "Bibliography of the Writings of Karl Jaspers to Spring 1957," in Paul Schilpp, ed., *The Philosophy of Karl Jaspers* (New York: Tudor Pub. Co., 1957), pp. 871-888.

1568. Rotenstreich, N., "The Ontological Status of History," *American Philosophical Quarterly,* IX (1972), pp. 49-58.

1569. Roth, L., "Albert Camus," *Philosophy* (October, 1955), pp. 291-303.

1570. Roubiczek, Paul. *Existentialism For and Against* (Cambridge: Cambridge University Press, 1964).

1571. –. *The Misinterpretation of Man: Studies in European Thought of the Nineteenth Century* (New York: 1947).

See especially pp. 108-137 on Nietzsche.

1572. de Rougemont, Denis, "Kierkegaard and Hamlet: Two Danish Princes," *The Anchor Review,* I (1955), pp. 109-127.

1573. Royce, Josiah, "Nietzsche," *Atlantic Monthly* (March, 1917), pp. 321-331.

1574. Rudolph, Arthur W. *Superhistorical Individuality in Nietzsche's Thought,* Ph.D. diss., University of Southern California (1963).

1575. Ruggiero, Guido de. *Existentialism: Disintegration of Man's Soul* (New York: Social Science Publishers, 1948).

1576. Rukavina, Thomas F., "Being and Things in Heidegger's Philosophy: A Rejoinder," *New Scholasticism,* XXXIII (1959), pp. 184-201.

1577. –. *Heidegger as a Critic of Western Thinking,* Ph.D. diss., Indiana University (1960).

1578. –, "Heidegger's Theory of Being," *The New Scholasticism,* XL (1966), pp. 423-446.

1579. Ruoff, J. E., "Kierkegaard and Shakespeare," *Comparative Literature,* XX (1968), pp. 343-354.

1580. Ruotolo, Louis, "Keats and Kierkegaard: The Tragedy of Two Worlds," *Renascence,* XVI (1964), pp. 175-190.

1581. –. *Six Existential Heros* (New York: 1972).

1582. Russell, Bertrand. *Power: A New Social Analysis* (New York: 1938).

Contains much on Nietzsche.

1583. Russell, John, "The Existentialist Theatre," *Horizon,* XI (May, 1945), pp. 319-328.

The theater in France.

1584. Ryle, Gilbert, "Martin Heidegger: 'Sein und Zeit'," *Journal of the British Society for Phenomenology,* I (1970), pp. 3-14.

1585. Sadler, W. A. *Existence and Love: A New Approach in Existential Phenomenology* (New York: Charles Scribner's Sons, 1969).

1586. Sainsbury, Geoffrey, "Nietzsche," in J. McMurray, ed., *Some Makers of the Modern Spirit* (London: 1933), pp. 152-165.

1587. St. Aubyn, F. C., "Rilke, Sartre and Sarraute: The Rôle of the Third," *Revue de Littérature comparée,* XLI, 2 (1967), pp. 275-284.

1588. Saisselin, R. G., "The Absurd, Death, and History," *The Personalist,* XLII (1961), pp. 165-177.

1589. Sallis, John. *The Concept of World: A Study in the Phenomenological Ontology of Martin Heidegger,* Ph.D. diss., Tulane University (1964).

1590. –, ed. *Heidegger and the Path of Thinking* (Pittsburgh: Duquesne University Press, 1970).

Collection of essays by a number of scholars; a Festschrift in honor of Heidegger's 80th birthday (September 26, 1969). Sallis has included an essay of his own entitled, "Towards the Movement of Reversal: Science, Technology, and the Language of Homecoming," pp. 138-168.

1591. –, "Language and Reversal," in Edward G. Ballard and Charles E. Scott, eds., *Martin Heidegger in Europe and America* (The Hague: Martinus Nijhoff, 1973), pp. 129-146.

1592. –. *Phenomenology and the Return to Beginnings* (Pittsburgh: Duquesne University Press, 1973).

1593. –, "The Problem of Judgment In Husserl's Later Thought," *Tulane Studies in Philosophy*, XVI (1967), pp. 129-152.

1594. –, "World, Finitude, and Temporality in the Philosophy of Martin Heidegger," *Philosophy Today*, IX (1965), pp. 40-52.

1595. Salter, Walter M., "An Introductory Word on Nietzsche," *Harvard Theological Review*, VI (1913), pp. 461-477.

1596. –. *Nietzsche the Thinker: A Study* (New York: F. Ungar, 1968).

1597. Salvan, Jacques. *The Scandalous Ghost: Sartre's Existentialism as Related to Vitalism, Humanism, Mysticism, Marxism* (Detroit: Wayne State University Press, 1967).

1598. –. *To Be or Not To Be: An Analysis of Jean-Paul Sartre's Ontology* (Detroit: Wayne State University Press, 1962).

1599. Samay, Sebastian. *Reason Revisited: The Philosophy of Karl Jaspers* (Notre Dame: University of Notre Dame Press, 1971).

1600. Sanborn, Patricia F. *Existentialism* (New York: Pegasus, 1968).

1601. Santayana, George. *Egoism in German Philosophy* (New York: Scribner's, 1916).

1602. –, "On Existentialism: An Unpublished Letter," *Partisan Review*, XXV (1958), pp. 632 ff.

1603. Santoni, Ronald E., "Sartre on 'Sincerity': Bad Faith or Equivocation?" *The Personalist,* LIII (1972), pp. 150-160.

1604. Sartre, Jean-Paul. *The Age of Reason,* tr. by Eric Sutton (New York: Alfred Knopf, 1947).

1605. –, "American Novelists in French Eyes," *Atlantic Monthly,* CLXXVIII, 2 (August, 1946), pp. 114-118.

1606. –, "Americans and Their Myths," *Nation,* CLXV, 16 (October 18, 1947), pp. 402-403.

1607. –. *Anti-Semite and Jew,* tr. by George Becker (New York: Schocken Books, 1948), and as *Portrait of the Anti-Semite,* tr. by Eric de Mauny (London: Secker and Warburg, 1948).

1608. –. *Baudelaire,* tr. by Martin Turnell (New York: New Directions, 1950).

1609. –. *Being and Nothingness,* tr. by Hazel Estella Barnes (New York: Philosophical Library, 1956).

Sartre's major systematization of his philosophy. Barnes has added a useful glossary of Sartrean terms at the end.

1610. –, "The Case for a Responsible Literature," *Horizon,* XI (May, 1945), pp. 307-311, and *Partisan Review,* XII (Summer, 1945), pp. 304-308.

1611. –. *The Emotions: Outline of a Theory,* tr. by Bernard Frechtman (New York: Philosophical Library, 1948), and as *Sketch for a Theory of the Emotions,* tr. by Philip Mairet (London: Methuen, 1962).

1612. –. *Essays in Aesthetics,* tr. by Wade Baskin (New York: Philosophical Library, 1963).

1613. –. *Existentialism,* tr. by Bernard Frechtman (New York; Philosophical Library, 1947). Translation of Sartre's famous *L'Existentialisme est une humanisme.*

1614. –, "Existentialist on Mobilist," *Art News,* XLVI (December, 1947), pp. 22, 55.

1615. –, "Forgers of Myths: The Young Playwrights of France," *Theatre Arts,* XXX (June, 1946), pp. 324-335.

1616. –, "For Whom Does One Write?" *Partisan Review,* XV, 3 (March, 1948), pp. 313-322; XV, 5 (May, 1948), pp. 536-544.

1617. –. *Imagination,* tr. by Forest Williams (Ann Arbor: University of Michigan Press, 1962).

1618. –, "Intentionality: A Fundamental Idea of Husserl's Phenomenology," *Journal of the British Society for Phenomenology,* I (1970), pp. 4-5.

1619. –. *Intimacy and Other Stories,* tr. by Lloyd Alexander (New York: New Directions, 1948).

1620. –. *Literary and Philosophical Essays* (New York: Criterion Books, 1955).

1621. –. *Literature and Existentialism (What is Literature),* tr. by Bernard Frechtman (New York: Philosophical Library, 1949).

1622. –, "Literature in Our Time," *Partisan Review,* XV, 6 (June, 1948), pp. 634-653.

1623. –, "Materialism and Revolution," *Politics,* IV (July-August, 1947), pp. 161-172.

1624. –. *Nausea,* tr. by Lloyd Alexander (New York: New Directions, 1949), and as *The Diary of Antoine Roquentin,* (London: John Lehmann, 1949).

1625. –, "New Writing in France," *Vogue* (May, 1945), pp. 84-86.

1626. –, "Paris Alive: The Republic of Silence," *Atlantic Monthly,* CLXXIV (December, 1944), pp. 39-40.

1627. –, "Portrait of the Inauthentic Jew," *Commentary,* V, 5 (May, 1948).

1628. –. *Psychology of the Imagination,* tr. by Bernard Frechtman (New York: Philosophical Library, 1948).

1629. –. *The Reprieve,* tr. by Eric Sutton (New York: Alfred Knopf, 1947).

1630. –, "The Responsibility of the Writer," in L. Allan Wingate, ed., *Reflections on Our Age* (New York: Columbia University Press, 1949), pp. 67-83.

1631. –. *Saint Genet, Actor and Martyr,* tr. by Bernard Frechtman (New York: Braziller, 1963).

1632. –. *Search for a Method,* tr. by Hazel E. Barnes (New York: Alfred Knopf, 1963).

1633. –, "The Situation of the Jew," *Commentary,* V, 4 (April, 1948), pp. 306-316.

1634. –. *The Transcendance of the Ego,* tr. by Forrest Williams and Robert Kirkpatrick (New York: Noonday Press, 1957).

1635. –. *Troubled Sleep,* tr. by Gerard Hopkins (New York: Alfred Knopf, 1950), and as *Iron in the Soul* (London: Hamish Hamilton, 1950).

1636. –. *The Wall and Other Stories* (New York: New Directions, 1948).

1637. –, "We Write for Our Own Time," *Virginia Quarterly Review,* XXIII (Spring, 1947), pp. 236-243.

1638. –, "What is Writing?" *Partisan Review,* XV (January, 1948), pp. 9-31.

1639. –, "The Word as Mirror," *Saturday Review of Literature,* XXX (December 6, 1947), pp. 25-26.

1640. –. *The Words,* tr. by Bernard Frechtman (New York:

Braziller, 1964).

1641. Sass, Hans-Martin. *Heidegger-Bibliographie* (Meisenheim am Glan: Verlag Anton Hain, 1968).

1642. –. *Materialien zur Heidegger-Bibliographie 1917-1972* (Meisenheim am Glan: Verlag Anton Hain, 1975).

1643. Scanlon, John D., "Consciousness, the Streetcar, and the Ego: *Pro* Husserl, *Contra* Sartre," *Philosophical Forum,* II (1971), pp. 332-354.

1644. –, "The Epoche and Phenomenological Anthropology," *Research in Phenomenology,* II (1972), pp. 95-109.

1645. Schacht, Richard. *Alienation* (New York: Doubleday, 1971).

1646. –, "Husserlian and Heideggerian Phenomenology," *Philosophical Studies,* XXIII (1972), pp. 293-314.

1647. –, "Nietzsche and Nihilism," in Robert Solomon, ed., *Nietzsche: A Collection of Critical Essays* (New York: Anchor press, 1973), pp. 58-82.

1648. –, "On 'Existentialism,' *Existenz*-Philosophy, and Philosophical Anthropology," *American Philosophical Quarterly,* XI (1974), pp. 291-305.

1649. Schaff, Adam. *A Philosophy of Man* (New York: Monthly Review Press, 1963).

1650. Schaldebrand, Mary Aloysius, "Freedom and the 'I': An Existential Inquiry," *International Philosophical Quarterly,* III (December, 1963), pp. 571-599.

1651. –. *Phenomenologies of Freedom* (Washington, D.C.: Catholic University of America, 1960).

1652. Schürmann, Reiner, "Situating René Char: Hölderlin, Heidegger, Char and the 'There Is'," Special Heidegger and Literature issue, *boundary 2,* IV, 2 (1976), pp. 513-534.

1653. Scharff, R. C., "On 'Existentialist' Readings of Heidegger," *Southwestern Journal of Philosophy,* II (1971), pp. 7-20.

1654. Shattuck, Roger, "Making Time: A Study of Stravinsky, Proust, and Sartre," *The Kenyon Review,* XXV (1963), pp. 248-263.

1655. Scheler, Max, "Ressentiment," in Robert Solomon, ed., *Nietzsche: A Collection of Critical Essays* (New York: Anchor Press, 1973), pp. 243-257.

1656. Schilpp, Paul Arthur, ed. *The Philosophy of Karl Jaspers* (New York: Open Court, 1957).

1657. Schmidl, G., "Psychoanalysis and Existential Analysis," *Psychoanalysis Quarterly,* XXIX (1960), pp. 344-354.

1658. Schmidt, Fritz, "Psychoanalysis and Existential Analysis," *Psychoanalytical Quarterly,* XXIX (1960), pp. 344-354.

1659. Schmidt, Paul F., "The Real Basis of Existentialism," *The Hibbert Journal,* LXIII (1964), pp. 12-15.

1660. Schmitt, Richard, "Heidegger's Analysis of 'Tool'," *The Monist,* XLIX (1965), pp. 70-86.

1661. –, "Husserl's Transcendental-Phenomenological Reduction," in Joseph J. Kockelmans, ed., *Phenomenology: The Philosophy of Edmund Husserl and Its Interpretation* (New York: Anchor Press, 1967), pp. 58-67.

1662. –. *Martin Heidegger on Being Human: An Introduction to Sein und Zeit* (New York: Random House, 1969).

1663. –, "Phenomenology," in Paul Edwards, ed., *The Encyclopedia of Philosophy* (New York: Macmillan and Free Press, 1967), vol. VI, pp. 135-151.

1664. –, "Transcendental Phenomenology Muddle or Mystery?" *Journal of the British Society for Phenomenology,*

II (1971), pp. 19-27.

1665. Schoenborn, A. *Being, Man, and Questioning: An Ontological Prolegomena to Heidegger's Existentialism,* Ph. D. diss., Tulane University (1971).

1666. –, "Heideggerian Analysis," *Southwestern Journal of Philosophy,* III (1972), pp. 103-110.

1667. von Schoenborn, Alexander, "Heidegger's Question: An Exposition," in Edward G. Ballard and Charles E. Scott, eds., *Martin Heidegger in Europe and America* (The Hague: Martinus Nijhoff, 1973), pp. 47-54.

1668. Schöfer, Erasmus, "Heidegger's Language: Metalogical Forms of Thought and Grammatical Specialties," in Joseph J. Kockelmans, ed., *On Heidegger and Language* (Evanston: Northwestern University Press, 1972), pp. 281-302.

1669. Schottlaender, Rudolf, "Two Dionysians: Emerson and Nietzsche," tr. by J. Campbell, *South Atlantic Quarterly,* XXXIX (1940), pp. 330-343.

1670. Schrader, George A., "Existence, Truth and Subjectivity," *Journal of Philosophy,* LIII (1956), pp. 759-771.

1671. –, "Existential Psychoanalysis and Metaphysics," *Review of Metaphysics,* XIII (1959), pp. 139-164.

1672. –, ed. *Existential Philosophers: Kierkegaard to Merleau-Ponty* (New York: McGraw-Hill, 1967).

1673. –, "Heidegger's Ontology of Human Existence," *Review of Metaphysics,* X (1956-1957), pp. 35-36.

1674. –, "Norman Mailer and the Despair of Defiance," *Yale Review,* LI (1961), pp. 267-280.

1675. Schrag, Calvin O. *Existence and Freedom: Towards an Ontology of Human Finitude* (Evanston: Northwestern University Press, 1970).

A well-written, important, original work which expands on Heidegger's everyday Existentielles.

1676. –, "Existence and History," *Review of Metaphysics,* XIII (1959), pp. 28-45.

1677. –. *Experience and Being: Prolegomena to a Future Ontology* (Evanston: Northwestern University Press, 1969).

1678. –, "Heidegger and Cassirer on Kant," *Kantstudien,* LVIII (1967), pp. 87-100.

1679. –, "Heidegger on Repetition and Historical Understanding," *Philosophy East and West,* XX, 3 (1970), pp. 287-296.

1680. –, "Kierkegaard's Existential Reflections on Time," *The Personalist,* XLII (1961), pp. 149-164.

1681. –, "The Main Types of Existentialism," *Religion in Life,* XXIII (1953), pp. 103-114.

1682. –, "Note on Kierkegaard's Teleological Suspension of the Ethical," *Ethics,* LXX (1959).

1683. –, "Phenomenology, Ontology, and History in the Philosophy of Heidegger," *Revue Internationale de Philosophie,* XII (1958), pp. 117-132.

1684. –, "The Structure of Moral Experience: A Phenomenological and Existential Analysis," *Ethics,* LXXIII (July, 1963), pp. 255-265.

1685. –, "Whitehead and Heidegger: Process Philosophy and Existential Philosophy," *Dialectica,* XIII (1959), pp. 42-56.

1686. Schrag, Oswald O. *Existence, Existenz, and Transcendence: An Introduction to the Philosophy of Karl Jaspers* (Pittsburgh: Duquesne University Press, 1971).

1687. –, "Existential Ethics and Axiology," *Southern Journal of Philosophy,* I (1963), pp. 39-47.

1688. Schuetz, Alfred, "Sartre's Theory of the Alter Ego," *Philosophy and Phenomenological Research,* IX (1948), pp. 181-199.

1689. Schulweis, Harold, "Crisis Theology and Martin Buber," *Review of Religion,* XIV, 1 (1949), pp. 38-42.

1690. –, "Martin Buber: An Interview," *The Reconstructionist,* XVII, 3 (March 21, 1952), pp. 7-10.

1691. Schutz, A., "Mozart and the Philosophers," *Social Research,* XXIII (1956), pp. 219-242.

1692. Schutz, Alfred. *On Phenomenology and Social Relations: Selected Writings,* ed. by Helmut B. Wagner (Chicago: University of Chicago Press, 1970).

1693. –, "Type and Eidos in Husserl's Later Philosophy," *Philosophy and Phenomenological Research,* XX (1959-1960), pp. 147-165.

1694. Schuwer, André, "Prolegomena to 'Time and Being': Truth and Time," in John Sallis, ed., *Heidegger and the Path of Thinking* (Pittsburgh: Duquesne University Press, 1970), pp. 169-190.

An important and illuminating study in the differences between the pre- and post-Kehre Heidegger.

1695. Scott, Charles E., "Daseinanalysis: An Interpretation," *Philosophy Today,* XIX (1974), pp. 182-197.

1696. –, "Heidegger and Consciousness," in Edward G. Ballard and Charles E. Scott, eds., *Martin Heidegger in Europe and America* (The Hague: Martinus Nijhoff, 1973), pp. 91-108.

1697. –, "Heidegger's Attempt to Communicate a Mystery," *Philosophy Today,* X (1966), pp. 132-141.

1698. –, "Heidegger, the Absence of God, and Faith," *Journal of Religion,* XLVI (1966), pp. 365-373.

1699. –. *Martin Heidegger's Concept of Man's Presence to Himself: Toward a Reconsideration of Religious Awareness,* Ph.D. diss., Yale University (1965).

1700. Scott, Nathan, "The Broken Center: A Definition of the Crisis of Values in Modern Literature," *Chicago Review,* XIII (Summer, 1959), pp. 182-202. Reprinted in Rollo May, ed., *Symbolism in Religion and Literature* (New York: 1961), pp. 178-200, and in William Spanos, ed., *A Casebook on Existentialism,* vol. 1 (New York: 1966), pp. 162-183.

1701. –. *Modern Literature and the Religious Frontier* (New York: Harper, 1958).

1702. –. *The Unquiet Vision: Mirrors of Man in Existentialism* (New York: World Publishing Co., 1969).

1703. Scudder, John, Jr., "Why Buber Would Not Endorse a Pseudo-Existentialist," *Educational Theory,* XXV (1975), pp. 197-201.

1704. Searles, H. L., "Kierkegaard's Philosophy as a Source of Existentialism," *The Personalist,* XXIX (1948), pp. 173-187.

1705. Sechi, Venina, "Art, Language, Creativity, and Kierkegaard," *Humanitas,* V (1969-1970), pp. 81-97.

1706. Sefler, G. F. *The Structure of Language and Its Relation to the World: A Methodological Study of the Writings of Martin Heidegger and Ludwig Wittgenstein,* Ph.D. diss., Georgetown University (1970).

1707. Seibert, Charles. *On Being and Space in Heidegger's Thinking,* Ph.D. diss., De Paul University (1972).

1708. Siedel, G. J., "Heidegger: Philosopher for Ecologists?" *Man and World,* IV (1971), pp. 93-99.

1709. –. *Martin Heidegger and the Pre-Socratics: An Introduction to His Thought* (University of Nebraska Press, 1964).

1710. Sellars, Roy W., "Existentialism, Realistic Empiricism, and Materialism," *Philosophy and Phenomenological Research,* XXV (March, 1965), pp. 315-322.

1711. Seyppel, J. H., "A Comparative Study of Truth in Existentialism and Pragmatism," *The Journal of Philosophy,* L (1953), pp. 229-241.

1712. –, "A Criticism of Heidegger's Time Concept with Reference to Bergson's Durée," *Revue Internationale de Philosophie,* X (1956), pp. 503-508.

1713. Shapiro, Gary, "Choice and Universality in Sartre's Ethics," *Man and World,* VII (1974), pp. 20-36.

1714. Shaw, George Bernard, "Nietzsche in English," in Robert Solomon, ed., *Nietzsche: A Collection of Critical Essays* (New York: Anchor Press, 1973), pp. 371-374.

1715. Sheehan, Thomas J., "Heidegger, Aristotle and Phenomenology," *Philosophy Today,* XIX (1975), pp. 87-94.

1716. –, "Notes on a 'Lover's Quarrel:' Heidegger and Aquinas," *Listening,* IX (1974), pp. 137-143.

1717. Shefner, Helena. *Spiritual Crisis in French Prose Literature, 1940-1944,* dissertation (Columbia University, 1962).

1718. Shepard, L. A., "Verbal Victory and Existential Anguish," *Philosophical Journal,* VI (1969), pp. 95-111.

1719. Shepherd, Leslie A. *The Implosion of Personality in the Modern European Novel,* dissertation (New York University, 1969).

1720. Sheridan, James M. *Sartre: The Radical Conversion* (Athens, Ohio: Ohio University Press, 1969).

1721. Sherover, Charles M. *Heidegger, Kant and Time* (Bloomington: Indiana University Press, 1971).

1722. –, "Heidegger's Ontology and the Copernican Revolution," *The Monist*, LI (1967), pp. 559-573.

1723. –. *The Kantian Source of Heidegger's Conception of Time*, Ph.D. diss., New York University (1966).

1724. –, "Kant's Transcendental Object and Heidegger's Nichts," *Journal of the History of Philosophy*, VII (1969), pp. 413-422.

1725. Sherover, Erica, "Nietzsche: On Yea- and Nay-Saying," *Journal of Existentialism*, XX (1965), pp. 423-427.

1726. Sherry, C. E. *The Poetics of Disclosure: Heidegger and Rilke*, Ph.D. diss., Rutgers University (1972).

1727. Shestov, Lev. *Dostoyevsky, Tolstoy and Nietzsche* (Athens, Ohio: Ohio University Press, 1969).

1728. –. *Kierkegaard and the Existential Philosophy*, tr. by Elinor Hewitt (Athens, Ohio: Ohio University Press, 1969).

1729. Shinn, Roger Lincoln, ed. *Restless Adventure: Essays on Contemporary Expressions of Existentialism* (New York: Charles Scribner's Sons, 1968).

1730. Shmuëli, Adi. *Kierkegaard and Consciousness*, tr. by Naomi Handleman (Princeton: Princeton University Press, 1971).

1731. Shoery, I., "Phenomenological Analysis of Waiting," *Southwestern Journal of Philosophy*, III (1972), pp. 93-101.

1732. –. *The Psychological Origins of Jean-Paul Sartre's Concept of Freedom*, Ph.D. diss., University of Oklahoma (1968).

1733. –, "Reduction in Sartre's Ontology," *Southwestern*

Journal of Philosophy, II (Spring-Summer, 1971), pp. 47-53.

1734. Siegfried, H., "Martin Heidegger: A Recollection," *Man and World*, III (1970), pp. 3-4.

1735. Sikes, Walter. *On Becoming the Truth: An Introduction to the Life and Thought of Soren Kierkegaard* (St. Louis: Bethany Press, 1967).

1736. Simon, John K., "Faulkner and Sartre: Metamorphosis and the Obscene," *Comparative Literature*, XV (1963), pp. 216-225.

1737. —. *The Glance of the Idiot: A Thematic Study of Faulkner and Modern French Fiction*, dissertation (Yale University, 1963).

1738. Simpson, L. V., "Tensions in the World of Albert Camus," *Modern Language Journal*, XXXVIII, pp. 186-190.

1739. Slaatte, Howard Alexander. *The Paradox of Existentialist Theology: The Dialectics of a Faith-Subsumed Reason-in-Existence* (New York: Humanities Press, 1971).

1740. Slochower, Harry, "The Function of Myth in Existentialism," *Yale French Studies*, I, 1 (1948), pp. 42-52.

1741. Slote, Michael A., "Existentialism and the Fear of Dying," *American Philosophical Quarterly*, XII (1975), pp. 17-28.

1742. Smart, R. N., "Being and the Bible," *Review of Metaphysics*, IX (1956), pp. 589-608.

1743. Smit, Harvey Albert. *Kierkegaard's Pilgrimage of Man: The Road of Self-Positing and Self-Abdication* (Delft: W. D. Meinema, 1965).

1744. Smith, Colin. *Contemporary French Philosophy: A Study in Norms and Values* (London: Methuen, 1964).

1745. –, "Sartre and Merleau-Ponty: The Case for a Modified Essentialism," *Journal of the British Society for Phenomenology,* I (1970), pp. 73-79.

1746. Smith, Constance I., "The Single One and the Other," *Hibbert Journal,* XLVI (1948), pp. 315-321.

1747. Smith, David W. and Ronald McIntyre, "Intentionality via Intensions," *Journal of Philosophy,* LXVIII (1971), pp. 541-560.

1748. Smith, F. J., "Heidegger's Kant Interpretation," *Philosophy Today,* XI (1967), pp. 257-264.

1749. –, "The Meaning of the 'Way' in Heidegger," *Church Quarterly,* III (1962), pp. 89-102.

1750. –, ed. *Phenomenology in Perspective* (The Hague: Martinus Nijhoff, 1970).

1751. --, "Two Heideggerian Analysis," in Edward G. Ballard and Charles E. Scott, eds., *Martin Heidegger in Europe and America* (The Hague: Martinus Nijhoff, 1973), pp. 171-182.

1752. Smith, Joyce Carol Oates, "The Existential Comedy of Conrad's Youth," *Renascence,* XVI (1963), pp. 22-28.

1753. –, "Ritual and Violence in Flannery O'Connor," *Thought* XLI (1966), pp. 545-560.

1754. Smith, J. E., "Revolt of Existence," *Yale Review,* XLIII (1954), pp. 364-371.

1755. Smith, P., "Heidegger's Critique of Absolute Knowledge," *New Scholasticism,* XLV (1971), pp. 56-86.

1756. Smith, Ronald Gregor, "Karl Jaspers on Theology and Philosophy," *Hibbert Journal,* XLIX (1950-1951), pp. 62-66.

1757. –, "Kierkegaard's Library," *Hibbert Journal,* L (1951), pp. 18-21.

1758. – and J. G. Hamanen. *A Study in Christian Existentialism* (New York: Harper & Bros., 1960).

1759. Smith, Vincent Edward, "Existentialism and Existence," *The Thomist,* XI (1948), pp. 141-196 and 297-329.

1760. –, "Philosopher of the Absurd," *The Shield,* XXVI (1946), pp. 27 ff.

1761. Snider, Nancy V. *An Annotated Bibliography of English Works on Nietzsche,* Ph.D. diss., University of Michigan (1962).

1762. Snyder, R., "The Role of Meanings in Personal Existence," *Journal of Existential Psychiatry,* I (1960), pp. 127-144.

1763. Soderquist, Harold Oliver. *The Person and Education: A New Approach to Philosophy of Education for a Democracy* (Columbus: C. E. Merrill Books, 1964).

1764. Sokel, W. H., "Kliest's Marquise of O, Kierkegaard's Abraham, and Musil's Tonko: Three Stages of the Absurd, or the Touchstone of Faith," *Wisconsin Studies in Contemporary Literature,* VIII (1967), pp. 505-516.

1765. Sokolowski, Robert. *The Formation of Husserl's Concept of Constitution* (The Hague: Martinus Nijhoff, 1964).

1766. Soll, Ivan, "Reflections on Recurrence: A Re-Examination of Nietzsche's Doctrine, *die Eqige Wiederkehr des Gleichen,*" in Robert Solomon, ed., *Nietzsche: A Collection of Critical Essays* (New York: Anchor Press, 1973), pp. 322-342.

1767. Solomon, Robert C. *From Rationalism to Existentialism: The Existentialists and Their 19th Century Backgrounds* (New York: Harper and Row, 1972).

1768. –, ed. *Nietzsche: A Collection of Critical Essays* (New York: Anchor Books, 1973).

1769. –, "Nietzsche, Nihilism, and Morality," see above item 1768, pp. 202-225.

1770. –, ed. *Phenomenology and Existentialism* (New York: Harper and Row, 1972).

A good collection of primary sources.

1771. Sonnemann, Ulrich. *Existence and Therapy: An Introduction to Phenomenological Psychology and Existential Analysis* (New York: Grune and Stratton, 1954).

Pp. 102-131 deal with Heidegger.

1772. Sontag, Frederick. *The Existentialist Prolegomena to a Future Metaphysics* (Chicago: University of Chicago Press, 1969).

1773. –, "Heidegger and the Problem of Metaphysics," *Philosophy and Phenomenological Research*, XXIV (1963-1964), pp. 410-416.

1774. –, "Heidegger, Time and God," *Journal of Religion*, XLVII (1967), pp. 279-294.

1775. –, "Kierkegaard and the Search for a Self," *Journal of Existentialism*," VII (1967), pp. 443-457.

1776. Soper, William W. *The Self and Its World in Ralph Barton Perry, Edgar Scheffield Brightman, Jean-Paul Sartre, and Soren Kierkegaard*, Ph.D. diss., Boston University (1962).

1777. Spanos, William V., "Breaking the Circle: Hermeneutics as Dis-Closure," *boundary 2*, V, 2 (1977), pp. 421-457.

1778. –. *A Casebook on Existentialism*, vol. 1 (New York: Thomas Crowell Co., 1966), vol. 2 (New York:

Thomas Crowell Co., 1976).

The two volumes of Spanos' *Casebook* form one large anthology designed for classroom use. All the major existential philosophers are represented with carefully selected essays, and there are several hard-to-find essays by critics applying Existentialism to works of literature. Included are works by Kafka, Sartre, Dürrenmatt, Ionesco, Unamuno, Dostoyevsky, and many others. Spanos has also provided an annotated bibliography, questions for discussions, and a section entitled "Topics for Writing Projects." The *Casebook* is fronted by a long essay by Spanos, "Abraham, Sisyphus, and the Furies: Some Introductory Notes on Existentialism."

1779. —, "The Detective and the Boundary: Some Notes on the Postmodern Imagination," *boundary 2,* I, 1 (1972), pp. 147-168.

1780. —, "Heidegger, Kierkegaard, and the Hermeneutic Circle: Towards a Postmodern Theory of Interpretation as Dis-closure," *boundary 2,* IV, 2 (1976), pp. 455-488.

1781. —, "Heidegger's Phenomenology of Time: Hermeneutics as Discovery," Paper No. 2, *University Seminar in Postmodernism* (University Seminars Council, State University of New York at Binghamton, n.d.)

1782. —. *Icon and Time* (forthcoming).

1783. —, "Modern Drama and the Aristotelian Tradition: The Formal Imperatives of Absurd Time," *Contemporary Literature,* XII, 3 (1971), pp. 345-372.

1784. —, "The Spatialization of Time in Modern Literary Criticism," *Journal of Aesthetics and Art Criticism,* XXIX (1970), pp. 87-104.

1785. Spencer, M., "Spinoza and Nietzsche: A Comparison," *The Monist,* XLI (1931), pp. 67-90.

1786. Spiegelberg, Herbert, "French Existentialism: Its Social

Philosophers," *Kenyon Review,* XVI (1954), pp. 448-454.

1787. –, "Husserl in England: Facts and Lessons," *Journal of the British Society for Phenomenology,* I (1970), pp. 4-15.

1788. –, "Husserl's Phenomenology and Existentialism," *Journal of Philosophy,* LVII (1960), pp. 62-74.

1789. –, "Husserl's Syllabus of the London Lectures: Notes," *Journal of the British Society for Phenomenology,* I (1970), pp. 16-17.

1790. –, "On the Misfortunes of Edmund Husserl's *Encyclopaedia Britannica* Article: 'Phenomenology'," *Journal of the British Society for Phenomenology,* II (1971), pp. 74-76.

1791. –. *The Phenomenological Movement: A Historical Introduction, Phaenomenologica Series,* vols. V and VI (The Hague: Martinus Nijhoff, 1959, 1960).

Vol. V deals with the Germans, Vol. VI with the French. Vol. V, pp. 271-357 are on Heidegger's phenomenology.

1792. –. *Phenomenology in Psychology and Psychiatry: A Historical Introduction* (Evanston: Northwestern University Press, 1972).

1793. Spier, J. M. *Christianity and Existentialism,* tr. by David Freeman (Philadelphia: Presbyterian and Reformed Pub., 1953).

1794. Spinka, Matthew. *Christian Thought from Erasmus to Berdyaev* (Englewood Cliffs: Prentice-Hall, 1962).

See especially the chapter "Soren Kierkegaard and the Existential Theology," pp. 146-155.

1795. –. *Nicholas Berdyaev: Captive of Freedom* (Philadelphia: Westminster Press, 1950).

1796. Spurling, Laurie, "Marx and the Existentialists," *Journal of the British Society of Phenomenologists,* VII (1976), pp. 135-137.

1797. Stace, Walter. *Destiny of Western Man* (New York: 1942).

Pp. 286-311 on Nietzsche.

1798. –, "Metaphysics and Existence," *Philosophy and Phenomenological Research,* IX (1949), pp. 458-462.

1799. Stack, George J., "Aristotle and Kierkegaard's Concept of Choice," *The Modern Schoolman,* XLVI (1968-1969), pp. 11-23.

1800. –, "The Being of the Work of Art in Heidegger," *Philosophy Today,* XIII (1969), pp. 159-173.

1801. –, "Concern in Kierkegaard and Heidegger," *Philosophy Today,* XII (1969), pp. 26-35.

1802. –, "Existence and Possibility," *Laval Théologique et Philosophique,* XXVIII (1972), pp. 149-170.

1803. –. *Kierkegaard's Existential Ethics* (Alabama University Press, 1976).

1804. –, "Kierkegaard and the Phenomenology of Repetition," *Journal of Existentialism,* VII (1966-1967), pp. 111-128.

1805. Stallknecht, Newton P., "Being in Becoming: A Theory of Human Freedom," *Review of Metaphysics,* VIII (1955), pp. 633-641.

1806. –, "Beyond the Concrete: Wahl's Dialectical Existentialism," *Review of Metaphysics,* VIII (1954), pp. 144-155.

1807. –, "Decision and Existence," *Review of Metaphysics,* VI (1952), pp. 31-44.

1808. –, et al, "Freedom and Existence: A Symposium," *Re-*

view of Metaphysics, IX (1955), pp. 27-57.

1809. –, "Gabriel Marcel and the Human Situation," *Review of Metaphysics,* VII (1954), pp. 661-668.

1810. –, "Mysticism and Existentialism," in A. P. Stiernotte, ed., *Mysticism and the Modern Mind* (New York: Liberal Arts Press, 1959).

1811. –, "The Quality of Man," *Review of Metaphysics,* IX (1956), pp. 531-547.

1812. Stambaugh, Joan, "Commentary on T. Umehara's Heidegger and Buddhism," *Philosophy East and West,* XX (1970), pp. 283-286.

1813. Stamps, A., "Shifting Focus from Sartre to Husserl," *Thought,* VIII (1973), pp. 51-53.

1814. Stark, W., "Kierkegaard on Capitalism," *Social Review,* XLII (1950), pp. 87-114.

1815. Starr, D. E. *Ousia and Dasein: An Ontological Investigation of Aristotle and Heidegger,* Ph.D. diss., Boston University (1972).

1816. Starrides, M. *The Concept of Existence in Kierkegaard and Heidegger* (New York: Columbia University Press, 1952).

1817. Stavrou, C. N. *Whitman and Nietzsche* (Chapel Hill: University of North Carolina Press, 1964).

1818. Steinberg, Milton, "Kierkegaard and Judaism," *Menorah Journal,* XXXVII (1949), pp. 163-180.

1819. Steiner, Rudolph. *Friedrich Nietzsche, Fighter for Freedom* (New York: Herman, 1960).

1820. Stern, A., "Existential Analysis and Individual Psychology," *Journal of Individual Psychology,* XIV (1958), pp. 38-50.

1821. Stern, Alfred, "Sartre and French Existentialism," *The Personalist,* XXIX (1948), pp. 17-31.

1822. –. *Sartre: His Philosophy and Psychoanalysis* (New York: Liberal Arts Press, 1953).

1823. –, "Some Philosophical Considerations of Literature," *The Personalist,* XLIX, 2(1968), pp. 163-181.

1824. Stern, Guenther Anders, "Emotion and Reality," *Philosophy and Phenomenological Research,* X (1950), pp. 353-362.

1825. –, "On the Pseudo-Concreteness of Heidegger's Philosophy," *Philosophy and Phenomenological Research,* VIII (1947-1948), pp. 337-370.

1826. Stern, K. *The Third Revolution* (New York: Harcourt, Brace, 1954).

1827. Stevens, Wallace. *The Necessary Angel: Essays on Reality and the Imagination* (New York: Vintage Books, 1951).

1828. Stewart, David and Algis Mickunas. *Exploring Phenomenology: A Guide to the Field and Its Literature* (Chicago: American Library Association, 1974).

1829. Stockwell, H. C. R., "Proust and Sartre," *Cambridge Journal,* VII (1954), pp. 476-487.

1830. –, "Sartre–His Existentialist Philosophy," *Cambridge Journal* (September, 1953), pp. 753-760.

1831. Strasser, St., "The Concept of Dread in the Philosophy of Heidegger," *The Modern Schoolman,* XXV (1957-1958), pp. 1-20.

1832. Strasser, Stephen. *The Idea of Dialogical Phenomenology* (Pittsburgh: Duquesne University Press, 1969).

1833. –. *Phenomenology and the Human Sciences: A Contribution for a New Scientific Ideal* (Pittsburgh: Duquesne University Press, 1963).

1834. Stratton, J. D. *The Hegelian Motif in Heidegger's Thought on Language*, Ph.D. diss., Southern Illinois University (1972).

1835. Straus, Erwin, "Norm and Pathology of I-World Relations," *Journal of Nervous and Mental Diseases*, Monograph Suplement (1961).

1836. –, "On the Form and Structure of Man's Inner Freedom," *Kentucky Law Journal*, XLV (1956), pp. 255-269.

1837. –. *Phenomenological Psychology: The Selected Papers of Erwin W. Straus*, tr. by Erling Eng (New York: Basic Books, 1966).

1838. – and Richard Griffiths, ed. *Aisthesis and Aesthetics: Fourth Lexington Conference on Pure and Applied Phenomenology* (Pittsburgh: Duquesne University Press, 1970).

1839. –, eds. *Phenomenology of Memory: The Third Lexington Conference on Pure and Applied Phenomenology* (Pittsburgh: Duquesne University Press, 1970).

1840. –, eds. *Phenomenology of Will and Action: Second Lexington Conference on Pure and Applied Phenomenology* (Pittsburgh: Duquesne University Press, 1967).

1841. –, eds. *Phenomenology: Pure and Applied: The First Lexington Conference on Pure and Applied Phenomenology* (Pittsburgh: Duquesne University Press, 1964).

1842. –, Maurice Natanson and Henri Ey. *Psychiatry and Philosophy*, tr. by Erling Eng and Stephen C. Kennedy (New York: Springer, 1969).

1843. Streller, Justus. *To Freedom Condemned: A Guide to the Philosophy of Jean-Paul Sartre*, tr. and with an introduction by Wade Baskin (New York: Philosophical Library, 1960).

1844. Strickland, Ben, "Kierkegaard and Counseling for Individuality," *Personnel and Guidance Journal,* XLIV (1966), pp. 470-474.

1845. Strong, Tracy, "Nietzsche and Politics: Parables of the Shepherd and the Herd," in Robert Solomon, ed., *Nietzsche: A Collection of Critical Essays* (New York: Anchor Press, 1973), pp. 258-292.

1846. Sutherland, Donald, "Time on Our Hands," *Yale French Studies,* X (1952-1953), pp. 5-13.

1847. Swenson, D. *Something About Kierkegaard* (Minneapolis: Augsburg, 1941).

1848. Sypher, Wylie, "Hamlet: The Existential Madness," *Nation,* CLXII (1946), pp. 750-751.

1849. –. *Loss of Self in Modern Literature and Art* (New York: Random House, 1962).

1850. Tagliacozzo, Giorgio and Hayden V. White, eds. *Giambattista Vico: An International Symposium* (Baltimore: The Johns Hopkins Press, 1969).

See item 496 of this Bibliography.

1851. Takeuchi, Y., "Buddhism and Existentialism: A Dialogue Between Oriental and Occidental Thought," in W. Leibrecht, ed., *Religion and Culture* (New York: Harper and Bros., 1959).

1852. Taubes, S. A., "The Gnostic Foundations of Heidegger's Nihilism," *The Journal of Religion,* XXXIV (1954), pp. 155-172.

1853. Tavard, George H., "Christianity and the Philosophy of Existence," *Theological Studies,* XVIII (1957), pp. 1-16.

1854. Taylor, Robert E., "The *Sex*pressive S in Sade and Sartre,"

Yale French Studies, XI (1953), pp. 18-24.

1855. Teo, W. K.-H. *Heidegger on Dasein and Whitehead on Actual Entities,* Ph.D. diss., Southern Illinois University (1969).

1856. Thalheimer, A. *Existential Metaphysics* (New York: Philosophical Library, 1960).

1857. Thévenaz, Pierre. *What is Phenomenology? And Other Essays,* ed. by James M. Edie (Chicago: Quadrangle, 1962).

Excellent short exposition of Husserl, Heidegger, Sartre, and Merleau-Ponty.

1858. Thibault, Herve J. *Creation and Metaphysics: A Genetic Approach to Existential Act* (The Hague: Martinus Nijhoff, 1970).

1859. Thielicke, H., "Nihilism and Anxiety," *Theology Today,* XII (1955), pp. 342-345.

1860. Thody, Philip. *Albert Camus: A Study of His Work* (New York: Grove Press, 1957).

1861. –, "Existential Psychoanalysis," *Journal of the British Society for Phenomenology,* I (1970), pp. 83-92.

1862. –, "French Novelists and the American Novel," *Modern Languages,* XXXVII (1955), pp. 7-10.

1863. –. *Jean-Paul Sartre: A Literary and Political Study* (London: Hamish Hamilton, 1960; New York: Macmillan, 1964).

1864. –, "Jean-Paul Sartre: A Writer's Politics," *Twentieth Century,* CLXV (1959), pp. 13-22.

1865. –, "A Note on Camus and the American Novel," *Comparative Literature,* IX (1957), pp. 243-249.

1866. –. *Sartre: A Bibliographical Introduction* (New York:

Scribner's, 1971).

1867. Thomas, J. H., "The Christology of Soren Kierkegaard and Karl Barth," *Hibbert Journal,* LIII (1955), pp. 280-288.

1868. –, "Kierkegaard on the Existence of God," *Review of Religion,* XVIII (1953), pp. 18-31.

1869. –. *Subjectivity and Paradox* (Oxford: Blackwell's, 1957).

1870. Thomas, J. M. Lloyd, "The Modernness of Kierkegaard," *Hibbert Journal,* XLV (1947), pp. 309-320.

1871. –, "Pascal and Kierkegaard," *Hibbert Journal,* XLVII (1948), pp. 36-40.

1872. Thompson, Josiah. *Kierkegaard: A Biographical Essay* (New York: Alfred Knopf, 1973).

1873. –, ed. *Kierkegaard: A Collection of Critical Essays* (New York: Anchor Books, 1972).

This collection includes essays by Sartre, Mackey, Updike, George Schrader, and others. Several essays were never published outside of this collection; it is a continually exciting and thought-provoking group of essays.

1874. –. *The Lonely Labyrinth: Kierkegaard's Pseudonymous Works* (Cambridge: Southern Illinois University Press, 1967).

1875. –, "The Existential Philosophy," *Studia Varia,* XVII (1958), pp. 95-111.

1876. Thompson, K. F., Jr., "Nietzsche's Religious Atheism," *Union Seminary Quarterly Review,* XIV (1959), pp. 27-34.

1877. Thompson, J. M., "Existentialism and Humanism," *Hibbert Journal,* XLVII (1949), pp. 170-174.

1878. Thomte, Reidar, "Kierkegaard in American Religious Thought," *Lutheran World,* II (1955), pp. 137-146.

1879. –. *Kierkegaard's Philosophy of Religion* (New York: Greenwood Press, 1969).

1880. Thyssen, Johannes, "The Concept of 'Foundering' in Jaspers' Philosophy," in Paul Schilpp, ed., *The Philosophy of Karl Jaspers* (New York: Tudor Pub. Co., 1957), pp. 297-336.

1881. Tibbetts, Paul, "Some Recent Philosophical Contributions to the Problem of Consciousness," *Philosophy Today,* XIV (1970), pp. 3-22.

1882. Tiebout, H. M., Jr., "Existentialism in Transit," *Christian Century,* LXXVI (1959), pp. 669-670.

1883. –, "Freud and Existentialism," *Journal of Nervous and Mental Diseases,* CXXVI (1958), pp. 341-353.

1884. –, "Subjectivity in Whitehead: A Comment on 'Whitehead and Heidegger'," *Dialectica,* XIII (1959), pp. 350-353.

1885. –, "Tillich, Existentialism, and Psychoanalysis," *The Journal of Philosophy,* LVI (1959).

1886. van Til, C., "The Later Heidegger and Theology," *Westminster Theological Journal,* XXXVI (1964), pp. 121-161.

1887. Tillich, Paul, "Being and Love," in Ruth N. Anshen, ed., *Moral Principles of Action* (New York: Harper & Bros., 1952).

1888. –. *Biblical Religion and the Search for Ultimate Reality* (Chicago: University of Chicago Press, 1955).

1889. –. *The Courage to Be* (New Haven: Yale University Press, 1952).

1890. –. *The Dynamics of Faith* (New York: Harper and Bros.,

1958).

1891. –, "Existential Philosophy," *Journal of the History of Ideas,* V (1944), pp. 44-70.

1892. –, "Existential Thinking in American Theology," *Religion in Life,* X (1941), pp. 452-455.

1893. –. *The Interpretation of History* (New York: Charles Scribner's Sons, 1936).

1894. –, "Jewish Influences on Contemporary Christian Theology," *Cross Currents,* II, 3 (1952), pp. 38-42.

1895. –. *Love, Power and Justice* (New York: Oxford University Press, 1954).

1896. –, "Martin Buber and Christian Thought," *Commentary,* V, 6 (June, 1948), pp. 515-521.

1897. –, "The Meaning and Sources of Courage," *Child Study,* XXXI (1954), pp. 7-11.

1898. –, "The Nature and Significance of Existentialist Thought," *Journal of Philosophy,* LIII (1956), pp. 739-748.

1899. –. *The New Being* (New York: Charles Scribner's Sons, 1955).

1900. –, "Nietzsche and the Bourgeois Spirit," *Journal of the History of Ideas,* VI, 3 (1945), pp. 307-309.

1901. –. *The Protestant Era,* tr. by James Luther Adams (Chicago: University of Chicago Press, 1948).

1902. –, "Psychoanalysis, Existentialism and Theology," *Faith and Freedom,* IX (1955), pp. 1-11.

1903. –, "Relation of Metaphysics and Theology," *Review of Metaphysics,* X (1956), pp. 57-64.

1904. –. *The Religious Situation* (New York: Meridian Press,

1958).

1905. –. *Systematic Theology,* 3 vols. (Chicago: University of Chicago Press, 1953-1964).

1906. –, "Heidegger and the 'Irrational'," *Proceedings of the Aristotelian Society,* LVI (1956-1957), pp. 253-268.

1907. Tiryakian, Edward A. *Sociologism and Existentialism: Two Perspectives on the Individual and Society* (Englewood Cliffs: Prentice-Hall, 1962).

1908. Topitsch, Ernst, "The Sociology of Existentialism," *Partisan Review,* XXI, 3 (May-June, 1954), pp. 289-304.

1909. Toussaint, B. J. *The Interpretation of the 'Self' in the Early Heidegger,* Ph.D. diss., De Paul University (1971).

1910. Trevor-Roper, Hugh, "The Denazification of Nietzsche," *New Statesman,* LXIX (1965), pp. 443-444.

1911. Trivers, Howard, "Heidegger's Misinterpretation of Hegel's Views on Spirit and Time," *Philosophy and Phenomenological Research,* III (1942-1943).

1912. Troisfontaines, Roger. *Existentialism and Christian Thought,* tr. by M. Jarrett-Kerr (London: A. & C. Black, 1950).

1913. –, "What is Existentialism?" *Thought,* XXXII (1957), pp. 516-532.

1914. Tulloch, Doreen M., "Sartrean Existentialism," *Philosophical Quarterly,* II, 6 (January, 1952), pp. 31-52.

1915. Turienzo, S. A., "Absence of God and Man's Insecurity," *Philosophy Today,* III (1959), pp. 135-139.

1916. Turnball, R. G., "Heidegger on the Nature of Truth," *Journal of Philosophy,* LIV (1957), pp. 559-565.

1917. Tursman, Richard A. *Nietzsche's View of Science and*

Art, Ph.D. diss., University of Illinois (1964).

1918. Tuska, John, "Thomas Mann and Nietzsche: A Study in Ideas," *Germanic Review,* XXXIX (1964), pp. 281-299.

1919. Tweedie, D. F. *Logotherapy and the Christian Faith: An Evaluation of Frankl's Existential Approach to Psychotherapy* (Grand Rapids, Michigan: Baker Book House, 1961).

1920. –. *The Significance of Dread in the Thought of Kierkegaard and Heidegger* (Boston: 1954).

1921. Tymieniecka, Anna-Teresa, "Cosmos, Nature and Man and the Foundations of Psychiatry," in John Sallis, ed., *Heidegger and the Path of Thinking* (Pittsburgh: Duquesne University Press, 1970), pp. 191-220.

On the Hiedeggerian existential analytic and its meaning for psychiatry.

1922. –, ed. *For Roman Ingarden: Nine Essays in Phenomenology* (The Hague: Martinus Nijhoff, 1959).

1923. –. *Phenomenology and Science in Contemporary European Thought* (New York: Farrar, Straus, & Cudahy, 1962).

1924. Uffelmann, H. W. *Towards and Ontology of Social Relations,* Ph.D. diss., Northwestern University (1967).

1925. Umehara, Takeshi, "Heidegger and Buddhism," *Philosophy East and West,* XX (1970), pp. 271-282.

See the reply to this by J. Stambaugh.

1926. Unger, E., "Existentialism (Sartre and Heidegger)," *19th Century,* I (1948), pp. 28-37.

1927. Ungersma, A. J. *The Search for Meaning* (Philadelphia: Westminster Press, 1961).

1928. Updike, John, "The Fork," *The New Yorker* (February 26, 1966), pp. 115-134.

On Kierkegaard.

1929. Ussher, Arland, "The Existentialism of J.-P. Sartre," *The Dublin Magazine*, XXI, 2 (1946), pp. 32-35.

1930. –. *Journey through Dread: A Study of Kierkegaard, Heidegger, and Sartre* (New York: Biblo and Tannen, 1955).

1931. Vahanian, Gabriel. *The Death of Our Post-Christian Era* (New York: Braziller, 1961).

See especially the chapter "Existentialism and the Death of God," pp. 203-227.

1932. Vaihinger, Hans, "Nietzsche and His Doctrine of Conscious Illusion," in Robert Solomon, ed., *Nietzsche: A Collection of Critical Essays* (New York: Anchor Press, 1973), pp. 83-104.

1933. –. *The Philosophy of 'As-If'*, tr. by C. K. Ogden (New York: Harcourt Brace, 1924).

1934. Vail, L. M. *Heidegger and Ontological Difference* (University Park: Pennsylvania State University Press, 1972).

1935. –, "Heidegger's Conception of Philosophy," *The New Scholasticism*, XLII (1968), pp. 470-496.

1936. Vandenberg, Donald. *Being and Education: Essays in Existential Phenomenology* (Englewood Cliffs, New Jersey: Prentice-Hall, 1971).

1937. Van Den Berg, J. H. *The Phenomenological Approach to Psychiatry: An Introduction to Recent Phenomenological Psychopathology* (Springfield: Thomas, 1955).

1938. Van de Pitte, M. M., "On Bracketing the Epoch," *Dialogue*, XI (1972), pp. 535-545.

1939. –, "Sartre as Transcendental Realist," *Journal of the British Society for Phenomenology,* I (1970), pp. 22-26.

1940. Van de Leeuw, Gerardus. *Religion in Essence and Manifestation: A Study in Phenomenology,* tr. by J. E. Turner (London: Allen & Unwin, 1938).

1941. Van Dusen, Wilson, "Adler and Existence Analysis," *Journal of Individual Psychology,* XV (1959), pp. 100-111.

1942. –, "Existential Analytic Psychotherapy," *American Journal of Psychoanalysis,* XX (1960), pp. 35-40.

1943. –, "The Theory and Practice of Existential Analysis," *American Journal of Psychotherapy,* II (1957), pp. 310-322.

1944. Van Kaam, Adrian. *Existential Foundations of Psychology* (Pittsburgh: Duquesne University Press, 1966).

1945. –, "The Impact of Existential Phenomenology on the Psychological Literature of Western Europe," *Review of Existential Psychology and Psychiatry,* I (1961), pp. 63-92.

1946. –, "Person and Personality in the Light of Existential Psychology," *Existential Inquiry,* I (1959), pp. 7-8.

1947. –. *The Third Force in European Psychology* (Greenville, Delaware: Psychosynthesis Research Foundation, 1960).

1948. Vatai, L. *Man and His Tragic Life* (New York: Philosophical Library, 1954).

1949. Versényi, L. *Heidegger, Being and Truth* (New Haven: Yale University Press, 1965).

1950. Vial, Fernand, "Existentialism and Humanism," *Thought,* XXIII (1948), pp. 17-20.

1951. –, "New Tendencies in the French Novel of Today," *American Society Legion of Honor Magazine*, XXIX (1958), pp. 89-101.

1952. Vick, G. R., "Heidegger's Linguistic Rehabilitation of Parmenides' 'Being'," *Philosophical Quarterly*, VIII (1971), pp. 139-150.

1953. Vietta, E., "Being, World, and Understanding: A Commentary on Heidegger," *Review of Metaphysics*, V (1952), pp. 157-172.

1954. Voelkel, Thomas S. *Heidegger and the Problem of Circularity*, Ph.D. diss., Yale University (1971).

1955. Volkmann-Schluck, K.-H., "The Problem of Language," in Edward G. Ballard and Charles E. Scott, eds., *Martin Heidegger in Europe and America* (The Hague: Martinus Nijhoff, 1973), pp. 121-128.

1956. Votow, A., "Literature of Extreme Situations," *Horizon*, XX (1949), pp. 150-153.

1957. Vycinas, Vincent. *Earth and Gods: An Introduction to the Philosophy of Martin Heidegger* (The Hague: Martinus Nijhoff, 1961).

1958. de Waelhens, A., "Reflexions on Heidegger's Development: A propos of a Recent Book," *International Philosophical Quarterly*, V (1965), pp. 475-502.

1959. Wagner, Roland C., "The Idea of Nothingness in Wallace Stevens," *Accent*, XII (1952), pp. 111-121.

1960. Wahl, Jean, "Existentialism: A Preface," *The New Republic* (October 1, 1945), pp. 442-444.

1961. –, "Freedom and Existence in Some Recent Philosophies," *Philosophy and Phenomenological Research*, VIII (1947-1948), pp. 538-556.

1962. –, "Notes on Some Relations of Jaspers to Kierkegaard and Heidegger," in Paul Schilpp, ed., *The Philosophy of Karl Jaspers* (New York: Tudor Pub. Co., 1957), pp. 393-406.

1963. –. *Philosophies of Existence: An Introduction to the Basic Thought of Kierkegaard, Heidegger, Jaspers, Marcel, Sartre*, tr. by F. M. Lory (New York: Schocken Books, 1968).

1964. –, "Realism, Dialectic, and the Transcendant," *Philosophy and Phenomenological Research*, IV (1944), pp. 496-507.

1965. –. *A Short History of Existentialism*, tr. by Forrest Williams and Stanley Maron (New York: Philosophical Library, 1949).

Two short lectures, very informal.

1966. Waidson, H., "Durrenmatt: The Comedy of Despair," *The Nation*, CXC (1960), pp. 34-35.

1967. Walker, I. H., "Camus at the Crossroads," *Twentieth Century*, CLXVI (1959), pp. 73-77.

1968. Walker, Leslie, "Gilbert Ryle and Jean-Paul Sartre," *Month*, CLXXXIX (1950), pp. 432-443.

1969. Walsh, J. H. *A Fundamental Ontology of Play and Leisure*, Ph.D. diss., Georgetown University (1968).

1970. –, "Heidegger's Understanding of No-Thingness," *Cross Currents*, XII (1963), pp. 305-323.

1971. Walton, W. M., "Is Existence a Valid Philosophical Concept?" *Philosophy and Phenomenological Research*, XII (1952), pp. 557-561.

1972. Wang, Joan Parsons. *Joseph Conrad, Proto-existentialist: A Comparative Study of Conrad, Camus, and Sartre*, dissertation (Indiana University, 1965).

1973. Warbeke, J. M., "Friedrich Nietzsche: Antichrist, Superman, and Pragmatist," *Harvard Theological Review*,

II (1909), pp. 366-385.

1974. Warnock, Mary, "The Concrete Imagination," *Journal of the British Society for Phenomenology,* I (1970), pp. 6-12.

1975. —. *Ethics Since 1900* (London: Oxford University Press, 1960).

See especially the chapter, "Existentialism: Jean-Paul Sartre," pp. 162-196.

1976. —. *Existentialism* (New York: Oxford University Press, 1970).

1977. —, "The Moral Philosophy of Sartre," *The Listener,* VIII (January 8, 1959), pp. 64 ff., and (January 15, 1959), pp. 105 ff.

1978. —. *The Philosophy of Sartre* (London: Hutchinson; New York: Hillary House, 1965; Barnes and Noble, 1967).

1979. van de Water, L., "The Work of Art, Man, and Being: A Heideggerian Theme," *International Philosophical Quarterly,* IX (1969), pp. 214-235.

1980. Watson, J. R., "Heidegger's Hermeneutic Phenomenology," *Philosophy Today,* XV (1971), pp. 30-43.

1981. Watson, P. S., "Existentialism and Christian Faith," *London Quarterly and Holborn Review,* I (1953), pp. 67-69.

1982. Weatherhead, A. *A Reading of Henry Greene* (Seattle: University of Washington Press, 1964).

1983. Webber, R. H., "Kierkegaard and the Elaboration of Unamuno's *Niebla,*" *Hispanic Review,* XXXII (1964), pp. 118-134.

1984. —, "A Critique of Heidegger's Concept of 'Solicitude'," *The New Scholasticism,* XLII (1968), pp. 537-560.

1985. –, *Individual and Social Being in Heidegger's Being and Time*, Ph.D. diss., Columbia University (1966).

1986. Weigel, G., "Humani Generis: Existentialism and Catholic Doctrine," *Commonweal*, LIV (1951), pp. 525 ff.

1987. Wellwarth, George. *The Theater of Protest and Paradox* (New York: New York University Press, 1964).

1988. Weber, Eugene. *Paths to the Present: Aspects of European Thought from Romanticism to Existentialism* (New York: Dodd, Mead, 1960).

1989. Weigert, E., "Existentialism and its Relations to Psychotherapy," *Psychiatry*, XII (1949), pp. 399-412.

1990. –, "Soren Kierkegaard's Mood Swings," *International Journal of Psychoanalysis*, XLI (1960), pp. 521-525.

1991. Weil, Eric, "The Strength and Weakness of Existentialism," *The Listener* (May 8, 1952), pp. 473-477.

1992. Weiler, G., "On Heidegger's Notion of Philosophy," *Hermathena*, XCIII (1959), pp. 16-25.

1993. Wein, Hermann, "The Concept of Ideology in Sartre: 'Situatedness' as an Epistemological and Anthropological Concept," *Dialogue*, VII (1968), pp. 1-15.

1994. Weiss, Helen, "The Greek Conceptions of Time and Being in the Light of Heidegger's Philosophy," *Philosophy and Phenomenological Research*, II (1941), pp. 173-187.

1995. Weiss, Paul, "Existenz and Hegel," *Philosophy and Phenomenological Research*, VIII (1947-1948), pp. 206-216.

1996. Welch, E. *The Philosophy of Edmund Husserl: The Origin and Development of his Phenomenology* (New York: Columbia University Press, 1941).

1997. Wells, Norman, "Thomistic Existentialism," *Listening*, IX

(1974), pp. 178-181.

1998. Wenkart, Antonia, "Creativity in the Light of Existentialism," *Journal of Existential Psychiatry,* I (1960), pp. 367-379.

1999. –, "Irrational Trends in Contemporary Psychotherapy: Cultural Correlates," *Psychoanalysis and the Psychoanalytic Review,* XLV (1958), pp. 1-4.

2000. Werkmeister, W. H., "Hegel and Heidegger," in W. E. Steinkraus, ed., *New Studies in Hegel's Philosophy* (New York: Holt, Rhinehart, 1971), pp. 142-155.

2001. –, "Heidegger and the Poets," *The Personalist,* LII (1971), pp. 5-22.

2002. –, "An Introduction to Heidegger's Existential Phenomenology," *Philosophy and Phenomenological Research,* II (1941-1942), pp. 79-87.

2003. Whitcomb, H. W., "The Dilemma in Kierkegaard's Either/ Or," *Journal of Philosophy,* XLII (1945), pp. 216-219.

2004. White, D. A., "Revealment: A Meeting of Extremes in Aesthetics," *Journal of Aesthetics and Art Criticism,* XXVIII (1970), pp. 515-520.

2005. –, "World and Earth in Heidegger's Aesthetics," *Philosophy Today,* XII (1968), pp. 282-286.

2006. White, V. E., "Existentialism and Experience," *The Thomist,* XI (1951), pp. 171-183.

2007. Whiting, Charles G., "The Case for 'Engaged' Literature," *Yale French Studies,* I, 1 (1948), pp. 84-89.

2008. Whittemore, Robert C., "Metaphysical Foundations of Sartre's Ontology," *Tulane Studies in Philosophy,* VIII (1959), pp. 111-121.

2009. –, "Pro Hegel, Contra Kierkegaard," *Journal of Religious*

Thought, XIII (1956), pp. 131-144.

2010. Widmer, Kingsley, "The Existential Darkness: Richard Wright's *The Outsider,*" *Wisconsin Studies in Contemporary Literature,* I, 3 (1960), pp. 13-21.

2011. Wieczynski, Joseph, "A Note on Jean-Paul Sartre: Monist or Dualist," *Philosophy Today,* XII (1968), pp. 184-189.

2012. Wiegand, William, "Salinger and Kierkegaard," *Minnesota Review,* V (1965), pp. 137-156.

2013. Wienpahl, P. D., "Philosophy and Nothing," *Chicago Review,* XIII (1959), pp. 59-74.

2014. Wilburn, Ralph G., "The Philosophy of Existence and Faith-Relation," *Religion in Life,* XXX (1961), pp. 497-517.

2015. Wilcocks, Robert, comp. *Jean-Paul Sartre: A Bibliography of International Criticism* (Alberta: University of Alberta Press, 1975).

A massive work listing almost every book or article that even mentions Sartre (797 pages).

2016. Wild, John Daniel, "Authentic Existence," *Ethics,* LXXV (1965), pp. 227-239.

2017. –. *The Challenge of Existentialism* (Bloomington: Indiana University Press, 1955).

2018. –, "Contemporary Phenomenology and the Problem of Existence," *Philosophy and Phenomenological Research,* XX (1959), pp. 166-181.

2019. –. *Existence and the World of Freedom* (Englewood Cliffs: Prentice-Hall, 1963).

2020. –, "Existentialism: A New View of Man," *University of Toronto Quarterly,* XXVII (1957), pp. 79-95.

2021. –, "Existentialism as a Philosophy," *The Journal of Philosophy,* LVII (1960), pp. 45-62.

2022. –, "Heidegger and the Existential A Priori," in John Sallis, ed., *Heidegger and the Path of Thinking* (Pittsburgh: Duquesne University Press, 1970), pp. 221-234.

2023. –. *Human Freedom and Social Order* (Durham: Duke University Press, 1959).

2024. –, "Kierkegaard and Classic Philosophy," *The Philosophical Review* (1940).

2025. –, "Kierkegaard and Contemporary Existentialist Philosophy," *Anglican Theological Review,* XXXVIII (1956), pp. 15-32.

2026. –, "The New Emprism and Human Time," *Review of Metaphysics,* VII (1953-1954), pp. 537-557.

2027. –, "The Philosophy of Martin Heidegger," *Journal of Philosophy,* LX (1963), pp. 664-677.

2028. –, "William James and Existential Authenticity," *Journal of Existentialism,* V (1964-1965), pp. 243-256.

2029. Wilde, Jean T. and William Kimmel, eds. and trs. *The Search for Being: Essays from Kierkegaard to Sartre on the Problem of Existence* (New York: Twayne Pub., 1962).

2030. Wilhelmsen, F. D., "The Aesthetic Act and the Act of Being," *The Modern Schoolman,* XXIX (1952), pp. 227-291.

2031. Will, Frederic A., "A Confrontation of Kierkegaard and Keats," *The Personalist,* XLIII (1962), pp. 338-351.

2032. –, "Heidegger and the Gods of Poetry," *The Personalist,* XLIII (1962), pp. 157-167.

2033. –, "Sartre and the Question of Character in Literature,"

PMLA, LXXVI (1961), pp. 455-460.

2034. Williams, F., "Cezanne and French Phenomenology," *Journal of Aesthetics and Art Criticism*, XII (1954), pp. 481-492.

2035. Williams, J. R., "Heidegger, Death, and God," *Studies in Religion*, I (1972), pp. 298-320.

2036. Williams, M. E., "Gabriel Marcel's Notion of Personal Communication," *Modern Schoolman*, XXXV (1958) pp. 107-116.

2037. Williams, Martha E. *The Problems of Man and his Justification in the Philosophy of Friedrich Neitzsche*, Ph.D. diss., Bryn Mawr College (1959).

2038. Wilshire, Bruce W., "Kierkegaard's Theory of Knowledge and New Directions in Psychology and Psychoanalysis," *Review of Existential Psychology and Psychiatry*, III (1963), pp. 249-261.

2039. Wilson, Colin. *Introduction to the New Existentialism* (Boston: Houghton Mifflin, 1967).

2040. –. *The Outsider* (London: Gollancz; Boston: Houghton Mifflin, 1956).

2041. –. *Religion and the Rebel* (London: Gollancz, 1957).

2042. Wilson, Edmund. *Classics and Commercials* (New York: Farrar, Straus, 1950).

Includes a chapter on Sartre's existentialism.

2043. Wimsatt, W. K., "Battering the Object: The Ontological Approach," in Malcolm Bradbury and David Palmer, eds., *Contemporary Criticism*, Stratford-Upon-Avon Studies 12 (London: Edward Arnold Pub., Ltd., 1970).

2044. Winn, R. *A Concise Dictionary of Existentialism* (New York: Philosophical Library, 1960).

2045. Winthrop, Henry, "The Sartrean Typology: Those Who Deny Freedom and Those Who Ignore It," *Journal of Existentialism,* V (1965), pp. 265-276.

2046. Wirkus, Brenda, "Reply to Spurling's 'Marx and the Existentialists'," *British Journal of Phenomenology,* VII (1976), p. 138.

See item 1796 of this Bibliography.

2047. Wodehouse, Helen, "Martin Buber's 'I and Thou'," *Philosophy,* XX (1945), pp. 17-30.

2048. Wolfe, P., "Image and Meaning in Thus Spake Zarathustra," *Modern Language Notes,* LXXIX (1964), pp. 546-552.

2049. Wollheim, R., "The Political Philosophy of Existentialism," *Cambridge Journal* (October, 1953), pp. 3-19.

2050. Wolter, A. B. "Jean-Paul Sartre: Philosophy of Thought and Nausea," in J. K. Ryan, ed., *Twentieth Century Thinkers* (New York: Alba House, 1965), pp. 331-352.

2051. Woodbridge, Hensley Charles, "A Bibliography of Dissertations Concerning Kierkegaard Written in the U.S., Canada, and Great Britain," *American Book Collector,* XII (1961), pp. 21-22.

2052. –, "Soren Kierkegaard: A Bibliography of His Works in English Translation," *American Book Collector,* XII (1961), pp. 17-20.

2053. Wren, T. E., "Heidegger's Philosophy of History," *Journal of the British Society for Phenomenology,* III (1972), pp. 111-125.

2054. Wright, W. H. *What Nietzsche Taught* (New York: Huebach, 1917).

2055. Wright, Walter E., "Existentialism, Idealism, and Fichte's Concept of Coherence," *Journal of the History of*

Philosophy, XIII (1975), pp. 37-42.

2056. Wyschograd, M. *Kierkegaard and Heidegger: The Ontology of Existence* (London: 1954).

2057. Yolton, John W., "The Metaphysic of En-soi and Pour-soi," *Journal of Philosophy*, XLVIII (1951), pp. 548-556.

2058. Zaner, Richad M. and Don Ihde, eds. *Phenomenology and Existentialism* (New York: Putnam, 1973).

2059. –. *The Problem of Emobidment: Some Contributions to a Phenomenology of the Body* (The Hague: Martinus Nijhoff, 1964).

2060. –. *The Way of Phenomenology* (New York: Pegasus, 1970).

2061. Zeigler, Leslie, "Personal Existence: A Study of Buber and Kierkegaard," *Journal of Religion*, XL (1960), pp. 80-94.

2062. Zimmerman, Eugenia N., "*La Nausée* and the Avatars of Being," *Mosaic*, V, 3 (1972), pp. 151-157.

2063. –, "Some of these days. Sartre's 'Petite Phrase'," *Contemporary Literature*, XI (1970), pp. 375-388.

2064. Ziolkowski, T., "Max Frisch: Moralist Without a Moral," *Yale French Studies*, XXIX (1962), pp. 132-141.

2065. Zuboff, Arnold, "Nietzsche and Eternal Recurrence," see Robert Solomon, ed., *Nietzsche: A Collection of Critical Essays* (New York: Anchor Press, 1973), pp. 343-357.

2066. Zuidema, S. U., "The Idea of Revelation with Karl Barth and with Martin Heidegger: The Comparability of Their Patterns of Thought," *Free University Quarterly*, IV (1955), pp. 71-84.

2067. –. *Kierkegaard* (Philadelphia: Presbyterian and Reformed

Publishing Co., 1960).

SELECTIVE SUBJECT INDEX

The Selective Subject Index is divided into the following categories: *Bibliographies, Buber and Jewish Existentialism, Camus, Christian Existentialism, Education, Heidegger, Husserl, Introductions and Anthologies, Kierkegaard, Literature and Literary Criticism, Merleau-Ponty, Nietzsche, Phenomenology, Political and Economic Systems, Psychology*, and *Sartre.*

The user of the Index should keep in mind that this Index is necessarily arbitrary and limited, and none of the categories exclude most of the other categories. This is meant more as a point-of-departure for further investigation, rather than as an inclusive listing.

Bibliographies

140, 144, 149, 206, 457, 518, 811, 852, 924, 929, 1084, 1087, 1088, 1089, 1157, 1311, 1452, 1511, 1554, 1567, 1641, 1642, 1761, 2015, 2051, 2052.

Buber and Jewish Existentialism

4, 14, 87, 91, 212, 248, *254, 255, 256, 257, 258, 259, 260, 261,* 335, 336, 441, 442, 580, 581, 582, 583, 584, 585, 586, 710, 711, 786, 802, 803, 804, 805, 921, 940, 1145, 1148, 1458, 1472, 1563, 1689, 1690, 1703, 1818, 1894, 1896, 2047, 2061.

Camus

3, 6, 56, 81, 102, 140, 142, 149, 170, 173, 192, 225, 226, 227, 228, 229, 230, 231, 232, 233, 234, 241, 242, 243, 253, 271,

276, *285, 286, 287, 288, 289, 290, 291,* 300, 320, 321, 322, 325, 334, 339, 340, 388, 403, 404, 405, 450, 474, 475, 502, 520, 593, *624, 629,* 721, 722, 723, 852, 1070, 1085, 1113, 1114, 1135, 1143, 1228, 1267, 1315, 1320, 1322, 1325, 1369, 1391, 1447, 1461, 1482, 1498, 1554, 1566, 1569, 1738, 1860, 1865, 1967, 1972.

Christian Existentialism

10, 15, 30, 32, 33, 43, 76, 123, 135, 151, 152, 153, 154, 155, 156, 157, 158, 159, 160, 161, 162, 163, 165, 172, 248, 264, 265, 266, 269, 277, 312, 329, 337, 353, 373, 411, 420, 421, 428, 448, 451, 454, 476, 487, 537, 548, 581, 606, 657, 658, 684, 704, 721, 741, 745, 746, 793, 797, 821, 833, 870, 879, 887, 898, 899, 905, 918, 921, 948, 962, 966, 976, 977, 1008, 1010, 1048, 1054, 1075, 1087, 1130, 1132, 1138, 1139, 1141, 1142, 1143, 1152, 1201, 1202, 1203, 1206, 1208, 1210, 1230, 1231, 1232, 1233, 1234, 1235, 1236, 1238, 1239, 1240, 1241, 1242, 1243, 1252, 1255, 1298, 1304, 1307, 1350, 1393, 1417, 1428, 1473, 1522, 1548, 1549, 1550, 1551, 1717, 1739, 1758, 1793, 1794, 1795, 1809, 1853, 1894, 1901, 1902, 1903, 1904, 1905, 1912, 1919, 1981, 1986.

Education

224, 246, 252, 307, 308, 433, 665, 786, 808, 809, 1020, 1276, 1311, 1340, 1388, 1763, 1936.

Heidegger

8, 9, 11, 19, 20, 21, 22, 23, 24, 25, 41, 42, 57, 74, 80, 90, 93, 94, 95, 120, 121, 122, 123, 141, 174, 175, 182, 183, 203, 215, 216, 239, 240, 248, 282, 292, 293, 294, 295, 296, 306, 326, 337, 354, 387, 396, 418, 421, 422, 430, 431, 455, 456, 459, 462, 463, 489, 510, 511, 512, 524, 530, 540, 541, 542, 544, 575, 588, 589, 590, 601, 603, 607, 608, 616, 617, 619, 621, 622, 626, 646, 648, 649, 654, 656, 660, 661, 662, 663, 664, 666, 679, 681, 696, 697, 699, 716, 719, 725, 734, 735, 736, 743, 747, *748, 749, 750, 751, 752, 753, 754, 755, 756, 757, 758, 759, 760, 761, 762, 763, 764, 765, 766, 767, 768, 769,*

770, 771, 772, 773, 801, 807, 814, 815, 819, 822, 827, 828, 848, 850, 851, 875, 880, 881, 927, 942, 944, 968, 978, 979, 1012, 1013, 1014, 1027, 1028, 1029, 1042, 1043, 1044, 1049, 1075, 1076, 1077, 1078, 1079, 1082, 1097, 1121, 1127, 1133, 1136, 1148, 1150, 1157, 1168, 1169, 1170, 1177, 1179, 1180, 1181, 1200, 1201, 1203, 1205, 1212, 1213, 1214, 1218, 1256, 1257, 1258, 1259, 1266, 1280, 1281, 1282, 1285, 1316, 1319, 1321, 1327, 1328, 1341, 1345, 1359, 1367, 1368, 1391, 1393, 1408, 1416, 1421, 1427, 1430, 1436, 1439, 1441, 1452, 1454, 1475, 1480, 1481, 1483, 1491, 1497, 1502, 1523, 1524, 1526, 1527, 1528, 1529, 1530, 1531, 1532, 1533, 1542, 1546, 1551, 1559, 1560, 1561, 1562, 1564, 1576, 1577, 1578, 1584, 1589, 1590, 1591, 1594, 1641, 1642, 1646, 1652, 1653, 1660, 1662, 1665, 1666, 1667, 1668, 1673, 1678, 1679, 1683, 1685, 1694, 1696, 1697, 1698, 1699, 1706, 1707, 1708, 1709, 1712, 1715, 1716, 1721, 1722, 1723, 1724, 1726, 1734, 1748, 1749, 1751, 1755, 1771, 1773, 1774, 1780, 1781, 1791, 1800, 1801, 1812, 1815, 1816, 1825, 1831, 1834, 1852, 1855, 1857, 1884, 1886, 1906, 1909, 1911, 1916, 1920, 1921, 1925, 1926, 1930, 1934, 1935, 1949, 1952, 1953, 1954, 1955, 1957, 1958, 1962, 1970, 1979, 1980, 1984, 1985, 1992, 1994, 2000, 2001, 2002, 2005, 2022, 2027, 2032, 2035, 2053, 2056, 2066.

Husserl

74, 86, 166, 218, 279, 302, 436, 452, 506, 508, 527, 529, 600, 790, *856, 857, 858, 859, 860, 861, 862, 863, 864, 865, 866, 867, 868,* 1014, 1025, 1026, 1031, 1032, 1096, 1123, 1124, 1279, 1285, 1342, 1364, 1379, 1425, 1426, 1474, 1476, 1505, 1539, 1593, 1643, 1646, 1661, 1693, 1765, 1787, 1788, 1789, 1790, 1813, 1857, 1996. See *Phenomenology.*

Introductions and Anthologies

1, 2, 27, 29, 31, 46, 66, 68, 84, 89, 101, 115, 117, 134, 139, 167, 176, 185, 199, 200, 202, 209, 211, 235, 351, 366, 371, 372, 374, 375, 384, 467, 515, 523, 562, 612, 655, 659, 678, 688, 729, 730, 776, 826, 837, 909, 939, 941, 952, 954, 964, 965, 1011, 1024, 1051, 1052, 1071, 1099, 1104, 1108, 1115, 1146, 1161, 1163, 1204, 1226, 1253, 1323, 1324, 1348, 1374, 1392, 1414, 1422, 1444, 1445, 1448, 1513, 1545, 1570, 1575,

1600, 1649, 1672, 1729, 1744, 1750, 1767, 1770, 1778, 1875, 1913, 1963, 1965, 1976, 1987, 1988, 2017, 2019, 2020, 2021, 2029, 2039, 2058.

Kierkegaard

13, 34, 36, 37, 38, 45, 55, 64, 65, 79, 85, 92, 113, 119, 138, 169, 190, 204, 205, 207, 220, 221, 236, 244, 245, 248, 280, 281, 284, 298, 301, 305, 315, 317, 324, 333, 337, 344, 352, 357, 358, 359, 360, 361, 367, 397, 399, 400, 401, 402, 432, 440, 443, 446, 447, 466, 469, 470, 471, 472, 486, 499, 500, 505, 518, 547, 609, 610, 611, 613, 623, 627, 680, 685, 689, 690, 691, 693, 708, 710, 711, 718, 722, 732, 774, 775, 779, 794, 804, 811, 829, 834, 835, 853, 872, 895, 919, 922, 923, 925, 929, 936, 937, 955, 973, *980, 981, 982, 983, 984, 985, 986, 987, 988, 989, 990, 991, 992, 993, 994, 995, 996, 997, 998, 999, 1000, 1001,* 1005, 1017, 1058, 1092, 1093, 1105, 1109, 1112, 1153, 1154, 1165, 1175, 1183, 1184, 1185, 1186, 1193, 1194, 1195, 1196, 1197, 1216, 1217, 1222, 1256, 1299, 1303, 1331, 1366, 1403, 1406, 1418, 1429, 1437, 1449, 1450, 1453, 1455, 1458, 1484, 1485, 1486, 1492, 1493, 1499, 1549, 1556, 1557, 1558, 1572, 1579, 1580, 1680, 1682, 1704, 1705, 1728, 1730, 1735, 1743, 1757, 1764, 1775, 1776, 1780, 1794, 1799, 1801, 1803, 1804, 1814, 1816, 1818, 1844, 1847, 1867, 1868, 1870, 1871, 1872, 1873, 1874, 1878, 1879, 1920, 1928, 1930, 1962, 1983, 1990, 2003, 2009, 2012, 2024, 2025, 2031, 2038, 2051, 2052, 2056, 2061, 2067. See *Christian Existentialism.*

Literature and Literary Criticism

3, 6, 7, 48, 55, 106, 107, 109, 114, 128, 148, 154, 168, 170, 175, 187, 192, 198, 242, 243, 251, 280, 281, 298, 310, 325, 327, 330, 331, 333, 341, 342, 343, 347, 387, 388, 403, 405, 407, 408, 427, 435, 444, 453, 460, 477, 497, 499, 507, 514, 517, 520, 525, 538, 539, 551, 554, 563, 568, 587, 591, 602, 616, 624, 629, 630, 635, 640, 642, 643, 644, 645, 656, 659, 671, 674, 694, 724, 732, 734, 736, 737, 780, 781, 782, 784, 788, 796, 799, 813, 818, 824, 830, 831, 839, 853, 854, 855, 881, 919, 941, 946, 957, 958, 963, 972, 973, 975, 976, 1003, 1008, 1018, 1023, 1056, 1070, 1102, 1103, 1106, 1109, 1110,

1114, 1116, 1134, 1135, 1140, 1166, 1171, 1173, 1176, 1198, 1209, 1222, 1229, 1262, 1312, 1318, 1330, 1336, 1344, 1353, 1361, 1362, 1369, 1375, 1383, 1386, 1389, 1390, 1403, 1407, 1413, 1434, 1435, 1438, 1446, 1447, 1451, 1462, 1463, 1465, 1467, 1482, 1484, 1487, 1488, 1498, 1508, 1509, 1510, 1516, 1543, 1564, 1565, 1566, 1572, 1579, 1580, 1581, 1583, 1587, 1652, 1669, 1674, 1700, 1701, 1702, 1717, 1719, 1727, 1736, 1737, 1740, 1752, 1753, 1764, 1777, 1779, 1780, 1781, 1782, 1783, 1784, 1817, 1823, 1827, 1829, 1848, 1849, 1854, 1862, 1865, 1918, 1951, 1956, 1959, 1966, 1972, 1982, 1987, 2007, 2010, 2012, 2031, 2033, 2040, 2043, 2062, 2063, 2064. See *Camus* and *Sartre.*

Merleau-Ponty

97, 112, 412, 628, 676, 933, 1061, 1062, 1063, 1080, 1084, 1088, 1089, 1097, 1162, *1286, 1287, 1288, 1289, 1290, 1291, 1292, 1293, 1294, 1295, 1296, 1297,* 1423, 1474, 1496, 1506, 1857. See *Phenomenology.*

Nietzsche

16, 28, 49, 60, 99, 150, 177, 195, 196, 197, 219, 222, 238, 319, 370, 377, 378, 379, 381, 390, 398, 409, 413, 414, 415, 424, 460, 462, 464, 486, 519, 549, 553, 555, 557, 558, 559, 560, 578, 633, 634, 636, 650, 705, 706, 712, 714, 715, 722, 732, 744, 746, 781, 783, 784, 785, 788, 793, 806, 808, 809, 830, 831, 832, 850, 853, 855, 869, 877, 879, 895, 896, 899, 900, 901, 918, 946, 949, 950, 956, 957, 958, 959, 960, 961, 962, 963, 1015, 1021, 1022, 1043, 1044, 1059, 1072, 1073, 1074, 1100, 1101, 1102, 1107, 1110, 1144, 1156, 1158, 1159, 1162, 1165, 1174, 1187, 1209, 1212, 1224, 1227, 1256, 1283, 1284, 1321, 1332, 1334, 1334, 1337, 1354, 1389, 1390, *1394, 1395, 1396, 1397, 1398, 1399, 1400,* 1401, 1411, 1413, 1442, 1443, 1450, 1457, 1468, 1469, 1488, 1510, 1511, 1518, 1521, 1547, 1555, 1571, 1573, 1574, 1582, 1586, 1595, 1596, 1601, 1647, 1655, 1669, 1714, 1727, 1761, 1768, 1769, 1785, 1797, 1817, 1819, 1845, 1876, 1900, 1910, 1917, 1918, 1932, 1973, 2037, 2048, 2054, 2065.

Phenomenology

27, 96, 171, 172, 237, 278, 308, 316, 410, 423, 425, 473, 488, 490, 491, 492, 493, 494, 495, 504, 509, 528, 531, 533, 534, 535, 700, 701, 702, 703, 720, 724, 798, 874, 875, 876, 932, 1014, 1030, 1031, 1032, 1036, 1055, 1086, 1097, 1098, 1099, 1125, 1160, 1161, 1162, 1163, 1164, 1278, 1317, 1329, 1371, 1374, 1378, 1380, 1381, 1382, 1432, 1459, 1474, 1500, 1535, 1536, 1537, 1538, 1539, 1585, 1592, 1644, 1646, 1651, 1663, 1664, 1692, 1731, 1745, 1750, 1770, 1791, 1828, 1832, 1833, 1838, 1839, 1840, 1841, 1857, 1922, 1923, 1936, 1938, 2058, 2059, 2060.

Political and Economic Systems

50, 54, 72, 272, 322, 381, 383, 639, 895, 1122, 1162, 1405, 1489, 1495, 1507, 1521, 1597, 1796, 1814, 1845, 1964, 2046, 2049.

Psychology

40, 47, 63, 70, 98, 100, 137, 145, 147, 171, 179, 180, 181, 191, 213, 214, 273, 275, 362, 353, 364, 365, 398, 406, 429, 483, 485, 503, 504, 522, 536, 569, 570, 571, 572, 573, 574, 579, 585, 595, 596, 597, 598, 599, 604, 562, 653, 686, 692, 703, 798, 810, 841, 842, 843, 844, 845, 486, 847, 891, 931, 969, 1015, 1025, 1031, 1034, 1035, 1037, 1039, 1050, 1066, 1067, 1068, 1083, 1090, 1111, 1219, 1260, 1261, 1263, 1268, 1269, 1270, 1271, 1272, 1273, 1274, 1275, 1300, 1314, 1317, 1355, 1365, 1409, 1456, 1485, 1505, 1513, 1657, 1658, 1671, 1688, 1695, 1732, 1771, 1792, 1820, 1835, 1836, 1837, 1842, 1844, 1861, 1883, 1885, 1902, 1919, 1921, 1937, 1941, 1942, 1943, 1944, 1945, 1946, 1947, 1989, 1990, 1998, 1999, 2038.

Sartre

5, 12, 18, 26, 35, 48, 52, 53, 54, 56, 58, 59, 73, 74, 77, 78, 82, 83, 98, 100, 103, 104, 105, 110, 116, 118, 125, 130, 144, 148, 169, 186, 187, 193, 194, 209, 230, 233, 234, 243, 246, 247, 249, 252, 262, 263, 267, 270, 283, 297, 303, 311, 312, 313,

318, 322, 328, 337, 340, 341, 342, 350, 368, 385, 389, 392, 393, 394, 395, 412, 416, 419, 429, 437, 449, 450, 452, 453, 454, 458, 465, 497, 498, 501, 503, 520, 545, 546, 561, 564, 585, 594, 614, 624, 630, 644, 647, 651, 669, 672, 675, 676, 682, 683, 686, 692, 695, 704, 709, 726, 727, 738, 379, 786, 789, 795, 798, 820, 840, 849, 882, 883, 884, 885, 886, 920, 921, 922, 926, 928, 933, 935, 971, 973, 974, 1007, 1046, 1050, 1056, 1065, 1069, 1093, 1094, 1097, 1114, 1121, 1140, 1153, 1162, 1167, 1178, 1188, 1189, 1192, 1211, 1225, 1229, 1244, 1254, 1256, 1264, 1267, 1277, 1298, 1306, 1308, 1309, 1326, 1338, 1339, 1350, 1356, 1363, 1367, 1372, 1377, 1379, 1383, 1384, 1387, 1415, 1433, 1434, 1447, 1460, 1463, 1465, 1466, 1474, 1477, 1479, 1482, 1485, 1487, 1492, 1495, 1498, 1503, 1504, 1506, 1512, 1534, 1549, 1553, 1587, 1597, 1598, 1603, *1604, 1605, 1606, 1607, 1608, 1609, 1610, 1611, 1612, 1613, 1614, 1615, 1616, 1617, 1618, 1619, 1620, 1621, 1622, 1623, 1624, 1625, 1626, 1627, 1628, 1629, 1630, 1631, 1632, 1633, 1634, 1635, 1636, 1637, 1638, 1639, 1640,* 1643, 1654, 1688, 1713, 1720, 1732, 1733, 1736, 1737, 1745, 1776, 1821, 1822, 1829, 1830, 1843, 1854, 1857, 1863, 1864, 1866, 1914, 1926, 1929, 1930, 1939, 1968, 1972, 1975, 1977, 1978, 1993, 2008, 2011, 2015, 2033, 2042, 2045, 2050, 2057, 2062, 2063. See *Literature and Literary Criticism,* and *Psychology.*